to study לדרש... to do לעשת... to teach ללמד...

Ezra 7: 10

Roots and Branches

Explorations into the Jewish Context of the Christian Faith

'You do not support the root, but the root supports you.'
Romans 11: 18

British Library Cataloguing in Publication Data. A catalogue record for this book is available from the British Library

Published by PWM Trust, The Park, Moggerhanger, Bedford, MK44 3RW and The Centre for Biblical and Hebraic Studies, The Park, Moggerhanger, Bedford, MK44 3RW

Typeset by Andrew Lewis, PWM Trust

Printed by Biddles Ltd, Guildford, UK

Front Cover photo: From a Ukranian Synagogue. The text reads 'She is a tree of life to those who embrace her' Proverbs 3: 18. Photo taken by Fred Wright

Back Cover photo: David Forbes, taken by Gary Clayton

Cover Design: Andrew Lewis

ISBN:

1-872395-40-6	Paperback Edition
1-872395-45-7	Hardback Edition

Contents

Editors' Preface

It has been a joy for us, in preparing this tribute to David, to work with such an international team of scholars.

David was a man of strong faith and clearly held beliefs. Yet he was also a man of broad sympathies and, within the purview of his interest in the 'Jewish Roots' theme, and especially in his interest in modern research into the Second Temple period, he held within his friendship circle, scholars representing a broad theological spectrum. This spectrum is well represented in these essays.

It is of the essence of this book, therefore, that there is variety of opinion represented here. Such is the breadth that they do not necessarily always represent the views of the Biblical and Hebraic Study Centre, or of the Editorial Team. Our editorial policy has been to use as light a touch as possible. This book of essays is produced, not to centre on a coherent theme or a progressive line of thought, but rather our aim has been to let each writer choose and present his material in his own way, as his own personal tribute to David. We have, however, aimed to present the essays in as coherent a sequence as possible and to present them in as consistent a 'house style' as possible, without diminishing the individuality of each essay.

The contributors are:

David Bivin	John Fieldsend
Joseph Frankovic	Simon Hawthorne
Dwight Pryor	Walter Riggans
John C P Smith	Fred Wright
Brad Young	

The editorial team comprised:

John Fieldsend	Jenny Forbes
Clifford Hill	Walter Riggans
John C P Smith	Fred Wright

We would like to express our appreciation to all the contributors for their willingness to contribute to this book, and for their co-operation, which has made our work such a pleasure.

By its very nature, a book of essays is not intended to present detailed exposition of theological or historical material. The essays are, in essence, exploratory and, hopefully, insightful introductions to their subject matter, and present an overview of up-to-date information as to research and directions of thought on their topics. In short, they are intended to be stimulants to the readers' own thinking, further reading and reflection. This was David's aim in founding the Centre, and if we have achieved this we shall have begun to serve our purpose.

However, we realise the importance of providing a forum where these themes can be given a wider exposure, and where our readers can be involved in a shared response and further exploration. This is where the Journal of our Centre, published four times per annum, comes in. It is our purpose that in the coming issues, different writers will respond to some of the themes of these essays, and develop their thinking from a variety of perspectives; and readers will be encouraged to share their own responses through the correspondence columns. In this sense this book will be a focus for David's original vision for the Centre. We invite you, therefore, to join with us in this continuing exploration. The journal may be obtained through membership of the Centre.

We would wish to express our gratitude to many people who have been involved in the production of this volume. Our special thanks are offered to Jenny Forbes for sharing her precious memories of David as she made her own special contribution to the editorial team. We would also like to thank Andy Lewis for all his detailed work in preparing the manuscripts for publication, and for designing the beautiful cover. Also Karen Hyland-Bennett, the Centre's administrator, has given much time to the administration that such a venture has required, and overseeing much of the proof reading, which was mainly undertaken by Jean Wolton, John McLaughlan and Val Lockhart.

I would also wish to express my personal thanks to all my fellow editors for their time so willingly given to prepare this book for publication. We have spent many hours, both being stimulated by the writing of the contributors, and in lively debate amongst ourselves as we discussed, revised and prepared the manuscripts in order to give the book a coherent pattern.

Inevitably, we didn't always agree amongst ourselves in all the detail, and any failings in the editorial process are my responsibility alone.

John Fieldsend,

Managing Editor, and Director of The Centre for Biblical and Hebraic Studies, The Park, Moggerhanger, Bedford, MK44 3RW.

Introduction

Clifford Hill

Roots and Branches is being published as a tribute to David Forbes who went to be with the Lord on 28 March 1997. He was the founder of *The Centre for Biblical and Hebraic Studies* based at The Park, Moggerhanger, Bedford, England. More is said about the work of the Centre in *Appendix 1*. It is an eloquent tribute to David and his work that such a distinguished company of scholars has been willing to contribute essays for this book. The study of the Hebraic Roots of the Christian faith has been given fresh life and impetus in the second half of the twentieth century through three significant developments.

The first is the founding of the modern State of Israel in 1948. Jewish scholarship has been advanced through having a territorial base in the ancient land once occupied by their ancestors in ancient Israel. The founding of scholarly institutions such as the University of Jerusalem and other academic research institutions has given considerable impetus to scholarly work. The discovery of the Dead Sea Scrolls has focused worldwide attention upon ancient Hebrew manuscripts, which in turn have shed new light upon the scriptures.

The vast increase in international travel during the second half of the twentieth century, with the growth of the tourist industry, has brought millions of visitors to Israel who have had the opportunity of seeing, at first hand, places they had read about in the Bible. This has created fresh interest in the study of scripture and the history of the people of Israel who were those called by God into a covenant relationship with himself. The fascination of the land of Israel, its ancient peoples and their faith which are vividly portrayed in the Bible through the Torah, the Psalms, the prophets and the writings, have gripped the attention of millions of Gentiles throughout the world. Even those who are only nominal in their observance of Christianity are often caught up in the desire to explore the origins of the faith which lie firmly rooted in ancient Israel and the writings of the Hebrew sages.

The second major development which has given rise to the current interest in exploring the Hebraic roots of the Christian faith is a renewed study of the wealth of material available for the study of the people and the culture into which Jesus was born. Much of this new interest was, of course, aroused by the discovery of the Dead Sea Scrolls. Until this point, students of Christian history and doctrine have worked along lines, both of which have been brought under serious questioning by these recent lines of research. One has been an over emphasis of what has been seen as 'a silence in revelation' between the close of the canon of the Hebrew scriptures and the beginning of the New Testament.

Because we have no scriptures which have been accepted as 'canonical' that cover this period, we have ignored the wealth of Jewish material that has been available, and which has been greatly enlarged by recent discoveries. Because of this we have tended to downplay the culture into which Jesus was born, and the religion which nurtured his life and by which he worshipped. Because of this, Jesus, the man for all people and all cultures (which expresses a vital truth) has been seen rather as the divine-man who was himself without, or at least beyond, a national people and culture.

There have, of course, been those who have sought to research Jesus' life and background, but until relatively recently, because of our greater acquaintance with Greek history and culture, Jesus, or at least the Gospel accounts which tell his story, have been interpreted in those categories. This is an imbalance which is now being rectified.

The third major development is the increasing number of Jewish people who have accepted Jesus as their Messiah since the founding of the modern State of Israel. There are today more than forty Messianic congregations in Israel and there are hundreds more scattered among the nations throughout the world.

The increasing number of Jewish believers in Jesus and the establishment of new Messianic congregations has not only encouraged the scholarly exploration of Hebraic roots, it has also brought an important new dimension to such studies. Jewish believers approach the New Testament from the background of their own culture and experience. This enables them to think with Jewish minds and to approach the Gospels from a Hebraic concept rather than from the largely Hellenistic dominated western Gentile culture which has pervaded the study of the Bible in Christian theological institutions for so many centuries.

This book of essays on Hebraic themes makes a significant contribution to the study of the roots of the Christian faith. It is a fitting tribute to the life and work of David Forbes. He had a great love for the Jewish people and for the land of Israel, both of which grew out of his love for the Bible as the word of God. David was a lifelong student of the scriptures. Nothing gave him greater joy than to be searching for new understanding of some passage in the Bible and looking for cross-references or historical and cultural contextualisation. His knowledge of the Bible was very extensive and he was an avid, though discerning, reader.

David grew up in Aberdeen in a God-fearing Scottish Brethren family where he learned to love and have great respect for the scriptures as the word of the living God. It was his thirst for knowledge and for greater understanding of the word that caused him to explore the Hebraic roots of the Christian faith. He enjoyed studying the history of Israel and the Jewish writings, but for David this was always a means to an end rather than the end in itself. He saw the study of Hebraic roots, Jewish traditions and Jewish culture as a means of bringing fresh understanding of the revealed word of God through the prophets of Israel or through the Torah. It was the Bible that was always David's first love. It was for this reason, when we began talking about establishing a Centre where the Hebraic roots of the faith could be explored. David insisted on it being called The Centre for **Biblical** and Hebraic Studies.

It is significant that the last words David wrote, at the end of his final Editorial for the Journal of the Centre, published in April 1997, were, *'we must never forget that the most important thing that we can offer Israelis and Jews throughout the world, is the good news that Jesus is their Messiah. We must always see this as a priority.'* For David, that was the heart of the matter. Jesus was Lord and Saviour and he longed to share his faith with everyone – both Jew and Gentile.

Clifford Hill
Director of Prophetic Word Ministries Trust

Introduction to Authors

David Bivin is Director of the Jerusalem School of Synoptic Research and publisher of *Jerusalem Perspective* magazine. A native of Oklahoma, David has lived in Israel since 1963. He and his wife, Josa, are members of Jerusalem's Narkis Street Congregation, where David and several other members of the Jerusalem School serve as teachers of the adult Bible class. A partial list of published works include: *A New Solution to the Synoptic Problem, Counting the Cost of Discipleship: Lindsey's Reconstruction of the Rich Young Ruler Complex, Understanding the Difficult Words of Jesus,* and *Aleph-Bet: A Beginner's Introduction to Reading and Writing Hebrew.*

John Fieldsend is a Messianic Jew who came to Britain from Czechoslovakia in 1939. After a short career in electrical engineering he was ordained into the Anglican Church in which he spent twenty-seven years in parochial ministry, and eight years as a director of the Church's Ministry Among Jewish People. He is a founder member of 'Kehilat Beit Shalom' a Messianic Congregation in North London. He is now Director of *The Centre for Biblical and Hebraic Studies* at The Park.

Joseph Frankovic holds a BA in Classical Studies from the University of Tulsa and BA and MA degrees in Biblical Literature from Oral Roberts University. He is currently teaching at Midwestern State University and working towards a PhD in Midrash at The Jewish Theological Seminary of America. Later this year he and his wife, Janet, will return to Jerusalem where Joseph will begin research on his dissertation project and fill the position of Managing Editor at *Jerusalem Perspective.* A partial list of published works include, *Reading the Book: a Popular Essay on Christian Bible Hermeneutics, Sermons from Narkis* (ed), *Celibacy and Charism in 1 Cor 7: 5-7.*

Simon Hawthorne is Midlands UK Regional Adviser for the Church's Ministry Among Jewish People and visiting lecturer in Biblical Hebrew at St John's College, Nottingham, where he formerly gained his Degree as Bachelor of Theology with specific reference to Jewish-Christian issues. His dissertation was on the subject *The Concept of God's love in the Hebrew Bible.*

Dwight Pryor is President and founder of the *Center for Judaic-Christian Studies* – established in 1984 to explore Jewish backgrounds to the life of Jesus, and to educate Christians about their full Hebraic heritage in Christ. A founding member of the *Jerusalem School of Synoptic Research in Israel*, Dwight also serves as teaching elder for the Church of the Messiah, in Dayton, Ohio.

Walter Riggans, the General Director of the Church's Ministry Among Jewish People, has a particular theological and pastoral commitment to the growing and maturing Messianic Jewish movement worldwide. Directing the ministry of CMJ is a full-time job, but he still finds time for writing and following cricket. In terms of his published works, he is best known for *Commentary on Numbers, God's Covenant with the Jews, Jesus Ben Joseph: An Introduction to Jesus the Jew*, and *Yeshua Ben David: Why do the Jewish People Reject Jesus as their Messiah.*

John C P Smith holds a BA Hons degree in Hebrew and Jewish Studies from the University College, London, which involved spending a year studying at the Hebrew University in Jerusalem. Since 1993 he has worked with Christian Friends of Israel, and has spoken at Pardes teaching days.

Fred Wright is the leader of the King David Fellowship and Study Centre in Essex, UK, and has worked extensively throughout Israel and Eastern Europe, including the former USSR. His most recent publications include *Words from the Scroll of Fire* and *The Cross Became a Sword.*

Brad Young, Associate Professor of Judaic-Christian Studies at Oral Roberts University, is the founder and president of the Gospel Research Foundation. Learned in both New Testament and Rabbinics, he earned MA and PhD degrees from the Hebrew University in Jerusalem. Brad is an internationally recognised speaker, author and scholar. His most recent publications include *Jesus the Jewish Theologian* and *Paul the Jewish Theologian*. A major scholarly work, *The Parables of Jesus in Light of Jewish Tradition and Christian Interpretation* is soon to be published as a companion volume to his *Jesus and His Jewish Parables.*

Section 1:

Jesus in his Hebraic Setting

Jesus the Rabbi

by David Bivin

1 Jesus' Jewish Education

A careful reading of the New Testament suggests that Jesus was a scholar learned in the scriptures and religious literature of the period, which was vast and varied. Yet the popular view of Jesus is that he was a simple, uneducated character from the provinces.

This misunderstanding is due in part to a number of disparaging statements made about Nazareth and the Galilee such as, 'Nazareth! Can anything good come from there?' (Jn 1: 46) and, 'Utterly amazed, they asked: "Are not all these men who are speaking Galileans?"' (Acts 2: 7).

These statements may reflect a Judean bias against Galileans. Some Judeans may have seen themselves as cultured and cosmopolitan. To them, the Galileans were provincials whose accent seemed coarse and unrefined.

Actually, however, the reverse may have been true: the Galileans were the more exposed to the outside world while the Judeans, living in the interior of the land, were partially sheltered from contact with foreign nations. The Galilee also was more urban, with many developed villages. Judea, by contrast, was generally more rural in character.

No doubt this same disdain towards Galileans prompted the assumption, preserved in John 7: 15, that Jesus had no education: 'The Jews were amazed and asked, "How did this man get such learning without having studied?"'

Conservative Galileans

Such passages have given rise to the idea that Jesus and his disciples were uneducated simply because they came from Galilee. Surprisingly, however, the standard of education and religious training in Galilee surpassed that of Judea.

According to Shmuel Safrai, Hebrew University Professor of Jewish History of the Mishnaic and Talmudic Periods, not only do the number of First Century Galilean sages exceed the number of Judean sages, but the moral and ethical quality of their teaching is still considered more highly than that of their Judean counterparts[1]. Such First Century Galilean sages as Yohanan ben Zakkai, Hanina ben Dosa, Abba Yose Holikofri of Tiv'on, Zadok and Jesus of Nazareth helped impart a deep understanding of the Torah to the residents of Galilee.

In addition to their high level of knowledge of and reverence for scripture, the Galileans could be seen as the religious conservatives of the period. Jewish messianic nationalism flourished in the Galilee. Judah the Galilean, for example, is considered by many to be the founder of the 'zealot' movement, and it was in Galilee, not Judea, that the great revolt against Rome broke out in 66 CE.[2]

Early Training

The New Testament says almost nothing about Jesus' life from after his birth until he appeared in the Temple at age twelve, and from then until he began his public ministry at about the age of thirty. Yet a good indication of what a young Jewish man in Jesus' day would have been doing may be found in Avot 5: 21, a tractate from a collection of rabbinic sayings called the Mishnah, which states:

> At five years of age, one is ready for the study of the Written Torah, at ten years of age for the study of the Oral Torah, at thirteen for bar mitzvah [the religious coming-of-age ceremony], at fifteen for the study of halachot [rabbinic legal decisions], at eighteen for marriage, at twenty for pursuing a vocation, at thirty for entering one's full vigour.

Although this statement cannot be dated with certainty, and may come some 100 years after the time of Jesus, there are many other passages in rabbinic works that indicate the importance placed upon the education of children and provide some insight into how the young Jesus was probably spending his time.

Certainly education was highly valued in Jewish society. In his apology for Judaism, *Against Apion*, written to counter antisemitism, the First Century Jewish historian Josephus states:

Above all we pride ourselves on the education of our children, and regard as the most essential task in life the observance of our laws and of the pious practices based thereupon, which we have inherited.[3]

The Talmud even suggests the preferred class size:

The maximum number of elementary pupils that should be placed under one teacher is twenty-five; if there are fifty, an additional teacher must be provided; if there are forty, a senior student should be engaged to assist the teacher. (Bava Batra 21a)

High Standard of Education

A synagogue in the first century usually had its own בֵּית סֵפֶר (bet sefer, elementary school) and בֵּית מִדְרָשׁ (bet midrash, secondary school) in which children and adults studied Torah and the oral traditions. Formal education ended at the age of twelve or thirteen when most children went to work. The more gifted students who so desired could continue their studies at the bet midrash together with adults who studied in their spare time.

A few of the most outstanding bet midrash students eventually left home to study with a famous sage, being encouraged and sometimes supported by their families. Only the very promising students were urged to continue studying since their assistance was usually needed in agricultural work at home.[4]

One might assume that the synagogue, as the place of worship, would be considered more important or more sacred than the schools, but this was not the case. To this day, the bet midrash is given more prominence than the synagogue – not because education is valued more highly than worship, but because Judaism does not make a distinction between the two. Indeed, Judaism has always held that study of Torah is one of the highest forms of worship.[5]

Diligent Study

Jewish tradition contains many statements enjoining continued and diligent study, such as the Mishnah passage, 'Discipline yourself to study Torah, for you do not acquire it by inheritance' (Avot 2: 12). This point of view is echoed throughout the New Testament in such passages as the following:

[The Jews of Berea] were more noble ... examining the scriptures daily
to see if these things were so. (Acts 17: 11)
Do your best to win God's approval as a workman who does not need
to be ashamed, because he knows how to interpret the word of truth
correctly. (2 Tim 2: 15)
Make every effort to add to your faith goodness, and to goodness,
knowledge.... (2 Pet 1: 5)

Memorisation

Although scrolls were used for reading publicly in the synagogue and
the practice of writing was highly developed, written material was
expensive because all manuscripts had to be hand-copied by trained
scribes. Scrolls, therefore, were relatively scarce, and even though in
Jesus' time every Jewish home had at least one of the approximately
twenty biblical scrolls, few people had immediate access to more than
a very small part of the entire library of sacred literature. Learning,
consequently, involved a great deal of memorisation. Professor Safrai
has written concerning educational methods of the period:

Individual and group study of the Bible, repetition of the passages,
etc, were often done by chanting them aloud. There is the frequent
expression, 'the chirping of children,' which was heard by people
passing close by a synagogue as the children were reciting a verse.
Adults too, in individual and group study, often read aloud; for it was
frequently advised not to learn in a whisper, but aloud. This was the
only way to overcome the danger of forgetting.[6]

In the eyes of the sages, repetition was the key to learning, as these
passages illustrate:

A person who repeats his lesson a hundred times is not to be
compared with a person who repeats it a hundred and one times.
(Babylonian Talmud, Hagigah 9b)
If [a student] learns Torah and does not go over it again and again, he
is like a man who sows without reaping. (Babylonian Talmud,
Sanhedrin 99a)

Many methods were used to assist the student in memorising his
lessons, and one passage in the Talmud (Shabbat 104a) even describes

in detail the mnemonic devices employed to teach small children the Hebrew alphabet. Elementary school students, who studied seven days a week, were given no new material on the Sabbath, but rather used that time to memorise material learnt earlier in the week.[7]

Students enjoyed memorising their lessons while strolling outdoors, but they were tempted to shift their attention to the surrounding scenery. The Mishnah specifically warns against this:

A person walking along the road repeating his lessons who interrupts his memorisation and exclaims: 'What a beautiful tree!' or 'What a beautiful field!' it is imputed to him as if he were guilty of a crime punishable by death. (Avot 3: 8)

Such peripatetic memorisation is still practised today in the Middle East, and is the foundation of the Muslim system of education. In the Arab world one can frequently see young men walking back and forth along the roads at the outskirts of villages and towns, apparently talking to themselves. They are actually repeating and memorising their lessons.

Jesus' Contemporaries

From accounts found in Jewish sources, such as those referred to above, one can form a reasonably accurate picture of what Jesus was doing in his childhood and adolescence. He was studying, committing to memory large amounts of material – scripture and commentary on scripture – all the available sacred literature of the day.

This was exactly what most of the other Jewish boys of Jesus' day were doing. The memorisation of Written Torah and Oral Torah was such a large part of Jewish education that most contemporaries of Jesus had large portions of this material – at the least almost all of the Written Torah – firmly committed to memory. As Professor Safrai has stated:

The scriptures were known almost by heart by everyone. From quite early in the Second Temple period, one could hardly find a little boy in the street who didn't know the scriptures. According to Jerome (342-420 CE) who lived in Bethlehem and learned Hebrew from local Jewish residents in order to translate the scriptures into Latin [producing the Vulgate]: 'There doesn't exist any Jewish child who doesn't know by heart the history from Adam to Zerubbabel [ie, from the beginning to the end of the Bible].' Perhaps this was a bit of an exaggeration on Jerome's part, but in most cases his reports have proved reliable. (Safrai, lecture on June 5, 1985)

Full-time Discipleship

The call to be a sage's disciple in First Century Israel often meant leaving relatives and friends and travelling the country under austere conditions. It also meant total commitment. A prospective disciple first had to be sure his priorities were in order.

Consider the words of the man who said to Jesus, 'I will follow you, Lord, but first let me go back and say goodbye to my family' (Lk 9: 61). Jesus' reply shows that only those who were prepared to commit themselves totally to him would be welcome, 'No one who puts his hand to the plough and then looks back is fit for the kingdom of God.'

This is emphasised in Jesus' response to another man who offered to follow him, but only after 'burying his father'. 'Let the dead bury their dead,' Jesus told him (Lk 9: 60; Mt 8: 22).

Apparently, Jesus' replies were directed towards persons whom he had invited to leave home and serve a full-time apprenticeship with him. This form of discipleship was a unique feature of ancient Jewish society.

Sacrifice

According to Peah 1: 1, there are certain things such as honouring one's father and mother of which a person 'benefits from the interest' in this world, while 'the principal' remains for him in the world to come. 'But,' the passage goes on, 'the study of Torah is equal to them all.' Jesus said something similar: as important as it is to honour one's parents, leaving home to study Torah with him was even more important.

To the rich man mentioned in Luke 18, the call to follow Jesus meant giving up all his wealth. The price was too high for him and he did not become one of Jesus' disciples. Peter reminded Jesus that he and the others who had accepted Jesus' call were different, 'We have left everything to follow you.'

'Amen!' said Jesus – in other words, 'Yes you have done that and it is commendable.' Jesus went on to promise that anyone who had made the sacrifice of total commitment for the sake of the Kingdom of God would receive something of much greater value than what he had given up, and eternal life in the world to come (Lk 18: 28–30).

Commitment

Jesus did not want his prospective disciples to have any false expectations, and he frequently stressed the need to count the cost before making a commitment to him:

> Which of you, if he wanted to build a tower, would not first sit down and estimate the cost to see if he had enough money to complete it? Likewise, any of you who is not ready to leave all his possessions cannot be my disciple. (Lk 14: 28–33)

Jesus was very clear about the degree of commitment that was required of a disciple:

> If anyone comes to me and does not hate his father, mother, wife, children, brothers, sisters, and himself as well, he cannot be my disciple. Whoever does not bear his cross and follow me cannot be my disciple. (Lk 14: 26–27)

In this context, the word 'hate' does not carry the meaning it normally has in English usage, but seems to be used in a Hebraic sense. In Hebrew 'hate' can also mean 'love less' or 'put in second place'. For example, Genesis 29: 31 states that Leah was 'hated,' but the context indicates that Leah was not unloved but rather loved less than Jacob's other wife, Rachel. Note that the preceding verse specifically says that Jacob loved Rachel more than Leah.

A second illustration of this particular Hebraic shade of meaning of the word 'hate' is found in Deuteronomy 21: 15: 'If a man has two wives, one loved and the other hated'. Here too, the context shows that the 'hated' wife is only second in affection and not really hated in the English sense of the word. Likewise in Jesus' statement, he was saying that whoever did not love him more than his own family or even his own self could not be his disciple.

Jesus also alluded to the rigours of the peripatetic life of a sage when he said, 'Foxes have holes and birds of the air have nests, but the Son of Man has nowhere to lay his head' (Lk 9: 57–58). The burden Jesus' disciples had to bear was a heavy one, but it was similar to what other First Century sages demanded of their disciples and would not have been considered extreme by the standards of First Century Jewish society.

Another hardship a disciple could face was being away from his wife. Disciples were commonly single, but since marriage took place at a relatively early age (usually by eighteen according to Avot 5: 21 in the Mishnah) many disciples had a wife and children. For example, the mother-in-law of one of Jesus' disciples is mentioned in Luke 4: 38. If married, a man needed the permission of his wife to leave home for longer than thirty days to study with a sage (Mishnah, Ketubot 5: 6).

Like a Father
Despite the many hardships, there was nothing to compare with the exhilaration of following and learning from a great sage and being in the circle of his disciples. A special relationship developed between sage and disciple in which the sage became like a father. In fact, he was more than a father and was to be honoured above the disciple's own father, as this passage from the Mishnah indicates:

> When one is searching for the lost property both of his father and of his teacher, his teacher's loss takes precedence over that of his father since his father brought him only into the life of this world, whereas his teacher, who taught him wisdom [ie, Torah], has brought him into the life of the World to Come. But if his father is no less a scholar than his teacher, then his father's loss takes precedence.
>
> If his father and his teacher are in captivity, he must first ransom his teacher, and only afterwards his father – unless his father is himself a scholar and then he must first ransom his father. (Bava Metsi'a 2: 11)

If it seems shocking that anyone could ransom his teacher before his own father, it is only because we do not understand the tremendous love and respect that disciples, and the community at large, had for their sages.

Similarly, it may seem cruel that Jesus would not allow a prospective disciple to say goodbye to his family before setting out to follow him. However, it would have seemed quite reasonable and normal to Jesus' First Century contemporaries. It would have been perfectly clear to them what Jesus meant when he said, 'No one can be my disciple who does not hate his father and mother, wife and children, brothers and sisters.'

2 Was Jesus Recognised as a Rabbi?

By the time Jesus began his public ministry, he not only had received the thorough religious training typical of the average Jewish man of his day, he had probably spent years studying with one of the outstanding sages in Galilee. Jesus thus appeared on the scene as a respected teacher himself. He was recognised as such by his contemporaries, as many passages in the New Testament illustrate:

- And Jesus answered and said to him, 'Simon, I have something to say to you.' And he said, 'Rabbi, what is it?' (Lk 7: 40)
- A lawyer asked him a question to test him: 'Rabbi, what is the greatest commandment in the Torah?' (Mt 22: 35–36)
- And behold, a [rich] man came up to him and said, 'Rabbi, what good thing must I do to have eternal life?' (Mt 19: 16)
- And someone in the crowd said to him, 'Rabbi, order my brother to divide the inheritance with me.' (Lk 12: 13)
- And some of the Pharisees in the crowd said to him, 'Rabbi, rebuke your disciples.' (Lk 19: 39)
- Some of the Sadducees came up to him ... and they asked him, saying, 'Rabbi ...' (Lk 20: 27–28)

Note the diversity of those who addressed Jesus as 'rabbi': a lawyer, a rich man, Pharisees, Sadducees and ordinary people. Clearly, there was a wide range of Jesus' contemporaries who respected him as a teacher.

Origin of 'Rabbi'

The term רַבִּי (rabbi) is derived from the Hebrew word רַב (rav), which in biblical Hebrew meant 'much, many, numerous, great'. It was also sometimes used to refer to high government officials or army officers (eg, Jer 39: 3, 13).

In Jesus' day, *rav* was used to refer to the master of a slave or of a disciple. Thus rabbi literally meant 'my master' and was a term of respect used by slaves in addressing their owner and by disciples in addressing their teachers.

Although it was only after 70 CE that rabbi changed from being a form of address and became a formal title for a teacher, and thus cannot correctly be applied to Jesus, this term may be more helpful than any other in conveying a correct image of Jesus to the average Christian reader. Although slightly anachronistic, it suggests that Jesus was recognised as a teacher in his day and that he was famous enough to draw students to himself.

Travelling Rabbi

To understand the full significance of Jesus being addressed as 'rabbi,' one must know what a sage of the first century was and how he functioned in the Jewish society of that time.

Jewish teachers of First Century Israel lacked the sophisticated methods of mass communication we have today. Consequently, the sages of Jesus' day spent much of their time travelling throughout the country, much like the biblical prophets, to communicate their teachings and interpretations of scripture.

The biblical prophets travelled with bands of followers called 'sons of the prophets' (eg, 2 Kings 2: 3, 5, 7, 15). These were not their physical sons, but rather their disciples. The use of 'son' as a synonym for 'disciple' still persisted in Hebrew during the time of Jesus, as illustrated by this saying of Jesus, 'If I cast out demons by [the power of] Beelzebul, by [the power of] whom do your sons cast them out?' (Lk 11: 19).

Itinerant Rabbis

According to Shmuel Safrai, an itinerating sage was the norm rather than the exception. Hundreds of such teachers circulated in the land of Israel in the first century. These sages did not hesitate to travel to the smallest of villages or the most remote parts of the country. In some instances they would conduct their classes in someone's home, but often classes would be held in the village square or out under a tree.

From the Gospels we learn that Jesus likewise moved from place to place a great deal, often accompanied by crowds. Mark 6: 6, for example, records that Jesus, 'went around from village to village teaching.' He travelled considerably in Galilee, especially in the vicinity of the Sea of Galilee.

Much of Jesus' teaching was done indoors, in homes (Lk 10: 38–42), synagogues (Mt 4: 23), even in the Temple (Mt 21: 23; Lk 21: 37). But we also find Jesus, like a typical First Century sage, teaching outside in impromptu situations. There is a picturesque account in Luke 5: 3 of Jesus teaching from a boat. The feeding of the five thousand occurred in 'a lonely place' (Mt 14: 13; Mk 6: 32; Lk 9: 12), and the Sermon on the Mount was so named because it was delivered in a rural location.

Disciples

Although classes tended to be crowded, the sages were perfectly willing to teach as few as two or three students. The sages were sincerely interested in changing people's lives, in leading more and more people to 'take upon themselves the yoke of Torah,' a rabbinic expression for accepting God's reign in one's life. To accomplish this, they not only trained advanced students as disciples, but also taught the masses.

Jesus had an inner circle of twelve disciples who received special training. He also called others to follow him, including Levi, a tax collector. According to Luke 5: 28, when Levi was challenged by Jesus to follow him, he immediately 'left everything' to respond.

We read in Matthew 8: 19 of another man who was warned by Jesus of the price he would have to pay after he perhaps too quickly and easily blurted out, 'Rabbi, I will follow you wherever you go!' Two would-be disciples were rebuked by Jesus when they asked his permission to tend to important family responsibilities before answering his call (Lk 9: 59–62). Jesus also called a rich man, demanding that he divest himself of his wealth before becoming his disciple (Mk 10: 21).

The Gospels show that there were others who studied with Jesus for varying lengths of time. Mary was one such disciple. As Jesus taught in her home, Mary shirked her kitchen duties to learn at his feet. She had chosen the 'best portion,' Jesus said, referring to her desire to listen to his teaching (Lk 10: 42). Luke 19: 37 notes that near the end of Jesus' life there was a 'multitude' of his disciples who rejoiced and praised God when he rode into Jerusalem on a colt, and it is recorded in Acts 1: 15 that following Jesus' death and resurrection Peter spoke to 120 disciples who were gathered in Jerusalem awaiting the promised Holy Spirit.

Tradesmen

Rabbinic literature contains many prohibitions against charging for teaching the scriptures, such as the following:

1 'He who makes a profit from the words of Torah has brought about his own destruction' (Mishnah, Avot 4: 5).
2 'Do not charge for teaching Torah. Accept no remuneration for it. One should not receive payment for the words of Torah which the Holy One, Blessed be he, has given *gratis*. If you take money for teaching Torah, you cause the destruction of the whole world' (Derech Eretz Zuta 3: 3).

Because of such interdictions, almost all sages practised a trade. Some were scribes, others sandal makers, leather workers or bakers. Jesus himself, according to Mark 6: 3, was a craftsman, and Acts 18: 3 notes that Paul supported himself by making tents (or working leather).

Hospitality

While travelling, however, the First Century sage could not easily set up a school due to the shortness of his stay in any given location. Nor would it have been fair when visiting smaller communities to take work away from a local resident in the same profession. Also, work could not readily be found for the large number of disciples who often accompanied a sage. Therefore the travelling rabbi and his disciples were necessarily dependent upon the hospitality and generosity of the communities they visited.

A sage's stay in a community might last from a few days to weeks or months. Although sages would not accept payment for teaching

Torah, most would accept lodging, and usually food as well, for themselves and their students.

Jesus clearly felt that his disciples should be entirely supported by their hosts when out teaching. In one instance, he sent out disciples commanding them to take nothing with them, neither food nor money. 'The labourer,' he said, 'deserves his wages' (Lk 10: 7). Paul apparently referred to this statement of Jesus when he wrote, 'The Lord commanded that those who preach the gospel should receive their living from the gospel' (1 Cor 9: 14). From the context, it seems that Paul viewed the receiving of monetary compensation as the legitimate right of a teacher or preacher of the gospel.

At the Feet of a Rabbi
For the long-term disciple, learning from a sage meant considerable travelling. One literally had to follow a teacher to learn from him. There is a rabbinic saying which supports this picture of the rabbi in the land of Israel:

> *Yose ben Yoezer said, 'Let your home be a meeting place for the sages, and cover yourself with the dust of their feet, and drink in their words thirstily.' (Mishnah, Avot 1: 4)*

Yose ben Yoezer, living in the first half of the second century BCE, was one of the earliest of the sages mentioned in the Mishnah. In the context of his statement, 'a meeting place for the sages' should be understood to mean a place where the sages could hold classes, not a place where the sages themselves could assemble. Had the people not opened their homes to the sages, it would have been impossible for them to reach others with their message.

The story of Mary and Martha in Luke 10: 38–42 offers a good example of a family who heeded Yose ben Yoezer's injunction to be hospitable to sages and their disciples. Not only did they make their home available as a meeting place for the sage Jesus, but Mary is described as 'sitting at the feet' of the sage – 'drinking in his words thirstily,' as ben Yoezer expressed it.

Covered in Dust
Note the continuation of Yose ben Yoezer's statement: 'and cover

yourself with the dust of their feet.' A number of translators of the Mishnah have rendered this, 'and sit amidst the dust of their feet.' However Prof Shmuel Safrai has suggested a different interpretation, upon which our translation above is based.

To this day the unpaved roads of Israel are covered with a fine dust. As a result, when people walk along these roads they invariably raise a considerable cloud of dust. Any group of disciples following a sage would be covered with dust at the end of a journey, and if one wanted to travel and study with a sage one literally had to cover oneself with the dust of his feet.

Incidentally, it was the dusty roads of Israel which gave rise to the practice of footwashing as a sign of hospitality to visitors and as a means of practical hygiene in the home (cf. Lk 7: 44).

Raising Disciples

'Make many disciples' is one of the three earliest sayings recorded in the Mishnah (Avot 1: 1), and a sage would often select and train large numbers of disciples. There is a tradition recorded in the Babylonian Talmud, Sotah 49b, that the apostle Paul's teacher Gamaliel, for instance, had 1,000 disciples who studied Torah with him.

Although Jesus had only twelve permanent students, there must have been many others who learned from him for shorter periods of time. Luke 19: 37 notes that near the end of Jesus' life, a 'multitude' of his disciples accompanied him as he entered Jerusalem. One can gain an idea of the size of that 'multitude' from the number of Galilean disciples – 120 – who remained in Jerusalem after Jesus' crucifixion (Acts 1: 15).

Jesus' twelve disciples were his inner circle who spent years of intensive study and practical training with their master. Later, they themselves were sent out to make disciples and pass on Jesus' teachings.

3 Jesus and the Oral Torah

The sages were the creators of the Oral Torah. This literature, still unwritten in Jesus' day, is of great value in understanding Jesus' sayings. It is also a rich treasure of spiritual wisdom.

As its name implies, the Oral Torah was transmitted orally and, in the time of Jesus, was still unwritten. Only after Jewish life in the land of Israel had been nearly extinguished did the weakened community feel the necessity of recording this literature in writing.

The first attempt to commit the Oral Torah to writing is called the Mishnah. This work was compiled by Rabbi Yehudah ha-Nasi around 200 CE. The Mishnah records the sayings of sages who lived and taught during the previous several hundred years and, except for isolated words and sentences, is written entirely in Hebrew.

Sayings of the Fathers

The best-known of the Mishnah's sixty-three tractates is titled 'Avot' (Fathers) or 'Pirke Avot' (Chapters of the Fathers), but often referred to in English as the 'Sayings of the Fathers' or 'Ethics of the Fathers'. Avot is a collection of the cherished sayings of more than sixty illustrious sages, beginning with sayings of the earliest known sages (third century BCE). According to Avot, there had been an unbroken chain of transmitters of Oral Torah since Moses' time. In its first chapter Avot traces the Oral Torah's transmission from its reception at Mount Sinai until the days of Hillel (last quarter of the first century BCE):

> *Moses received the [Oral] Torah at Sinai and handed it down to Joshua, Joshua to the elders, the elders to the Prophets, and the Prophets to the men of the Great Synagogue ... Shim'on the Righteous [c 300 BCE] was one of the survivors of the Great Synagogue ... Antigonus of Socho received [the Oral Torah] from Shim'on the Righteous ... Yose ben Yoezer of Tseredah and Yose ben Yohanan of Jerusalem received [the Oral Torah] from him ... Yehoshua ben Perahyah and Mattai [Matthew] of Arbel received [the Oral Torah] from them ... Yehudah ben Tabbai and Shim'on ben Shetah received [the Oral Torah] from them ... Shemayah and Avtalyon received [the Oral Torah] from them ... Hillel and Shammai received [the Oral Torah] from them ....*

Although the subject matter of the Mishnah is primarily halachic (legal), Avot is devotional in nature, dealing almost wholly with moral behaviour. Only six chapters in length (the last of which is a later addition), this tractate has some of the closest parallels to the sayings of Jesus known from rabbinic literature. Avot is so popular that it has become a custom to study a chapter of it in the synagogue following the afternoon prayers each Saturday between Passover and the Jewish New Year (a five month period). Consequently, the entire tractate is included in nearly all editions of the Prayer Book, a distinction that not even the Book of Psalms can claim.

Apart from the Bible, the Prayer Book and the Passover Haggadah, Avot is probably better known to religious Jews any other book, and more commentaries have been written on Avot than on any other rabbinic work. Even less religiously learned Jews are familiar with the maxims contained in Avot.

Jesus and the Fathers

Many sayings found in Avot have their counterparts in Jesus' teaching:

Do his will as if it were your will that he may do your will as if it were his will. Conform your will to his will that he may conform the will of others to your will. (Avot 2: 4)

There is a striking similarity between this saying and the sayings of Jesus in Matthew 6: 10 ('Let your will be done in heaven and on earth') and 7: 21 ('Not everyone who says to me, "Lord, Lord," enters the kingdom of Heaven, but only the person who does the will of my father who is in heaven').

Note the similarity between the following saying and the Golden Rule (Mt 7: 12).

Rabbi Eliezer said: 'Let the honour of your fellowman be as dear to you as your own.' (Avot 2: 10)

The saying of Rabbi Yose is similar:

Let the possessions [mammon] of your fellowman be as dear to you as your own. (Avot 2: 12)

Spiritual Depth

A number of sayings in Avot, although not directly parallel to sayings of Jesus, strongly remind us of the spiritual depth found in Jesus' teaching:

Rabbi Ya'akov said, 'This world is like an entry hall before the world to come. Prepare yourself in the entry hall that you may enter into the banqueting hall.' (Avot 4: 16)

Yehudah ben Tema said, 'Be as strong as the leopard, swift as the eagle, fleet as the gazelle and brave as the lion to do the will of your father in heaven.' (Avot 5: 20)

Do not be like slaves who serve their master in order to receive a reward; rather, be like slaves who do not serve their master in order to receive a reward. (Avot 1: 3)

Any love that depends on some passing thing, when the thing disappears, the love vanishes too; but a love that does not depend on some passing thing will last forever. Which love was it that depended on some passing thing? – the love of Amnon and Tamar [2 Sam 13: 1ff.]. And which love was it that did not depend on some passing thing? – the love of David and Jonathan [2 Sam 1: 26]. (Avot 5: 16)

Some Christian scholars read rabbinic literature only when searching for parallels to New Testament passages. This approach is sometimes referred to derisively as parallelomania. Surely, however, the sayings of the sages are a treasure that should be read first of all for their own sake.

Written and Oral Torah

Torah has always been the focus of rabbinic teaching. Unfortunately the Hebrew word תּוֹרָה (torah) is usually translated in English simply as 'law', which has created the impression that it has to do only with commandments. This is not the case at all. The Torah was given by God as instructions for following the path he outlined. A better translation would be 'God's instructions'.

The Written Torah, תּוֹרָה שֶׁבִּכְתָב (torah shebik'tav), consists of the instruction God gave to Israel at Sinai contained in the five books of Moses – Genesis, Exodus, Leviticus, Numbers and Deuteronomy. Israel's sages believed that in addition to this written revelation, Moses received further instructions that were communicated orally. These added instructions were the beginning of the Oral Torah, פֶּה תּוֹרָה שֶׁבְּעַל (torah sheb'al peh).

Living Tradition

The Orthodox Jewish view of Jesus' day was that this Oral Torah had been handed down from generation to generation from the time it was initiated with Moses. Along with forty-two verbal commandments given to Moses at Sinai, the Oral Torah included the precepts and interpretations implied in the Written Torah. It also came to include the legal decisions of rabbinical courts and the oral traditions which teachers had received from their predecessors.

The Oral Torah was a living tradition used for continuous interpretation of the written code as changing circumstances demanded. A contemporary analogy is found in the body of legal precedent that develops as judges hand down rulings that interpret the laws enacted by legislators. Such judges, like the early sages, apply the written law as cases are brought before them, and thus create a tradition of interpretations and precedents which is no less authoritative than the laws themselves.

The 'tradition of the elders', besides claiming an authority and continuity equal to that of the Written Torah, also claimed to be its authentic living interpretation and essential complement. It occupied a place above the Written Torah in the same sense that a house must be above its foundation. Each, however, was dependent upon the other.

Transcribing the Oral Torah

Rabbi Yehudah ha-Nasi was the first to compile the Oral Torah in written form for public use. His work is known as the Mishnah, and was completed in about 200 CE. Once he broke with tradition, other collections of the Oral Torah were made which incorporated material not included in the Mishnah, notably the Gemara, which is a commentary on the Mishnah. In time, the Gemara and Mishnah were printed together and known collectively as the Talmud.

The Talmud exists in two versions: the Jerusalem Talmud, compiled in Israel, and the Babylonian Talmud, compiled by Jewish sages in Babylonia. Being the work of different schools of scholarship, the Gemara in each version differs considerably, but the Mishnah in both is that of Rabbi Yehudah ha-Nasi.

The Babylonian Talmud, the Gemara of which is written mostly in

Aramaic, was completed about 500 CE and is a gigantic sea of rabbinic learning consisting of 2,500,000 words filling 5,894 pages approximately 27 by 36 centimetres (10.5 by 14 inches) in size. The Jerusalem Talmud preceded the Babylonian version by about 100 years. Only 574 pages of it has survived. Its Gemara is written mostly in Hebrew. Today, the Babylonian Talmud is the focus of Jewish religious education, and when the word 'Talmud' appears alone it refers to the Babylonian version.

The Written Torah is not viewed as something separate from the Talmud, but rather as the foundation upon which the 'house' of the Talmud is built. Therefore, a thorough knowledge of Written Torah is a prerequisite of Talmudic study. As in the days of Jesus, every Orthodox Jewish child today grows up learning the Bible, and familiarity with the five books of Moses is considered an important first step in studying the Talmud.

Jesus' Observance of the Oral Torah

Contrary to what many Christians believe, Torah is not a matter of laws and commandments, but rather instructions from God to man for living a life of blessing and joy. In the Jewish view, Torah consists of two elements – one written (the five books of Moses given to Israel at Sinai) and one oral (additional revelation given to Moses at Sinai, precepts and interpretations deduced from the Written Torah, and the legal decisions of rabbinical courts).

Jesus apparently attached great importance to the Oral Torah (unwritten in his day), and it seems he considered it to be authoritative. When he admonished his disciples to 'do and observe everything they [the scribes and Pharisees] command you' (Mt 23: 3), he was referring to the Pharisees' oral traditions and interpretations of the Written Torah. The Written Torah itself could not have been in question, for it was accepted by all sects of Judaism, and Jesus himself said, 'Heaven and earth would sooner disappear than one יוֹד [yod, the smallest letter in the Hebrew alphabet] or even one קוֹץ [kots, thorn, the long, thorn-like decorative stroke that First Century scribes added to the yod] from the Torah' (Mt 5: 18).

Many rabbinic statements express similar ideas, such as, 'Should all the nations of the world unite to uproot one word of the Torah, they would be unable to do it' (Leviticus Rabbah 19: 2).

Evidence of Jesus' Observance

To what extent did Jesus observe the practices of the Oral Torah?
Jesus was never charged with breaking any part of it, and although
his disciples were occasionally accused of disobeying aspects of the
Oral Torah (Lk 6: 1–2), only one such accusation was made against
Jesus – that he broke the Sabbath by healing the sick (Lk 14: 1–4).
However, even his Sabbath healings were permitted by rabbinic
ruling, as Hebrew University professor and Jerusalem School scholar
Shmuel Safrai notes in 'Religion in Everyday Life'.[8]

It may seem that there is a shortage of hard evidence in the New
Testament concerning Jesus' religious observance, but one must
remember that the New Testament was written by Jews for Jewish
readers. The normal Jewish religious practices were so well known
and followed both by the writers and first readers of the New
Testament, that it would have been considered superfluous to discuss
them. Nonetheless, one is able to gather enough evidence from the
Gospels to conclude that Jesus observed the biblical commandments
as they were interpreted in the Oral Torah.

Blessings

One of the most basic examples of a rabbinic command that Jesus
obeyed is in the realm of blessings. The sole scriptural basis for the
many blessings that an observant Jew still says daily is Deuteronomy
8: 10, וְאָכַלְתָּ וְשָׂבָעְתָּ וּבֵרַכְתָּ אֶת יְהוָה אֱלֹהֶיךָ (ve'akal'ta ve'sa'va'ta u'vey'rak'ta
et adonai eloheka), 'When you have eaten your fill, thank the LORD
your God' (literally, 'And you will eat and you will be full and you
will bless the LORD your God'). The sages found justification in this
verse for saying a blessing before the meal as well as after, and on
many other occasions – indeed, on almost every occasion.

The general rule, as delineated in the Babylonian Talmud,
Berachot 35a, was כָּל דָּבָר שֶׁנֶּהֱנֶה טָעוּן בְּרָכָה (kol davar she'ne'ha'neh ta'un
be'rakah), (Anything that is enjoyed requires a blessing). If a man
built a house or bought something new he was to say, 'Blessed is he
who has brought us to this moment.' If one saw a place where great
miracles had occurred in Israel's history, one was to say, 'Blessed is he

who in this place performed miracles for our ancestors.' In response to a shooting star, lightning, a storm or an earthquake, one was to say, 'Blessed is he whose strength fills the universe,' and a mountain, hill, lake, river or desert were to prompt, 'Blessed is he who fashions the works of creation.'

There was a blessing to be said before publicly reading from the Torah, and another at the completion of the reading; a blessing after immersing oneself in a mikveh (ritual immersion bath); a blessing upon seeing a great scholar. There was even a blessing to be said when one urinated:

> Blessed is he who formed man in wisdom and created in him
> numerous orifices and cavities. It is revealed and known before the
> throne of your glory that if even one of them should be opened or if
> even one of them should be obstructed, it would be impossible to exist
> and stand before you.

One was obligated to bless God for calamity and misfortune as well as for prosperity and good fortune. For rain and for good news one says, 'Blessed is he who is good and who gives good.' For bad news one says, 'Blessed is he who is the faithful judge.'

Jesus' Use of Blessings

There is evidence that Jesus adhered to the rulings of the Oral Torah in his use of various blessings. In conformity with the sages' interpretation of Deuteronomy 8: 10, Jesus not only recited a blessing after meals, but also said the blessing before meals, בָּרוּךְ הַמּוֹצִיא לֶחֶם מִן הָאָרֶץ (baruk ha'motsi lehem min ha'arets, Blessed is he who brings bread out of the earth). It is recorded that at the last Passover meal that Jesus ate with his disciples in Jerusalem, Jesus 'took bread and blessed and broke and gave to his disciples' (Mt 26: 26).

Since in the Greek text there is no direct object following the verbs 'blessed', 'broke' and 'gave', English translators have felt obliged to supply the word 'it' after each of these, or at least after 'broke' and 'gave'. The English reader therefore receives the impression that Jesus not only divided and distributed the bread, but blessed it as well. This is simply a misunderstanding.

One can find examples in scripture of people blessing people. Isaac blessed Jacob (Gen 27: 27–29), for instance; and Jacob, in turn, blessed his twelve sons (Gen 49: 28 cf Rom 12: 14; 1 Pet 3: 9.) However, in the context of taking a loaf of bread before beginning a meal, the blessing can only be a blessing directed towards God.

Saying 'Grace'

Before dining with the two disciples from Emmaus, Jesus 'blessed, broke and gave,' as he did before he fed the five thousand with five loaves and two fish. (In Luke's account, but not in Mark's or Matthew's, the text reads 'blessed them,' but one important Greek manuscript reads 'blessed for them' in Luke 9: 16). Because of the recurring 'blessed, broke and gave the bread' in the Gospels, it is a common Christian misunderstanding that Jesus blessed the bread. Consequently, Christians customarily 'bless the food' before they eat a meal.

The blessing that was said in Jesus' time before one ate was praise and thanksgiving to God who so wondrously provides food for his children, to him who 'brings bread out of the earth'. One does not bless the food, nor does one even ask God to bless the food. One blesses God who provides the food.

Similarly, it is a misunderstanding to assume that Jesus multiplied the loaves and fish by blessing them. Jesus, as usual, simply blessed God before beginning the meal. The miracle was not in the blessing, for food did not multiply on other occasions when Jesus offered a blessing before breaking bread.

Better Understanding

This is a good example of how Christians' lack of knowledge of Jewish custom has led to misunderstanding an act of Jesus. In this case, it has led to the development of a Christian practice that, though perhaps not harmful in itself, has no foundation whatsoever in Jesus' own practice or teaching.

Luke made it clearer for his Greek-speaking readers when he described Paul's practice of 'saying grace'. A literal translation of Acts 27: 35 reads, 'And taking bread, he gave thanks to God before all, and breaking, he began to eat.'

Use of God's Name

The original understanding of the third commandment, 'You shall not take the name of the LORD your God in vain' (Exod 20: 7; Deut 5: 11), was that one must be careful to keep one's vow when swearing by God's name. However, the sages eventually came to interpret this commandment to mean not using the LORD's name lightly or frivolously. To avoid the risk of employing the Divine Name irreverently, the sages ruled that one should not utter it at all.

The tetragrammaton יהוה (YHVH) could be pronounced only in the Temple – in the daily priestly blessing and in the confession of the High Priest on the Day of Atonement. When reading or reciting scripture, one was not to pronounce the Unutterable Name, but rather, to substitute Adonai (LORD).

This avoidance of the tetragrammaton began very early. Although there was no hesitation about pronouncing the Sacred Name in daily life during the First Temple period, already by the third century BCE Adonai was being substituted for YHVH.

Other Substitutes

In time, the substitute Adonai itself came to have such a sacred aura that it was used only in scripture reading and prayer. When it was necessary to refer to God in everyday speech, other substitutes were sought; *ha-Makom* (the Place), *ha-Gavoah* (the High), *ha-Lashon* (the Tongue), *ha-Shem* (the Name), *Shamayim* (Heaven), and others. Even Elohim (God), a plural form that could refer to the God of Israel or to false gods, was avoided in conversation.

So serious was the prohibition against pronouncing YHVH, that the sages included among those who have no share in the World to Come 'he who pronounces the Divine Name as it is spelled' (Mishnah, Sanhedrin 10: 1; 7: 5).

Divine Euphemisms

Jesus often used euphemisms for God – his audiences would have been shocked had he not. The most common word for reference to God used by Jesus was Shamayim (Heaven). This euphemism occurs frequently throughout the Gospel of Matthew in the phrase 'Kingdom of Heaven,' the term Jesus used for his community of disciples.

In Mark and Luke we find 'Kingdom of God,' possibly because most of their Greek readers might not have understood the euphemism. The original, however, is Malchut Shamayim (Kingdom of Heaven): 'Kingdom of Heaven' is common in Hebrew literature of the period, while 'Kingdom of God' is not attested.

Jesus asked those in the Temple who questioned his authority, 'Was the baptism of John from Heaven [that is, from God] or from men?' (Mt 21: 25). Similarly, in the so-called Parable of the Prodigal Son, Jesus has the prodigal say to his father, 'I have sinned against Heaven' (Lk 15: 21).

One other euphemism for God's name used by Jesus is *ha-Gevurah* (the Power). When interrogated by the high priests, Jesus was asked to admit that he was the Messiah. His answer, recorded in Luke 22: 69 (cf Mt 26: 64; Mk 14: 62), is a classic example of rabbinic sophistication: 'From now on the Son of Man will be sitting on the right of the Power,' which hints at two messianic passages from scripture, Daniel 7: 13 and Psalm 110: 1.

Tithing

Tithing is a biblical commandment set forth in Leviticus 27: 30–33, Deuteronomy 14: 22–29 and Deuteronomy 26: 12–14. Jesus must have observed this commandment since the New Testament clearly states, 'Having been born under the Torah, he committed no sin' (Gal 4: 4; 1 Pet 2: 22; Heb 4: 15). However, did Jesus observe this commandment as it was interpreted in the Oral Torah?

The Gospels give the general impression that Jesus dutifully adhered to the practices of observant Jews of his day, and that his attitude toward these practices was guided by the interpretations of the sages as expressed in the Oral Torah. There is no specific reference in the New Testament to Jesus tithing, yet, as discussed below, Jesus did make a statement that indirectly witnesses to his observance of this commandment.

Light and Heavy Commandments

It is sometimes suggested that Jesus criticised the Pharisees for being so pedantic as to tithe even the spices and herbs in their gardens (Mt 23: 23). The Mishnah confirms that the Pharisees did in fact tithe on 'everything that is used for food, that is looked after and that grows from the soil' (Ma'asrot 1: 1), that is, the Pharisees extended the biblical commandment – to tithe on grain, wine and olive oil – to include other cultivated crops used as food such as figs, grapes, pomegranates, walnuts, cucumbers and garden herbs.

Jesus, however, did not pronounce woe upon the Pharisees for tithing mint, dill and cumin, but rather for keeping only such 'light' or less serious commandments while failing to keep the 'heavy' commandments. To infer from this statement that Jesus was against tithing is an error similar to the misunderstanding that money is the root of all evil. Actually, the New Testament states that 'the *love* of money is the root of all evil' (1 Tim 6: 10).

Moreover, it would be wrong to conclude that a majority of the Pharisees did not keep the 'heavy' commandments such as 'Do not murder' and 'Do not commit adultery.' Jesus, like most teachers, often used general statements for didactic purposes, just as an American might say, 'We Americans are materialistic.' It would be a mistake to conclude from this generalisation that all Americans without exception are materialistic.

Internal Criticism

Jesus' criticism of the Pharisees was 'in-house,' constructive criticism. There *was* hypocrisy among the Pharisees – it was not unique to them – but they were just as critical of this hypocrisy as was Jesus. Jesus endorsed the Pharisees' doctrine, stating in Matthew 23: 3, 'Do and observe what they [the Pharisees] command you.'

What is frequently overlooked is that while Jesus criticised the Pharisees for their hypocrisy, he went on to say that the 'lighter' commandments, such as tithing even on the herbs grown in one's home garden, are 'necessary to do'. Jesus' statement leaves no doubt about how he felt regarding tithing. Additionally, the statement leaves no doubt about how he felt regarding the observance of the commandments as they were interpreted by the sages.

The parable of the Pharisee and the Tax Collector (Lk 18: 9–14) should also be noted in this regard. Jesus does not criticise the Pharisee for tithing on everything he got, but rather for his self-righteous attitude.

Almsgiving

Like tithing, almsgiving, or giving to the poor, is a biblical commandment (Deut 15: 8; Lev 25: 35). In the section of the Sermon on the
Mount in which Jesus criticises the hypocrites who fasted and prayed
'to be seen by men,' he also criticises those who made a public display
of giving to the poor (Mt 6: 2). One must be careful not to view Jesus'
criticism of the exaggerated observance of almsgiving as a general
condemnation of this biblical practice.

Jesus commanded his disciples to do their praying, fasting and
giving to the poor 'in secret' (Mt 6: 4; 6: 18). Most sages of Jesus' day
would have condemned ostentatious giving to the poor just as
strongly. According to the Talmud, 'Greater than our master Moses is
he who gives to the poor in secret' (Bava Batra 9b).

Secret Chamber

In the time of Jesus there was a 'Secret Chamber' in the Temple
(Mishnah, Shekalim 5: 6). The pious could anonymously leave money
there, and the poor members of well-to-do families were secretly
given money from this source, avoiding embarrassment to them.
There was a similar 'Secret Chamber' in every town in Israel (Tosefta,
Shekalim 2: 16).

Jesus must have been a generous giver himself: he taught his
disciples that they should 'lay up treasures in heaven', that is, give
alms to the poor (Mt 6: 20). He also taught them that to be full of the
Holy Spirit they must have a 'good eye', that is, give generously to the
poor (Mt 6: 22).

'*When* you give alms,' Jesus said (Mt 6: 2), not '*If* you give alms'.
Jesus assumed that his disciples were almsgivers, and we may confi-
dently assume that Jesus was as well.

Tsitsiyot (Tassels)

The New Testament makes it clear that Jesus, like all observant Jews
of the first century, wore צִיצִיּוֹת (tsitsi'yot). These are the tassels that
were attached to the four corners of one's robe as commanded in
Numbers 15: 37–41 and Deuteronomy 22: 12.

Jesus' observance of this commandment is dramatically illustrated
by the story, found in Matthew 9, Mark 5 and Luke 8, of the woman

who suffered from a haemorrhage for twelve years. She was healed when she came up behind Jesus and touched what the King James Version of the Bible refers to as the 'hem of his garment':

> *And behold, a woman which was diseased with an issue of blood twelve years came behind him and touched the hem of his garment. For she said within herself, if I but touch his garment, I shall be whole. (Mt 9: 20–21, KJV)*

If this story originally existed in Hebrew, as I suppose, then it seems certain that it was not the hem, but one of the tassels of Jesus' garment that the woman touched.

The Greek word that the King James translators rendered 'hem' is κράσπεδον (kraspedon). This is the same word that is used in the Septuagint, the ancient Greek translation of the Hebrew Scriptures, to translate צִיצִית (tsitsit, the singular of tsitsi'yot). It is found three times in Numbers 15: 37–41, where the wearing of tassels is commanded.

In Hebrew, therefore, the story would have spoken of the woman touching the צִיצִית טַלִּיתוֹ (tsitsit talito), that is the tsitsit (tassel) of his טַלִּית (talit, mantle).

Reminders

Apparently, most human beings need to be reminded of God and the observance of his commandments, and the wearing of tassels might be compared to tying a string around one's finger. According to Numbers 15: 39, these tassels serve as a sign to help the wearers 'recall all the commandments of the LORD and observe them so that you do not follow the lustful desires of your heart and eyes'.

Long Tassels

There was no fixed maximum length for the tassels, as the two major rabbinical schools in the half century before Jesus agreed:

> *The elders of the School of Shammai and the School of Hillel gathered in the upper chambers of Jonathan ben Bathyra and reached the decision that there is no prescribed length for tassels. (Sifre Numbers 115, to 15: 38).*

However, it seems there were some who, in an attempt to observe this commandment more fully, wore very long tassels. Shmuel Safrai has noted the wealthy Jerusalem resident mentioned in the Talmud in Gittin 56a, who received his nickname, בֶּן צִיצִית הַכֶּסֶת (Ben Tsitsit Hakeset), because of his long tassels[9]. He was remembered as being so devout that his tassels literally trailed behind him on the ground.

Naturally, there were also imitators who wished to appear more pious than they really were by wearing longer than normal tassels. Jesus condemned those who pretended to be pious by wearing long tassels (Mt 23: 5).

Two Garments

Like his Mediterranean contemporaries, Jesus wore two garments, a חָלוּק (haluk, tunic) and a talit (mantle). The lower garment, the tunic, was a lighter robe, usually made of linen. The upper garment, the mantle, which was draped over the tunic, was a heavy garment, usually woven from wool.

The mantle was a rectangular piece of cloth. It was the equivalent of the Roman *pallium* or the Greek *himation*, which were rectangular, not the Roman *toga*, which was semi-circular.

The heavier outer garment was the norm for public occasions. It was considered somewhat immodest in Jewish society to go out in public attired only in the under-robe or tunic, even though it extended to just above the ankles. The tunic alone could be worn around the house (unless guests arrived), or when one engaged in physical labour where the over-robe would be too cumbersome.

Everyday Dress

Under the influence of what is called tallit by Jews of today, some translators have understood that the mantle was a shawl-like covering draped over the upper part of a man's body during prayer. For instance, in Matthew 23: 5, the New International Version translates, 'They make ... the tassels of their prayer shawls long.'

This is misleading since, in the time of Jesus, the tallit or mantle was part of everyday dress and not a religious article. It is true that out of modesty one would not pray publicly in one's tunic, but the tallit was not itself a holy garment.

This clarification of the double robes worn in Jesus' time helps us understand his statement recorded in Matthew 5: 40, 'If someone wants to sue you for your tunic [haluk], let him also have your mantle [talit].'

In the privacy of one's home, the tunic could be worn without the mantle, but it was embarrassing to go out in public dressed in it alone. However, if necessary, the mantle could serve as one's only garment. Therefore, the mantle, not the tunic, was indispensable.

If someone tries to confiscate your tunic in a dispute, Jesus said, you should, for the sake of peace, even offer him your mantle.

Tefillin

The Gospels attest to the fact that Jesus had tassels on the four corners of his outer robe (Mt 9: 20; 14: 36; Mk 6: 56; Lk 8: 44). Although there is no explicit evidence in the Gospels, we have reason to suggest that he may also have worn phylacteries.

The word 'phylactery' is derived from the Greek *phylakterion*, and literally means a protecting charm or amulet. 'Phylacteries' is an unfortunate translation, as there is little if any evidence to suggest that they were regarded as amulets in Jesus' day. The Hebrew word is תְּפִלִּין (tefillin, the plural of tefilah, prayer).

Tefillin refers to either of the two small leather capsules containing tiny slips of parchment inscribed with the scriptural passages recorded in Exodus 13: 1–10, 11–16; Deuteronomy 6: 4–9; 11: 13–21.

Today, as in Jesus' day, the tefillin are strapped on the forehead and the arm. The arm tefillin consists of one compartment containing a parchment on which all four passages are written, while the head tefillin is divided into four compartments, each of which contains a parchment with one of the four passages written on it.

'As a Sign'

Wearing tefillin was an observance of the commandment to bind God's commandments 'as a sign on your arm and as a symbol on your forehead' (Deut 6: 4–9; 11: 18–21).

It might be argued that this is metaphorical language and simply means 'remember well'. For example, the same expression is used in Exodus 13: 16. There, following the commandment to sacrifice every

firstborn male animal and redeem every firstborn male child, the
Israelites are informed that 'it will be a sign on your arm and a
symbol on your forehead'. Obviously, this observance could not be
attached to one's body. However, by at least the second century BCE,
the biblical instructions to bind the commandments of the LORD to
one's arm and forehead were interpreted literally (Shmuel Safrai, *The
Jewish People in the First Century*, 2: 799).

Contemporaries of Jesus would have viewed the wearing of tefillin
as a biblical commandment, but in fact, the literal understanding of
this commandment is an interpretation, part of the Oral Torah. The
word תְּפִלִּין (tefillin) itself is not even found in the Bible.

Worn Every Day

In the first century, tefillin were part of ordinary everyday Jewish
dress. Putting on tefillin only during morning weekday prayers, as
normally practised today by observant Jews, is a later custom. In
Jesus' time, they were worn throughout the day, and removed only
when working or when entering a place that was ritually unclean
(Safrai, 2: 798).

Fragments of tefillin dating from the time of Jesus have been found
in the Judean Desert in caves near the Dead Sea. The most dramatic
find, head tefillin dating from the first half of the first century CE –
with three of the four parchment slips still folded and securely tied in
their original compartments.[10]

The head tefillin, including the strap, was quite modest and would
not have drawn attention to itself. The capsule found at Qumran is
rectangular and extremely small, approximately one-half by three-
fourths of an inch (13 by 20 mm). A small postage stamp would easily
cover it.

Hypocrisy Criticised

In Matthew 23: 5 Jesus criticised those who 'make their phylacteries wide.' As with his criticism of the public display of almsgiving
(Mt 6: 2), one must not view Jesus' words as a general condemnation of wearing tefillin. Rather, Jesus was condemning religious
hypocrisy that led to enlarging tefillin as a demonstration of
'higher spirituality'.

Just as Jesus faulted the ostentatious wearing of tsitsiyot (tassels), which he himself wore, he probably was also wearing tefillin while criticising those who wore them hypocritically. Had he not worn tefillin, it is unlikely that his criticism would have been directed only at the excesses. Criticising the *way* they were worn implies Jesus' acceptance of the practice and the sages' literal interpretation of this biblical command.

Jesus, a Contributor and Transmitter of Oral Torah
There are many literary parallels between the teaching of Jesus and the teaching of the sages of his day. A word of caution: the fact that one can find parallels between the sayings of Jesus and the sayings of the sages does not necessarily mean that they borrowed directly from each other. There was probably a general pool of motifs, words and expressions from which the ancient teachers of Israel chose.

Rabbinic Parallels to Jesus' Teaching
Common motifs and phraseology in parallel rabbinic literary contexts throw light on Jesus' sayings and *vice versa*. Take, for instance, the following saying of Jesus:

> The [work of] harvesting is great and the workers are few. Ask the owner of the harvest to bring [more] workers for his harvest. (Mt 9: 37–38).

Jesus' saying is echoed by a saying of Rabbi Tarfon (born c 50–55 CE):

> The day is short and the work is great, but the workers are lazy; however, the wages are high since the owner is in a hurry. (Mishnah, Avot 2: 15).

Note that while 'short' never appears in Jesus' saying, 'harvest' appears three times. In Hebrew the two words have the same root. The word 'harvest' is not mentioned in the rabbinic saying, although it is probably implied; 'work' is its replacement. The rabbinic saying speaks of the 'master of the house' (ie owner), while Jesus refers to 'master of the harvest' (ie owner of the field being harvested). Both terms refer to God.

'Workers' are mentioned in both sayings, as is 'great' or 'much,' which appears once in Jesus' saying and twice in the rabbinic passage. In Avot it is the 'work' and the 'pay' that are 'much'. In Jesus' saying it is the 'harvesting'. In each saying difficulty is caused by 'the workers': Jesus says they are too 'few', while in Avot they are too 'lazy'.

There is a basic similarity between the two sayings: both teach spiritual truths by analogy to an owner who needs labourers to complete his work quickly. Jesus' saying deals with harvesting, and although the rabbinic saying does not use the word 'harvest', its reference to the owner's urgency may suggest a harvest scene.

Each of the above sayings is more understandable when compared with the other. The rabbinic saying in Avot contributes to Jesus' saying the added dimensions of the urgency of the task and the shortness of the time.

Jesus' efforts were directed toward bringing more and more people under God's reign – or, in the rabbinic parlance he often used, getting them into the 'Kingdom of Heaven.' That is what he is referring to in this saying. Although he uses different words, Jesus stresses the same point as the rabbinic saying: the work of the kingdom of Heaven is all-important but difficult, and God is interested in the urgent completion of the work.

A Measure of Humility

Jesus said, 'With the measure you measure, it will be measured to you' (Mt 7: 2; Lk 6: 38), a saying that was used by the sages to teach the moral principle that the way we treat others will be the way God treats us. The fuller context of Jesus' saying is:

> Judge not, that you be not judged. For with the judgment you judge you will be judged, and with the measure [literally, measuring vessel] you [use to] measure, it will be measured to you. Why do you see the splinter in your brother's eye, but do not notice the log in your own eye? (Mt 7: 1–3).

In other words, the standard of justice we use will be the same standard used by God in meting out reward and punishment to us. The context in which the almost identical rabbinic version of this saying appears provides further insight into the saying's meaning:

> With the measure that a man uses to measure, they measure to him ...

*Samson went after [the desire of] his eyes, therefore the Philistines put
out his eyes ... Absalom gloried in his hair, therefore he was hanged by
his hair... (Mishnah, Sotah 1: 7–8).*

An exhaustive list of the similarities between rabbinic literature and
the Synoptic Gospels would fill a book of its own, but the sampling
presented here should provide some idea of the rabbinic quality of
Jesus' teaching. From these and many other examples, it seems clear
that Jesus, like the other sages of his day, not only helped to preserve
the sayings that had been transmitted to him by his teachers, but also
contributed to the tradition he had inherited by making innovations
of his own.

General Pool of Motifs
The existence of parallels does not necessarily mean in each case that the
sages and Jesus borrowed directly from each other. There was a general
pool of literary motifs, stock stories, phrases and words from which the
ancient teachers of Israel chose. Although a saying was transmitted in
the name of a sage who lived several generations after Jesus, the sage
may have independently preserved a rabbinic tradition that predates
Jesus, perhaps the very same tradition upon which Jesus drew.

Rabbinic Teachings
According to Luke 14: 11, Jesus said, 'Whoever exalts himself will be
humbled, and he who humbles himself will be exalted'. Rabbinic literature preserves very similar statements in at least two places.

Hillel, who lived a generation before Jesus, used to say, 'My
humiliation is my exaltation and my exaltation is my humiliation'
(Leviticus Rabbah 1: 5 [ed Margulies, p 17]). Hillel's disciples and the
disciples of his disciples, referred to collectively as 'the house of
Hillel' (bet hilel), were noted for their humility:

*For three years there was a dispute between the house of Shammai and
the house of Hillel, the former asserting, 'The halachah [rabbinic legal
ruling] is in accordance with our opinion', and the latter contending,
'The halachah is in agreement with our views'. Then a bat kol
[heavenly voice] issued this decree, '[The words of] both are the words
of the living God, but the halachah is in agreement with the rulings of*

*the house of Hillel.' Since, however, both are the words of the living
God, what was it that entitled the house of Hillel to have the halachah
fixed in agreement with their rulings? – Because they were gracious
and modest, they studied their own rulings and those of the house of
Shammai, and were even so humble as to mention the rulings of the
house of Shammai before theirs ... This teaches you that whoever
humbles himself, the Holy One, blessed be he, raises him up, but
whoever exalts himself, the Holy One, blessed be he, humbles him
(Babylonian Talmud Eruvin 13b) .*

Preceding Jesus' exhortation to humility in Luke 14 are these instructions:

*When you are invited by someone to a wedding feast, do not sit down
in the place of honour, for a person more distinguished than you may
have been invited. In that case, the person who invited you both might
come and say to you, 'Give this man your place.' Then, humiliated,
you would have to take the lowest place. But when you are invited, go
and take the lowest place, so that when your host comes he will say to
you, 'Friend, move up higher.' Then you will be honoured in the
presence of all your fellow guests. (Lk 14: 8–10).*

Significantly, Hillel's words in Leviticus Rabbah about the importance
of humility are also preceded by instructions concerning where to
seat oneself:

*Rabbi Yehoshua of Sikhnin in the name of Rabbi Levi expounded the
verse, '[Do not exalt yourself in the king's presence, and do not claim a
place among great men;] it is better for him to say to you, 'Come up
here,' than for him to humiliate you before a nobleman' [Prov 25: 7].
Rabbi Akiva taught in the name of Rabbi Shim'on ben Azzai: 'Move
two or three places lower and there sit down. Move down so that you
will be told, "Move up", rather than move up and be told, "Move
down". It is better for you to be told, "Move up, move up" than for you
to be told, "Move down, move down"'. (Leviticus Rabbah 1: 5 [ed
Margulies, pp 16–17]).*

The Lord's Prayer

The prayer that Jesus taught his disciples (Mt 6: 9–13; Lk 11: 2–4) is viewed by Christians as a model prayer. It is even sometimes suggested that since the Lord's Prayer be can easily prayed in about half a minute, prayers should be kept to that length. A little Jewish background provides an important perspective on the Lord's Prayer and removes the notion that all prayers should be short.

Central Prayer

The central prayer in Jewish life and liturgy is known by a number of names: Shemoneh Esreh (Eighteen), since it originally consisted of eighteen benedictions; Amidah (Standing), because it is said standing; or simply Tefilah (Prayer), the prayer *par excellence*. It is very ancient, its final version dating from around 90–100 CE when a nineteenth benediction was added.

The prayer is composed of three opening benedictions of praise which include, 'We will hallow your name in the world as it is hallowed in the highest heavens'; thirteen petitions including petitions for wisdom, healing, forgiveness, deliverance from want and affliction, and for the sending of the Messiah, 'the branch of David'; and three concluding benedictions which include thanksgiving to the 'rock of our lives and shield of our salvation' whose 'miracles are daily with us', whose 'wonders and benefits occur evening, morning and noon', and whose 'mercies and kindnesses never cease'. A person who is fluent in Hebrew can pray this prayer in about five minutes.

Every Jew is religiously obligated to pray the Eighteen Benedictions daily. Rabbi Gamaliel said: 'One must say the Eighteen every day' (Mishnah, Berachot 4: 3). In times of emergency, however, this obligation is fulfilled by praying a shortened form of the Eighteen:

> *Rabbi Yehoshua says, 'If one is travelling in a dangerous place, he says a short prayer, namely, "O LORD, save your people the remnant of Israel. In every time of crisis may their needs not be lost sight of by you. Blessed are you, O LORD, who answers prayer."' (Mishnah, Berachot 4: 4).*

Abbreviated Prayers for Emergencies

The Babylonian Talmud, (Berachot 29b) explains that 'a dangerous place' is 'a place infested with wild animals or bands of robbers' and provides additional examples of abbreviated prayers:

Rabbi Eliezer [a younger contemporary of Jesus] says: 'May your will be done in heaven above, grant peace of mind to those who fear you [on earth] below, and do what seems best to you. Blessed are you, O LORD, who answers prayer.'

Note the phrases 'your will be done' and 'in heaven above ... [on earth] below' as in the Lord's Prayer. Also note the parallel between 'grant peace of mind' in the prayer Eliezer taught and 'deliver us from evil' in the Lord's Prayer.

Rabbi Yehoshua says: 'Hear the supplication of your people Israel and quickly fulfil their request. Blessed are you, O LORD, who answers prayer.'

Rabbi Eleazar son of Rabbi Zadok says: 'Hear the cry of your people Israel and quickly fulfil their request. Blessed are you, O LORD, who answers prayer.'

Other sages say: 'The needs of your people Israel are many but they do not know how to ask for their needs. May it be your will, O LORD our God, to sustain each and every one and to supply each person what is needed. Blessed are you, O LORD, who answers prayer.'

The petitions for God's provision for livelihood and his supply of what is needed are strongly reminiscent of the request for 'daily bread' in the Lord's Prayer.

The sages taught their disciples abbreviated versions of the Eighteen Benedictions such as those above, and it seems likely that Jesus similarly gave his disciples a prayer for occasions when there was not time to say the full form of the prayer. Far from being proof that customarily one should pray very brief prayers, the Lord's Prayer points us to the Eighteen. It can be assumed that in normal times Jesus and his disciples prayed daily the much longer Eighteen.

Parables

Rabbinic parallels enhance our understanding of the sayings of Jesus, and *vice versa*. For instance, Jesus' parable about those who hear and do his words and those who hear and do not do his words, are more understandable when compared with their rabbinic parallels.

Jesus was not the only ancient sage to teach with parables. Nor was he the only sage to speak of 'two kinds of foundations,' the theme that good deeds are necessary along with knowledge. Many sages expressed this theme straightforwardly. Hanina ben Dosa, who taught around the middle of the first century CE, said, 'He who has more deeds than knowledge, his knowledge endures; but he who has more knowledge than deeds, his knowledge does not endure' (Mishnah, Avot 3: 10).

Stones and Mud

The same idea is presented more elaborately in the following parable attributed to Elisha ben Avuyah (c 120 CE):

> A person in whom there are good deeds and who has studied Torah extensively, what is he like? A man who builds first of stones and then afterwards of mud bricks. Even if a large quantity of water were to collect beside the stones, it would not destroy them. But a person in whom there are not good deeds, though he has studied Torah, what is he like? A man who builds first of mud bricks and then afterwards of stones. Even if only a little water collects, it immediately undermines them. *(Avot de-Rabbi Natan 24, Version A).*

Cup and Base

The simile of a cup is used to convey the same theme in another parable ascribed to Elisha ben Avuyah:

> A person in whom there are good deeds and who has studied Torah extensively, what is he like? A cup that has a base. But a person in whom there are not good deeds and who has studied Torah extensively, what is he like? A cup that has no base. When the cup is filled it falls on its side and all its contents are spilled. *(Avot de-Rabbi Natan 24, Version A).*

Branches and Roots

Anyone familiar with Jesus' parables will see how similar they are to those quoted above. Let us look at two more parables, one by Eleazar ben Azariah, who was active at the end of the first century CE, and one by Jesus:

*A person whose knowledge is greater than his deeds, what is he
like? A tree whose branches are many but whose roots are few: the
wind comes and uproots and overturns it. But a person whose
deeds are greater than his knowledge, what is he like? A tree whose
branches are few but whose roots are many: even if all the winds
were to come and blow against it, they could not move it.
(Mishnah, Avot 3: 18).*

Bedrock and Sand

Jesus' parable in Matthew 7: 24–27 presents this theme in much the
same way:

*A person who hears these words of mine and does them, what is he
like? A wise man who builds his house on bedrock: the rain comes
down, the rivers overflow, the winds blow and buffet the house, yet it
does not collapse because it has its foundations on bedrock. But a
person who hears these words of mine and does not do them, what is
he like? A foolish man who builds his house on sand: the rain comes
down, the rivers overflow, the winds blow and buffet the house, and it
collapses in total ruin.*

King Parables

The 'king parable' is a special form of parable often used by Jesus.
The Reform rabbi and scholar Ignaz Ziegler collected 937 'king
parables' from rabbinic literature and published them in 1903[11]. The
following is an example, preceded by a typical dialogue between a
teacher and his disciples:

*Rabbi Eliezer [last half of first century CE] said: 'Repent one day
before your death.'*
*His disciples asked him: 'But can a man know on what day he will
die?'*
*He said: 'All the more reason for him to repent today; perhaps he will
die tomorrow. It follows that a man should repent every day. Thus in
his wisdom Solomon said: "Let your garments always be white, and
never let your head be without ointment" [Ecclesiastes 9: 8].'*
*Rabban Yohanan ben Zakkai [Eliezer's teacher] told a parable: 'It is
like a king who invited his servants to a feast and did not set the time
for them to arrive. The wise adorned themselves and waited by the*

door of the palace, for they said: "Is there anything lacking in a palace?" The foolish continued working, for they said: "Is a feast ever given without preparation?"'

'Suddenly the king summoned his servants. The wise entered the palace adorned as they were, and the foolish entered in their work clothes.

'The king rejoiced when he saw the wise, but was angry when he saw the foolish, and said: "Those who adorned themselves for the feast shall sit down and eat and drink; but those who did not adorn themselves for the feast shall stand and look on."' (Babylonian Talmud, Shabbat 153a)

Note the striking similarity between the above parable and the parable of the Ten Virgins in Matthew 25: 1–12:

It will be like ten virgins who took their lamps and went to meet the bridegroom. Five of them were foolish, and five were wise, for when the foolish took their lamps, they took no oil with them, but the wise took flasks of oil with their lamps. As the bridegroom was delayed, they all slumbered and slept.

But at midnight there was a cry, 'The bridegroom is coming! Come out to meet him.'

Then all those virgins got up and trimmed their lamps. And the foolish said to the wise, 'Give us some of your oil, for our lamps are going out.'

But the wise replied, 'There may not be enough for both us and you. Go to those who sell oil and buy for yourselves.'

While they went to buy, the bridegroom came, and those who were ready went in with him to the marriage feast, and the door was shut.

Afterward, the other virgins also came, and said, 'Lord, lord, open the door to us.'

But he replied, 'I tell you, I do not know you.'

Below is another example of a 'king parable' from rabbinic literature, followed by its interpretation:

The matter may be compared to a king who arranged a banquet and invited guests to it. The king issued a decree that stated, 'Each guest must bring something on which to recline.'

Some brought carpets, others brought mattresses or pads or cushions or stools, while still others brought logs or stones.

The king observed what they had done, and said, 'Let each man sit on what he brought.'

Those who had to sit on wood or stone murmured against the king. They said, 'Is it respectful for the king that we, his guests, should be seated on wood and stone?'

When the king heard this, he said to them, 'It is not enough that you have disgraced with your wood and stone the palace that was erected for me at great cost, but you dare to invent a complaint against me! The lack of respect paid to you is the result of your own actions.'

Similarly, in the hereafter the wicked will be sentenced to Gehenna and will murmur against the Holy One, blessed be he: 'We sought his salvation. How could such a fate befall us?'

He will answer them, 'When you were on earth did you not quarrel and slander and do evil? Were you not responsible for strife and violence? That is why it is written, "All you that kindle a fire, that encircle yourselves with firebrands, walk in the flame of your fire and among the brands that you have kindled" [Isa 50: 11]. If you say, "This we have from your hand," it is not so. You have brought it upon yourselves, and therefore, "you will lie down in torment" [Isa 50: 11].' (Ecclesiastes Rabbah 3: 9).

Note the similarities between the above parable and Jesus' parable about a banquet:

A certain man once prepared a large banquet and invited many guests. When it was time for the banquet, he sent his slave to say to those who had been invited, 'Come, for everything is now ready.'

One after another they began to make excuses. The first said, 'I have just bought a field, and I must go and see it. I beg of you, have me excused.'

Another said, 'I have just bought five yoke of oxen, and I am on my way to try them out. I beg of you, have me excused.'

Still another said, 'I have just got married, and therefore I cannot come.'

The slave came back and reported this to his master. Then the house-holder in anger ordered his slave, 'Go out quickly into the streets and

*alleys of the town and bring in the poor, the crippled, the blind and
the lame.'*
*'Master,' the slave said, 'what you ordered has been done, and there is
still room.'*
*Then the master ordered his slave, 'Go out to the roads and hedges
and force people to come, so that my house will be full. I tell you, not
one of those men who were invited will taste my banquet.' (Lk
14: 16–24).*

Like the rabbinic parable, Jesus' parable mentions the preparation of a
banquet and guests being invited. In the Matthean version of the
parable (Mt 22: 2–14), there is an interesting addition:

*When the king came in to see the guests, he saw there a man who had
no wedding garment. And he said to him, 'Friend, how did you get in
here without a wedding garment?' And he was speechless. Then the
king said to the servants, 'Tie him hand and foot, and throw him into
the outer darkness, where there is weeping and gnashing of teeth.' For
many are invited, but few are chosen. (Mt 22: 11–14).*

Here, as in the rabbinic parable, the king observes that some of the
guests have disgraced him. He therefore has them punished. In both
the rabbinic passage and Matthew's version of Jesus' parable, the dis-
respectful guests represent the wicked and their punishment
symbolises eternal damnation.

In the rabbinic passage, note the response of the wicked to their
sentence, 'We sought his salvation. How could such a fate befall us?'
This strongly reminds us of the evildoers who on the day of judgment
protest to Jesus at the unfairness of their sentence: 'On that day many
will say to me, "Lord, lord, didn't we prophesy in your name, cast out
demons in your name, and in your name perform many miracles?"
And then will I declare to them, "I never knew you. Away from me,
you evildoers!"' (Mt 7: 22–23).

A similar protest is made by the unrighteous Gentiles at their
judgment:

*Then he [the Son of Man] will say to those on his left, 'Depart from
me, you accursed, into the eternal fire prepared for the devil and his
angels. For I was hungry and you gave me no food, I was thirsty and*

you gave me no drink, I was a stranger and you did not entertain me,
I needed clothes and you did not clothe me, sick and in prison and you
did not come to visit me.'
They will answer and say, 'Lord, when did we see you hungry or
thirsty or a stranger or needing clothes or sick or in prison, and did
not help you?'
He will answer them and say, 'I say to you, whatever you did not do
for one of these little brothers of mine, you did not do for me.'
And these will go away to eternal punishment, but the righteous to
eternal life. (Mt 25: 41–46).

Jesus' Use of Rabbinic Principles of Interpretation

Throughout the history of Judaism, the Torah has been investigated
and analysed by means of various rules of interpretation. These
hermeneutic (interpretative) principles are simply statements of
deductive reasoning.

The sage Hillel, a contemporary of Herod the Great, compiled a
list of seven such rules. We will focus upon the first in the list, kal
va'ho'mer (simple and complex). This is a logical deduction that can
be drawn from a simple truth and applied to a less obvious situation,
or from something known applied to something unknown. For
example, 'Silence becomes a scholar; how much more a fool' (Tosefta,
Pesahim 9: 2). Notice the key phrase, 'how much more', which
appears in most examples of rabbinic simple-to-complex reasoning.

In the Mishnah

The Mishnah preserves a halachah, or rabbinic legal ruling, inferred
from Deuteronomy 23: 3 and 23: 7 by means of this principle:

No Ammonite or Moabite may be admitted into the congregation of
the LORD, and this is a permanent prohibition. Ammonite and ·
Moabite women, however, may be admitted immediately [after con-
version]. Egyptians and Edomites are prohibited only until the third
generation, regardless of whether they be males or females.
Rabbi Shim'on said, 'This is deduced by the kal va'ho'mer principle.
If, where Scripture permanently prohibited the males, it permitted the
females immediately, how much more should the females be permitted
immediately where scripture prohibited the males only until the third

generation?' (Yevamot 8: 3).

Non-Legal Contexts

Two further examples from the Mishnah illustrate this type of reasoning in non-legal contexts:

If, speaking of a 'light' commandment, which deals with something that is worth only an issar, the Torah says, 'in order that you may prosper and have long life,' how much more for 'heavier' commandments in the Torah? (Hullin 12: 5).

Once again the phrase 'how much more' signals the use of simple-to-complex reasoning, used here to urge the observance of all the commandments, whether they are major or relatively insignificant. The specific commandment referred to, found in Deuteronomy 22: 6–7, commands that a mother bird be released when caught with her young. In Mishnaic times, a bird was valued at one issar, about one twenty-fourth of a day's wage.

In the following passage, simple-to-complex reasoning is used to teach something about the nature of God:

Rabbi Meir said, 'While the man is in agony, what does the Tongue [a euphemism for God] say? 'My head is hurting! My arm is hurting!' If the scripture has thus spoken – 'I agonise over the blood of the wicked' – how much more over the blood of the righteous that is shed?' (Sanhedrin 6: 5).

This Mishnah passage refers to Deuteronomy 21: 22–23, which speaks of a criminal who is being put to death. Rabbi Meir expounds the Hebrew words ki'le'lat e'lo'him as 'a painful thing of God', rather than 'a curse of God', and the inference therefore is that when even a criminal is enduring pain, God says, 'I am in pain.'

In Jesus' Teachings

The use of simple-to-complex reasoning is proportionately as frequent in the teaching of Jesus as it is in the teaching of other sages. The Mishnah is approximately six times the size of the Gospels, and it has exactly six times as many occurrences of this hermeneutic principle: eighteen in the Mishnah to three in the teachings of Jesus.

The key phrase, 'If ... how much more,' generally appears in rabbinic simple-to-complex reasoning. We find this phrase at the heart of the following teaching in which Jesus speaks of God's great care for his children:

Which of you would give his son a stone if he asked for bread, or a snake if he asked for a fish? If you, then, who are bad, know how to give good gifts to your children, how much more will your Father in Heaven give good gifts to those who ask him. (Mt 7: 9–11).

There is another passage in which Jesus employs simple-to-complex logic to prove God's reliable care for his children. Worrying about the concerns of everyday life, Jesus warns, is distrust of God and an affront to a heavenly father who is unfailing in providing for his children:

Look at how the wild flowers grow. They don't toil or spin. I tell you, even Solomon in all his splendour was not dressed like one of these. If God thus clothes grass in the fields, which is here today and tomorrow is used to stoke an oven, how much more can he be expected to clothe you, O men of little faith. (Mt 6: 28–30).

Master of the House

A third example of Jesus' use of simple-to-complex reasoning comes from Matthew 10: 24–25, and is so Hebraic that in translating it from Greek to Hebrew, the syntax need not be altered except in the case of one word. A literal English translation of the Greek will help illustrate how non-Greek are these words of Jesus:

Not is a pupil above the teacher, and not a slave above the master of him. [It is] enough for the pupil that he be like the teacher of him, and the slave like the master of him. If the ba'al ha'ba'yit ba'al ze'vul they have called, how much more the sons of the house of his.

The references to ba'al ha'ba'yit and ba'al ze'vul create a Hebrew word-play, in this case a play on the word ba'al. (ba'al ha'ba'yit master of the house, householder) is a term often used by sages to refer to God; ba'al ze'vul ('master of splendour', a title for Baal; Beelzebul) refers to Satan. In idiomatic English the passage would be expressed as follows:

A pupil is no better than his teacher, nor a slave better than his master. What is good enough for the teacher is good enough for the pupil, and a slave should not expect to receive better treatment than his master. If the householder has been called 'Satan,' it is only natural that the members of his household will be called the same.

The Green Tree

There is a fourth passage in which Jesus uses simple-to-complex reasoning, although the key phrase 'how much more' does not actually appear in it:

Daughters of Jerusalem, do not weep for me. Weep for yourselves and for your children. For a time is coming when the cry will be, 'How fortunate are the women who are childless, the wombs that have never borne and the breasts that have never nursed!' Then they will call to the mountains, 'Cover us!' and to the hills, 'Fall on us!' If this is done to the 'Green Tree,' what will happen to the 'dry trees'? (Lk 23: 28–31).

Not only does Jesus make use of the rabbinic 'simple-to-complex' principle of interpretation in this passage, he also uses the rabbinic teaching technique of scripture allusion. The expression 'Cover us, fall on us!' is from Hosea 10: 8, and points toward the events of Jerusalem's destruction. The 'Green Tree,' taken from Ezekiel 20: 47, similarly hints at the impending catastrophe, but beyond that at Jesus' role as Messiah.

The people who heard Jesus say these words as he was on his way to be crucified certainly understood that his oblique reference to himself as the 'Green Tree' was a bold messianic claim. It was also a warning, for Jesus was telling the people, 'If this terrible thing can happen to me, *how much more* to you.'

As in the preceding example, Jesus contrasts himself to others: if he is called 'Satan,' his disciples will certainly be called 'Satan'; if he is crucified, those who are weeping for him can only look forward to the same fate, or worse.

It is worth noting that another sage made a similar statement some 150 years prior to Jesus, while also on his way to be crucified. Yose ben Yoezer, one of the earliest sages known in rabbinic literature, was not only a great scholar but was referred to as the 'most pious in the priesthood' (Mishnah, Hagigah 2: 7). The statement he made while carrying his cross to the place of execution is structurally identical to that of Jesus, and it explicitly contains the key words of the kal va·ḤO·mer formula:

If it is thus for those who do his will, how much more for those who anger him. (Midrash Psalms 11: 7)

4 Conclusion

From the Gospel accounts, Jesus clearly appears as a typical First Century sage. He was addressed 'Rabbi' by his contemporaries, suggesting that he was recognised as a teacher. He travelled from place to place; he depended upon the hospitality of the people; he taught outdoors, in homes, in villages, in synagogues and in the Temple; he had disciples who followed him as he travelled. This is the very image of a Jewish sage in the land of Israel at that time.

Perhaps the most convincing proof that Jesus was a rabbinic sage was his style of teaching, for he used the same methods of scripture interpretation and instruction as the other sages of his day. A simple example of this is Jesus' use of parables to convey his teachings. Parables such as Jesus used were extremely prevalent among the teachers of First Century Israel and over 4,000 of them have survived in rabbinic literature.

The rabbis were the creators of the Oral Torah, and it appears that Jesus was also engaged in this monumental task. Many of his sayings are closely parallel to those we find in rabbinic literature, especially to those in its non-legal portions (eg, the Mishnah tractate Avot). Moreover, Jesus apparently considered the Oral Torah, as it existed in his day, to be authoritative – he taught his disciples to 'do and observe everything they [the scribes and Pharisees] command you' (Mt 23: 3). Jesus himself seems to have observed the rulings of the Oral Torah: he said a blessing before meals; he used euphemisms such as 'Heaven' to refer to God.

New archaeological discoveries and recent research have revolutionised our understanding of Jesus. The church, conservative by nature, has not yet adequately incorporated this knowledge into its teaching and preaching. The few examples provided in this article demonstrate how far we Christians still have to go in recovering the full meaning of Jesus' teaching. Paradoxically, many Christians are not even willing, for theological reasons, to use rabbinic literature in rounding out their picture of the life and times of Jesus. After all, they say, didn't Jesus speak against the Pharisees?

Let us hope that as we approach the next millennium, we will redouble our efforts to learn more about Jesus. May we not ignore him as a teacher within First Century Jewish society.

Notes

1   *The Jewish Cultural Nature of Galilee in the First Century*, Immanuel 24/25 [1990], 147–186.

2   For a full discussion see **Martin Hengel**, *The Zealot*, T&T Clark, Edinburgh.

3   *Against Apion* 1: 60, Loeb ed.

4   **Shmuel Safrai**, *Education and the Study of the Torah, The Jewish People in the First Century* 2: 953.

5   cf. Babylonian Talmud, Shabbat 30a.

6   *Education and the Study of the Torah, The Jewish People in the First Century* 2: 953.

7   *Education and the Study of the Torah, The Jewish People in the First Century* 2: 954.

8   *Religion in Everyday Life, The Jewish People in the First Century*, 2: 805.

9   *Religion in Everyday Life, The Jewish People in the First Century*, 2: 798, note 3.

10 Published by Israeli archaeologist Yigael Yadin in *Tefillin from Qumran*, Israel Exploration Society, 1969.

11 In his *Die Koenigsgleichnisse des Midrasch* (The King Parables in the Midrash), Breslau, Poland.

Jesus – The Fullness of Tanakh

by Dwight Pryor

Once when Jesus was praying in private and his disciples were with him, he asked them, 'Who do the crowds say I am?' And they replied, 'Some say you are Yohanan (John), the Baptiser. Others say you are Eliyahu (Elijah). And still others, that one of the prophets of long ago has come back to life.' 'But what about you?' he asked. 'Who do you say I am?' (Luke 9: 18-20)

'Who do the crowds say I am?' Jesus asked his disciples. With all the research going on today in the quest for the 'real' Jesus, perhaps we should rephrase the question, 'Who do the *scholars* say I am?' What diverse and varied responses we would get! The answers would range from the sublime and the philosophical, to the silly and the absurd. Consider a few examples of the current speculation, both scholarly and sensational, about the 'historical Jesus'.

Some hold to the view that Jesus was a sage, a philosopher perhaps of the Stoic school, who went about teaching the virtue of self- control and, like Socrates, came to a tragic end. Others see him as a social activist who sided with the poor against a vile and corrupt establishment, both political and religious, which conspired to crucify this popular rebel. This view, as you might imagine, has gained currency among some third-world theologians. Many see Jesus as a kind of apocalyptic sectarian who, convinced that the end of the age was imminent, believed that offering himself up as a sacrifice would be the catalyst for precipitating God's judgment at the end of the age and inaugurating the Kingdom. Was this not, after all, the urgent prophetic message proclaimed by John the Baptiser? Had not John warned that, 'The axe is already laid to the root, so you had better repent! The day of the Lord is at hand, and depending on your response, it will be either a Pentecost or a holocaust!'

One view of growing popularity today is that the real Jesus was a psychic mystic or enlightened master. This 'New Age' Jesus lived here in the Land until the age of twelve (when we see him discoursing with the sages at the Temple); then during his so-called 'lost years' he journeyed to the Far East in search of mystic enlightenment. There he studied with the gurus and avatars of India and learned the 'secret knowledge of the kingdom of God'. At the age of thirty he returned to Israel to share with the more advanced disciples of his inner circle the 'hidden' knowledge about meditation – to focus on the 'single eye' so as to be filled with light – so they, too, might come to the realisation that one's true self really is God. Jesus taught that the 'Christ consciousness' that came upon him at his baptism in the Jordan by John (the reincarnation of Elijah!), could also be theirs through esoteric knowledge and mystic technique. The 'religious' people of the day (ie, those legalistic Jews) knew nothing about true spirituality, and therefore, they found a way to silence Jesus for promoting such blasphemy.

Some views get even more bizarre. Consider the current political propaganda that the real Jesus was a Palestinian. Chairman Arafat and the Palestinians are the true descendants of the first Christians according to this revision of history, which many in the press seem to take seriously. Jesus really was a Palestinian from the Galilee who spoke Arabic, not Hebrew, and was persecuted by the 'Judeans' – in the very same way that Jews even today oppress Palestinians. Challenging Jewish hegemony, as Jesus learnt, is to come to an untimely end! Another political agenda perhaps lies behind the view claiming that Jesus was homosexual, a gentle and loving man who eschewed marriage because he preferred the company of other men (especially John, the disciple 'whom he loved'). Some are even proposing that Jesus was a gay magician, who went about with his companions performing the 'signs and wonders' of magic to astonish the masses. His greatest feat, it should be noted, was making his apparently deceased body vanish from a sealed and guarded tomb!

So who was Jesus, really? Was he a Hellenised sage, a mystic psychic, a social activist or a befuddled apocalyptic sectarian? Was he a Stoic philosopher, a Mediterranean peasant or an oppressed Palestinian? Or was he a gay activist with a disposition toward prestidigitation (sleight of hand)? My response to these proposals must be negative.

Surely, if we have learnt anything from the work of Dr Lindsey and other esteemed members of the *Jerusalem School*, it is the following foundational truth. To accurately analyse and fully appreciate the life and teachings of Jesus of Nazareth, we must place him squarely within the *Jewish* milieu of the first century, not the western world of the nineteenth and twentieth centuries. In other words, to do Jesus justice we must employ Hebraic categories of thought and rabbinic ways of interacting with the Hebrew scriptures. The sacred Hebrew text and the fertile theological world of the sages are invaluable tools for our inquiry. They permit us to look at our inspired Gospel accounts with fresh perspective, renewed clarity, and deeper understanding.

If, then, we were to paint a portrait of Jesus in Hebraic hues and rabbinic tones, what would be the image? I propose to summarise and offer a 'synopsis' – of the *Jerusalem School's* view of the man, Jesus of Nazareth, in six categories:

1   His mission
2   His method
3   His message
4   His call
5   His command, and
6   His commission.

Jesus operated under the 'great commission' of his day. He went about, making disciples. For centuries, especially from the time of Ezra and the restoration of the Land, the people and the Temple, the motto and motive of every Jewish sage was *'Ha'amidu talmidim harbeh.'* 'Raise up many disciples' (*Avot 1: 1*). If one's mission was to bring life to others – and 'life' was indeed the greatest Jewish value of all – then one's highest priority was to make them disciples or students of God's word, for the word gives life. Teach them to hear and to do the word of the Lord. If obedience is the offering most esteemed by God, then study which leads to obedience must be a high form of worship. This was the world of Jesus, and he was, in many ways, typical of this world. As an itinerant rabbi-type figure, or respected teacher, he would travel from place to place, always with the *mission* of making disciples. 'Follow me!' (literally, 'walk after me') was the auspicious invitation to become his disciple, to learn of him and to come into a knowledge of the truth that would set you free.

Secondly, Jesus' *method* of teaching was typically rabbinic and his language of instruction usually Hebrew. Jesus was multi-lingual (like most Israelis today). He spoke Aramaic and Greek, as circumstances dictated, but the preferred language of religious discourse was the revived Hebrew tongue. His teaching manner was thoroughly sage-like, in the best of Jewish tradition. He routinely employed rabbinic modes of biblical exposition. The extensive use of parables, the subtleties of rabbinic argumentation, like *kal v'homer, gezera shava*, etc, – all these were used by the master teacher, Jesus. His most characteristic technique was the use of *remez*. He would refer to or hint at passages from the Hebrew Bible, sometimes just with the slightest verbal allusion or other times by bold and prophetic actions. Jesus' mission, therefore, was to raise up many disciples. His method, to expound upon the word of God, utilising well-known rabbinic techniques of instruction, especially *remez*.

Thirdly, the *message* that Jesus consistently proclaimed was the good news of the Kingdom – that the time of the Kingdom of Heaven/God (*malkhut ha-shamayim*) was 'at hand'. This 'announcement' meant that God's redemptive and supernatural rule was presently active in the person of the King or Messiah, and gave abundant evidence of itself in his words and deeds. Jesus proclaimed the Kingdom in his preaching; he explained the Kingdom in his teaching, and he acclaimed the Kingdom by his signs, wonders and miracles.

Fourthly, to all who had hearts to repent, Jesus invited them to turn around and follow him, to become part of the 'Kingdom of Heaven' movement by submitting to his authority, obeying his teachings, and doing the will of his Father in heaven. The *call* of Rabbi Jesus, therefore, was consistently one of *teshuva* – of repentance. This meant turning from sin, self-centredness, and selfishness, and walking after Jesus in the paths of righteousness and the ways of life, as illuminated so brilliantly in his own life and words.

Fifthly, Jesus' *command* to his followers – the toughest command-ment of all – was to love, even as he had loved. This is the 'Great Commandment', the 'Mega Mitzva'. Unlike Jesus, we Christians have failed to understand that the aim of the Torah ultimately is love. That is why God commands it (for example, in the Shema – Deuteronomy 6: 4-5). He teaches us *how* to love, because the goal of his teaching or Torah *is* love. It is not surprising, then, that the Torah-incarnate Jesus renewed that commandment when he said to his disciples, 'This is my command: Love each other' (John 15: 17).

Finally, Jesus' call was to repentance; his command, to love one another. His *commission*, to those who would follow him, was to carry on his mission – in other words to imitate him in raising up many disciples. 'Therefore, in *your* going, make disciples ... teaching them to obey everything I have commanded you' (Matthew 28: 19-20). The New Testament is a book *about* disciple-making, authored *by* disciples, and written *for* disciples. It reflects the Jewish world and world-view of the most remarkable Jew of all, Jesus of Nazareth.

This is the 'historical Jesus' I find to be the most fruitful for us to study, to obey, and to follow. He came as God's Messiah, to reveal God's will, to explain God's wisdom, and to show us how to walk in God's ways. One who did follow him was a fisherman named Peter (*Petros*). And when Jesus posed the question, Peter was ready with a bold reply.

> 'But what about you?' he asked. 'Who do you say I am?' Peter answered, 'The Christ of God'. (Luke 9: 20)

Peter's pronouncement, 'You are the Christ, the Messiah of God', Dr Lindsey notes, has some linguistic parallels, even in the Dead Sea Scrolls. He suggests that this auspicious statement in Hebrew might be reconstructed as, 'Attah Meshiach-El.' The construct form of 'Meshiach-El' ('Messiah-God') emphasised the supernatural or divine character of Jesus' identity. To say, 'You are the Messiah of God' was to say, 'You are the Divine Messiah' or, 'You are God-Messiah!' Jesus was pleased with this bold, revelatory declaration.

This memorable confession of the apostle Peter occurred at Caesarea Philippi. That is where the Jordan ('descender') river issues out of springs at the base of the Golan mountains and begins its journey, some seventy miles downward, traversing the length of the land of Israel, and emptying into the Dead Sea. From this place of revelation, Jesus now takes his disciples on an ascent, to a high place of transfiguration. He takes them up, probably to the highest peak in Israel, Mt Hermon.

> He took Peter, John and James with him and went up onto a mountain to pray. As he was praying, the appearance of his face changed, and his clothes became as bright as a flash of lightning. Two men, Moshe (Moses) and Eliyahu (Elijah), appeared in glorious splendour, talking with Jesus. They spoke about his departure, which he was about to bring to fulfilment at Jerusalem... While he (Peter) was speaking, a cloud appeared and enveloped them, and they were afraid as they entered the cloud. (Luke 9: 28-31, 34)

If you read this text with a Hebraic mindset, immediately you would connect it with the story of the giving of the Torah at Sinai – another high mountain, on which a 'cloud' also descended and enveloped the mountain and Moses upon it. The 'cloud', of course, represents the very dwelling, the very presence, the *shekhinah* of God Almighty, coming with revelation. Similarly, the Cloud of Glory enveloped Jesus and his inner circle of disciples.

> A voice came from the cloud, saying, 'This is my Son, whom I have chosen; listen to him.' When the voice had spoken, they found that Jesus was alone. (Luke 9: 35-36)

Rabbinic literature abundantly attests to the phenomenon known as a *Bat Kol*, a voice from heaven that gives decisive revelation. I want to draw your attention to what the heavenly voice said, for I believe it is extraordinarily revelatory. Remember, earlier Jesus asked an important question, 'Who do the crowds say I am?' Then he turns to Peter, 'Who do *you* say I am?' We also asked, 'Who do the *scholars* say Jesus is?' Now, I suggest to you that what we have here is *God's* answer to the question! 'Almighty God, who do *You* say Jesus is?' He answers from his Cloud of Glory with a voice that solemnly declares, 'This is my Son, my chosen; you must listen to him!' I have come to cherish this answer because there is more to it than first meets the eye. There is a subtlety and sophistication to this divine declaration that bears profoundly on the identity of Jesus.

First, let us note that we see Jesus standing in the midst of Moses and Elijah – in the context, in other words, of the law and the prophets – and they are discoursing with him. We must always remember that Jesus stands right in the middle of the stream of revelation that began at Sinai. He stands in continuity with – never in opposition to – the law and the prophets. He is informed by the Torah and inspired by the prophets, and his ministry functions wholly within that great tradition.

A lovely midrash suggests that when the God of heaven and earth came down to Mt Sinai, he wrapped himself in a *tallit* (a prayer shawl), he sat down upon a rock and began to teach his disciple, Moshe, the words of life. In other words, Adonai is the Great Teacher. 'Torah' after all is 'teaching' – it is guidance, instruction, or direction – that aims you to hit the mark of the fullness of life our Father in heaven intends for his children. And so Yahweh is a Teacher. It is no surprise, therefore, that when his son, Yeshua, came, he came as a rabbi. He came in the spirit and in the instruction of the Lord, doing only that which he saw his Father doing. Nor should you be surprised to learn that when God answers the question, 'Who do you say I am?' he does so by citing scripture! He answers with a voice from heaven, hinting in a typically rabbinic way at three Messianic passages from the Hebrew Bible!

'The Book' was at the core of Jewish life, and so it was for Jesus himself. The holy scriptures defined his identity, directed his ministry, and served as the source for his teachings. Indeed, we cannot understand Jesus apart from biblical categories, like the 'Suffering Servant', the 'Son of Man', 'God's Anointed' etc. The Jewish people in the first century highly esteemed and eagerly studied the sacred scriptures. One of the great accomplishments of the Pharisees was to encourage and enliven people to lay hold of God's word. They viewed the Torah as 'a tree of life to those who embrace her; and those who lay hold of her will be blessed' (Proverbs 3: 18). Because of their familiarity with the Hebrew Bible, the people could grasp a biblical reference when alluded to by a rabbi like Jesus, or when uttered by a voice from heaven. Unfortunately, we Christians of the twentieth century do not possess that sophistication or familiarity with the Hebrew Bible – which is why we fail to notice the full significance of the *Bat Kol* recorded in Luke 9: 35. We do not recognise that God cites three texts in rabbinic fashion, that tell us much about the identity, mission, and purpose of Jesus.

First, the voice declares, 'This is my Son' – a reference or *remez* to the Psalms:

> *I will proclaim the decree of the LORD: He said to me, 'You are my son. Today I have become your father. Ask of me, and I will make the nations your inheritance, the ends of the earth your possession.' (Psalm 2: 7-8)*

Note that the *Bat Kol* uses some of the same language here as when the heavenly voice spoke at the inauguration of Jesus' ministry, at his baptism by John (cf Matthew 3: 17). Then, Jesus was at the lowest point, physically, in the land of Israel – in the wilderness of Judea, near the Dead Sea. Now, he is probably at the highest point of the land of Israel, Mt Hermon, and approaching the end of his ministry (for from here he will go up to Jerusalem to be handed over as a sacrificial offering). Again God, the loving Father of Jesus, speaks words of affirmation and approval over his son by alluding to Psalm 2, 'You are my son. Today I have begotten you' or, 'become your father'. Actually, an alternative reading of this text is noted by Dr Lindsey, 'Today I am presenting you.' The image is that of a midwife taking delivery of a child, and then holding him up for all to see. God in effect is saying, 'Here, this is my son. Look at him, isn't he impressive!'

So the first *remez* God makes from the Cloud of Glory is to Psalm 2: 7 – a text that is highly Messianic. (See, for example, the reference to God's 'Anointed One' in verse 2.) The sages of Israel recognised this as a text that speaks of the Messiah being God's son in some special sense. The Messiah will have such intimacy with God that – even like the twelve-year old Jesus at the Temple – he will speak of God as more than just *Avinu* ('our Father'); he will address him in the first person, as *Avi* ('my Father'). On this mountain of transfiguration, God proudly presents Jesus as his son and declares him to be the promised Messiah, indeed *'Meshiach-El'*! Jesus comes in the fullness of Psalm 2, verse 7.

Secondly, the voice declares, 'This is my chosen one' – a reference or *remez* to Isaiah:

Here is my servant, whom I uphold, my chosen one in whom I delight;
I will put my Spirit on him and he will bring justice to the nations.
(Isaiah 42: 1)

In answer to the question, 'Who do you say I am?' God again alludes to a clearly Messianic text, this time from the prophet Isaiah. Again he shows fatherly approval of his son, whom he lifts up or upholds as his 'servant' and delights in as his 'chosen one.' Jesus is the one chosen to be God's anointed, bringing justice-salvation-righteousness to all peoples. Jesus himself referred to this Messianic identity when, from the *bimah* (platform) of the Nazareth synagogue, he read from the Isaiah scroll, 'The Spirit of the Sovereign LORD is on me, because the LORD has anointed me to preach good news ... ' (Isaiah 61: 1). The voice from Heaven now affirms that Jesus comes in the fullness of Isaiah 42, verse 1.

Thirdly, the voice declares, 'Listen to him' – a reference or *remez* to Deuteronomy:

The LORD your God will raise up for you a prophet like me from
among your own brothers. You must listen to him. (Deuteronomy
18: 15)

For his last word, God draws upon a Messianic text from the Torah, the most authoritative portion of all the Hebrew scriptures. The sequence is not coincidental. There is a progression of increasing authority in the Bat Kol's witness, from the Psalms, to the Prophets, and now to the Law. We might compare it to a lawyer arguing a case, who marshals his evidence in such a way as to make stronger and stronger impressions on the jury, saving the most impressive piece of evidence until last. To the ears of the apostles, indeed to any first-century Jewish ear well versed in scripture, 'listen to him' would be an unmistakable *remez* to the Torah and the prophetic promise of Moses recorded in Deuteronomy 18. 'Prophet' is a code word for Messiah. Moses in effect was the first Messiah of Israel, but he declares that another is yet to come, the last Messiah, if you will. And when God raises him up, we must 'listen to him'. The command 'to listen' or 'to hear' in Hebrew has the connotation of 'to obey'. It is 'listening obedience'. When Jesus came, though many heard him, not all 'listened' to him. They did not understand that he came in the fullness of Deuteronomy 18, verse 15.

We know what the crowds have said about Jesus. We have heard Peter's confession about Jesus as 'Messiah-God'. And now we have God's answer to the question, 'Who do you say that I am?' From his Cloud of Glory the Lord God declares in a heavenly voice that Jesus is the fulfilment of Psalm 2 – his 'Son', the Messiah to whom the Father will give the nations as an inheritance. He is the fulfilment of Isaiah 42 – the 'Chosen One' anointed as Messiah to bring justice and salvation to the nations. And he is the fulfilment of Deuteronomy 18 – the Prophet or Messiah like unto Moses, to whom we must 'listen'. What we have here is not only profound but utterly delightful. Yahweh the Teacher cites three texts from the Hebrew Bible, in the rabbinic manner of *remez*, to point to the identity of his son, Yeshua, the Rabbi from Nazareth. Out of the mouth of three witnesses God has established the identity of Jesus and expressed his approval and affection for him!

But there is even more to this story... From this high place of revelation and transfiguration, atop Mt Hermon, Jesus begins a literal and spiritual descent. Halvar Ronning teaches that Jesus departs this high mountain and begins a journey downward. He descends the Golan, down through the Galilee, following the Jordan river and traversing the Jordan valley, until finally he reaches the lowest point in the land of Israel, at Jericho, near the Dead Sea. But he must go yet even lower. He must go up to Jerusalem, to be handed over for crucifixion, and go all the way down to the depths of death and the grave. There is good news, however. In the kingdom of God, the way down is really the way up! So on the third day, in fulfilment of scripture, and after taking his Sabbath rest in the tomb, Jesus arose from the grave and was seen of many witnesses!

We pick up the story in the 24th chapter of Luke's gospel. The resurrected Lord encounters some disciples on the road to Emmaus. We can see here Jesus' sense of humour in this incident. Jesus poses a question to the discouraged disciples:

'What are you discussing together as you walk along?' They stood still, their faces downcast. And one of them named Cleopas, asked him, 'Are you the only one living in Jerusalem who doesn't know the things that have happened there in these days?' 'What things?' he asked. (Luke 24: 17-19)

Along with the humour, note the typically Jewish character of this exchange. Jesus asks a question – Cleopas answers with a question – Jesus responds with another question. This 'question-for-question' style of communication is typical of Jewish tradition. We see it, for instance, when the precocious child Jesus is 'sitting among the teachers' at the Temple Mount (Luke 2). There is a popular Jewish saying, 'Rabbi, why do you always answer a question with a question?' The rabbi smiled and said, 'Why not?'

He said to them, 'How foolish you are, and how slow of heart to believe all that the prophets have spoken. Did not the Messiah have to suffer these things and then enter his glory?' And beginning with Moses and all the Prophets, he explained to them what was said in all the scriptures concerning himself... Then he opened their minds so they could understand the scriptures. (Luke 24: 25-27, 45)

What are the scriptures referred to here? Let us be very clear about this. They are the scriptures of the Hebrew Bible. The New Testament was not written yet. These are the same holy scriptures, the apostle Paul reminded Timothy, that made him 'wise unto salvation in Messiah Jesus' and are 'God-breathed' (2 Timothy 3: 15-16). From the Jewish point of view of the first century, to say that the scriptures were 'inspired' was not to engage in the 'inspiration' debates of many evangelicals in the twentieth century. For Paul the issue was not 'verbal inerrancy', 'plenary inerrancy', or 'infallibility' – all these typically Hellenistic categories of analysis that occupy our western minds. No, when Paul says scriptures are 'God-breathed' or 'inspired' he is suggesting that they are 'in-Spirited'! In other words, they are life-giving. For where the spirit is, there is life. God breathed upon the dust – that glorified mud ball called Adam – and he became a living being. He came alive because God's breath was in him. God promises that same breath for the 'dry bones' of Ezekiel's vision, 'I will put my spirit in you and you will live ...' (Ezekiel 37: 14). When Paul writes, therefore, that the scriptures are inspired he emphasises that they are living and life-giving. To those who lay hold of them, they are a tree of life. They bear much fruit, and that is why they are profitable for 'teaching, rebuking, correcting, and training in righteousness' – so that the man or woman of God 'may be thoroughly equipped for every good work' (2 Timothy 3: 17):

> He said to them, 'This is what I told you while I was still with you "Everything must be fulfilled that is written about me in the Law of Moses, the Prophets and the Psalms."' (Luke 24: 44)

Scripture, for Jesus, for Paul, and for the emergent church, was the Hebrew Bible. These words of Jesus in Luke 24 reflect the prevailing tripartite division of those scriptures in the first century – a tradition that continues to this day in Jewish Bibles – of the Law, the Prophets, and the Psalms. The sequence of books within these three sections differs somewhat from our Christian Old Testament. The first section is the *Torah*, or the five books of Moses that we refer to (regrettably) as The Law. The second section is the *Nevi'im*, or The Prophets (*Nevi'im* is the plural of *navi*, prophet). The third group is the *Ketuvim*, or The Writings (*Ketuvim* relates to the verb *katav*, to write). Within The Writings, the first and pre-eminent book is the Psalms. The canon as such was not formally established in Jesus' day; and this third division especially was in a fluid state. But the Psalms were treasured and popular, and were often joined to the inspired Prophets and the Law. The Torah, of course, was venerated as fully authoritative and the final arbiter of faith and practice in Jewish tradition.

Luke tells us that the resurrected Jesus enlightened his discouraged disciples by reminding them that the entirety of the holy scriptures – Torah, Nevi'im, and Ketuvim – spoke of him and came to their fullness in him. He opened their eyes to see all that was written about him in the life-giving scriptures of the Hebrew Bible. Indeed, to use later New Testament language, he is the goal or end toward which all the Hebrew scriptures point. He is the *telos* of the Torah. He is the *Logos* made flesh. He is the fullness of Torah, Nevi'im and Ketuvim.

If you take the first letter of each of the three sections of Jewish scripture – ie, 'T' for Torah, 'N' for Nevi'im, and 'K' for Ketuvim – you can combine them into an acronym *TaNaKh.* This term, 'Tanakh,' is used in Judaism as the title for what we Christians call the Old Testament. Jesus said that the scriptures of the Tanakh speak of him. And indeed they do, even in ways you may not have noticed. Did it occur to you, for instance, that God alludes to these three portions of the Hebrew Bible – Torah, Nevi'im, and Ketuvim, in reverse sequence – in the Bat Kol of Luke 9: 35? First the voice from heaven declares, 'You are my son' – a reference to the writings (Psalm 2: 7). Then come the words, 'My chosen one' – a reference to the prophets (Isaiah 42: 1). And finally, the exhortation, 'Listen to him' – a reference to the last book of the Torah (Deuteronomy 18: 15). How clever of God! If anybody should know the scriptures, he should!

We have, therefore, God's answer to the question, 'Who do you say that I am?' In a striking and sophisticated way, he reveals the fuller dimensions of the identity of the Jewish Messiah, Jesus, by alluding to three biblical texts, one from each of the three-fold divisions of the Jewish scriptures. Jesus comes in the fullness, not just of Psalm 2, Isaiah 42, and Deuteronomy 18, but of the entirety of biblical revelation that they represent – Torah, Nevi'im and Ketuvim. In other words, Jesus of Nazareth, when transfigured in the radiance of God's glory, is seen as nothing less than the fullness of Tanakh!

Jesus, Son of Man, and the Temple

Brad Young

Jesus' favourite title for himself is 'Son of Man'.[1] This quintessential designation Jesus used for himself is most certainly connected to Daniel 7: 13-14.

The Son of Man in Daniel

I saw in the night visions, and behold, with the clouds of heaven there came one like a Son of Man, and he came to the Ancient of Days and was presented before him. And to him was given dominion and glory and kingdom, that all peoples, nations and languages should serve him; his dominion is an everlasting dominion, which shall not pass away, and his kingdom one that shall not be destroyed.

The apocalyptic description of the Son of Man in Daniel is only one example of a widely circulated perspective on the coming of the Messiah. Ancient Judaism was characterised by diversity of thought. Different views of the future actions of the coming Messiah were developed. A royal Messiah, priestly Messiah, military leader, or one like unto Moses, were just a few perspectives on the future deliverance. The prophecy of Daniel, however, describing the judgment of the nations and the ultimate triumph of God's plan, captured the apocalyptic imagination and won wide support. The rabbinic literature also reveals a strong vision of redemption which was connected to Daniel 7: 13. For example:

Rabbi Alexandri said: Rabbi Joshua ben Levi discussed a contradiction. It is written, 'in its time [will the Messiah come], while it is also written, 'I [the Lord] will hasten it!' If they are worthy, I will hasten it, if not, [he will come] at the due time. Rabbi Alexandri said: Rabbi Joshua opposed two verses: it is written, 'And behold, one like the Son of Man came with the clouds of heaven' while [elsewhere] it is written, '[behold, your king comes unto you ...] lowly, and riding upon a donkey!' If they are worthy, [he will come] 'with the clouds of heaven;' if not, 'lowly and riding upon a donkey'.[2]

Here the rich diversity of Jewish thought emerges from a discussion of the contradictory nature of various texts which could describe the redemptive plan. The coming of the Messiah could happen in more than one way. The preparedness of the people, or lack thereof, may influence the way in which the Messiah will appear. If the people are worthy, he will come as a judge, as described in Daniel 7: 13. If not, humbly he will ride into Jerusalem on a donkey. Fascinatingly, both streams of thought find echoes in the Gospels. Jesus rode into Jerusalem on a donkey fulfilling Zechariah 9: 9 (Luke 19: 28-40 and parallels). He also taught about his Second Coming as the Son of Man when he would appear with the clouds of glory (Matthew 25: 31-46; Luke 21: 27).

The Dead Sea Scrolls, moreover, describe the priestly role of Melchizedek as one who in the future will atone for the sins of the people. Like the Son of Man in Daniel 7: 13, he will execute judgment and bring about the deliverance of the people. The eminent Jewish scholar, David Flusser, has linked this Dead Sea Scroll passage with the theme of the Son of Man in ancient Jewish expectations concerning the coming of the Messiah:

Then the 'D[ay of Atone]ment shall follow af[ter] the [te]nth [ju]bilee period, when he shall atone for all the Sons of [Light] and the peopl[e who are pre]destined to Mel[chi]zedek ...

Therefore Melchizedek will thoroughly prosecute the veng[ea]nce required by Go[d's] statu[te]s. [Also, he will deliver all captives from the power of B]elial, and from the power of all [the spirits predestined to him.] ...

This vi[sitation] is the Day of [Salvation] that He has decreed [through Isai]ah the prophet [concerning all the captives,] inasmuch as scripture sa[ys, 'How] beautiful upon the mountains are the fee[t of] the messeng[er] who [an]nounces peace, who brings [good] news, [who announces salvat]ion, who [sa]ys to Zion, 'Your [di]vine being [reigns'' (Isaiah 52: 7).] This scripture's interpretation: 'the mounta[ins' are the] prophet[s], they w[ho were sent to proclaim God's truth and to] proph[esy] to all I[srael]. 'The messenger' is the [An]ointed of the spirit, of whom Daniel[iel] spoke, ['After the sixty-

two weeks, an Anointed one shall be cut off' (Daniel 9: 26). The 'messenger who brings] good news, who announ[ces salvation'] is the one of whom it is wri[tt]en, ['to proclaim the year of the LORD's favour, the day of vengeance of our God;] to comfo[rt all who mourn' (Isaiah 61: 2). This scripture's interpretation:] he is to inst[r]uct them about all the periods of history for eter[nity... and in the statutes of] [the] truth. [...] [...dominion] that passes from Belial and ret[urns to the Sons of Light...] [...] by the judgment of God, just as it is written concerning him, ['who says to Zi]on 'your divine being reigns'' (Isaiah 52: 7). ['Zi]on' is [the congregation of all the sons of righteousness, who] uphold the covenant and turn from walking [in the way] of the people. 'Your di[vi]ne being is [Melchizedek, who will del]iv[er them from the po]wer of Belial.[3]

The future deliverance will break the power of Belial, *ie* Satan, and destroy the force of evil. The essence of Jesus' teachings concerning the coming of the Messiah reveals two comings, one as the suffering servant (Isaiah 53) and the other as the superhuman eschatological judge as portrayed by one like the Son of Man (Daniel 7: 13). The term Son of Man, literally means 'human being'. In Daniel 7: 13 the construction is unique in the scriptures, he is 'kevar enash' (*like* a son of man). David Flusser pointed out here, 'The Son of Man has a superhuman, heavenly sublimity. He is the cosmic judge at the end of time. Sitting upon the throne of God, judging the entire human race with the aid of the heavenly hosts ...'[4]

Strong emphasis, however, is placed upon constant preparedness for the unknown time of the Second Coming. He rivets attention to the actions in the present (Matthew 25: 31-46). Jesus' followers are called to feed the hungry, clothe the needy, visit the prisoner and minister to the sick. The day of the coming of the Son of Man, which will break decisively the power of evil, is yet to be revealed. This imminence of the Second Coming of Jesus must be examined in the larger context of Paul's message of the Man of Lawlessness and the Temple.

The Man of Lawlessness and the Temple

No prophecy in the New Testament predicts the rebuilding of the Temple. Although this is true, some teachers of prophecy continue to explain how the rebuilding of the Third Temple in Jerusalem is soon to take place. When the new Jewish Temple is rebuilt in Jerusalem, according to their teachings, the way will then have been prepared for the Second Coming of the Lord. The Third Temple is a sign of fulfilled prophecy for the Second Coming. Since no prophecy in the Bible speaks about the rebuilding of the Third Temple, why is there such a passionate interest in its construction?

The answer to this question is rooted in Paul's epistle to the believers in Thessalonica.[5] The apostle Paul was addressing a serious crisis in the church. He had established the church on his second missionary journey (Acts 17: 1). Not long after the congregation began, a false teaching penetrated the inner circles of the believers. False teachers told them that Jesus Christ had already returned. Many of the new believers in Thessalonica were accepting this new doctrine. There was some confusion. Had Jesus already returned, or not? (2 Thessalonians 2: 2). The erroneous conviction that Christ had already come back was infiltrating the church and capturing the minds of some of the people.

At the time of Paul's writing in 51 CE, the Second Temple was still standing. Paul fulfils the role of a loving pastor when he writes his letter to the church at Thessalonica. He yearns to see the people return to sound doctrinal principles in which the church was established. Paul reminds the people about Jesus' promise to come again. For the Jewish apostle to the Gentiles, the Second Coming of Christ was a major doctrine. Paul rooted his message in the teachings of Jesus.

When the apostle composed his letter to the believers at Thessalonica, one prediction made by Jesus had not yet come to pass. Jesus had prophesied the destruction of the Second Temple. Clearly Paul wanted them to understand the plan of God for Jesus' Second Coming. The apostle explains to the believers he knew and loved so well:

Now concerning the coming of our Lord Jesus Christ and the assem-
bling to meet him, we beg you, brethren, not to be quickly shaken in

mind or excited, either by spirit or by word, or by letter purporting to be from us, to the effect that the day of the Lord has come. Let no one deceive you in any way; for that day will not come; unless the rebellion comes first, and the Man of Lawlessness is revealed, the son of perdition, who opposes and exalts himself against every so-called god or object of worship, so that he takes his seat in the temple of God, proclaiming himself to be God (2 Thessalonians 2: 1-4).

The firm belief that a Third Temple will be built and that the Antichrist will appear within her sacred precincts continues to dominate the message of Bible prophecy teachers. 'The Temple must be rebuilt', they proclaim, 'before the Lord returns'. They attempt to view the future through the eyes of Paul. The Temple will be rebuilt and the Antichrist will appear (2 Thessalonians 2: 1-4). Although this interpretation of Bible prophecy has gained adherence in some circles, the historical context and the foundation of Paul's message in the teachings of Jesus do not clearly outline these events as future predictions. Paul is more concerned with correcting the false teachings which had been accepted by many believers in Thessalonica. He never predicted the building of a Third Temple. The day of the Lord, Paul explains, has not yet taken place. But the coming of the Lord is an awesome event which will happen in the future. No believer should fail to grasp the urgency of the time. The ultimate judgment of God will come suddenly whether everyone is prepared or not.

The words of Paul must be carefully pondered in the light of the apostle's historical situation. When he wrote, the Second Temple had not yet been destroyed. The apostle anchors his message within the context of Jesus' teachings. In fact Paul may well be referring to the events leading up to the destruction of the Second Temple, a prophecy of Jesus yet to be fulfilled at the time of his writing in 51 CE. While it is true that most prophecy teachers place all the events described in 2 Thessalonians 2: 1-11 into the future, in my opinion they seem quite recognisable because of a prediction made by Jesus. The events are incredibly similar to the historical accounts of Jerusalem's tragic destruction in 70 CE. Could the 'son of perdition' (2 Thessalonians 2: 3) be identified with Titus the Roman emperor who desecrated the Holy of Holies? Titus was worshipped as a god.

Sometimes stories circulated about how the emperor may even have performed a miracle cure. After all, the Caesar was considered to be god even if many had began to doubt his deity in Paul's day. Tacitus tells how Vespasian, the father of Titus who preceded him on the imperial throne, healed a blind man.[6] Josephus, the Jewish historian, speaks of unusual signs which occurred leading up to the Roman attack against Jerusalem in 70 CE.[7] These were signs which should have been heeded by the people. At the coming of Jesus, Paul explains, the power of lawlessness will be completely overcome.

Paul warned the believers at Thessalonica that the Second Coming of Christ had not yet taken place. One of the reasons, were the teachings of Jesus concerning the Temple. The history of the Temple complex gives rich insight into Paul's epistle to the church at Thessalonica.

The Temple of God

In the Bible, God's Temple in Jerusalem has been the centre for Israel's worship. The celebration of the three major pilgrimage feasts of Passover, Pentecost and Tabernacles focused on the prayers and sacrifices in the Temple. Today, without a Temple and animal sacrifices, Judaism has stressed prayer and good works. The living prayers of God's people fill the place of animal sacrifices which have ceased. In biblical history, nonetheless, the Temple signifies God's blessing upon his people.

Today much attention has been focused upon the issues surrounding the ancient Jewish centre of worship and sacrifice. The Temple from the time of Jesus was destroyed by the Romans in 70 CE, and today a venerated Muslim shrine is the centre of worship for devout followers of Islam from around the world. Many earnestly believe that a Third Temple must be constructed before the Second Coming of Jesus or the appearance of the Messiah. According to this approach, the Third Jewish Temple must be rebuilt, in the place of, or next to, the present Muslim shrine. In fact, some prophecy teachers suggest that four Temples are needed. A third will be reconstructed and used by the Antichrist. It will be destroyed and a fourth Temple will be built in the exact dimensions of Ezekiel's Temple (Ezekiel 40-44).

No prophecy, however, anywhere in the Bible, speaks about the

construction of a Third Temple. Nowhere did Jesus foretell the reconstruction of a Temple. Paul never prophesied that a Third Temple
would be constructed after the second had been destroyed. The book
of Revelation is silent in regard to the construction of another Temple.

Rebuilding the Temple is a project which would require enormous
expense, major planning, a great deal of time, concentrated efforts
and nothing short of a major political miracle. Why then do some
prophecy teachers advocate rebuilding the Temple? Many dispensa-
tionalist Christians, and a small number from among nationalistic
and/or ultra-religious Jewish groups advocate the construction of a
Third Temple. According to their interpretations of 2 Thessalonians 2,
many dispensationalists believe that the Antichrist must appear in the
Temple before the return of Jesus can take place. Some nationalist
and/or ultra-religious Jews, moreover, view the rebuilding of the
Temple as a sign of God's blessing upon the people in their national
homeland.

Much of the New Testament was written before the destruction of
the Second Temple. So it is not surprising that the apostle Paul
mentions the Temple of God in 2 Thessalonians 2: 4. Jesus, moreover,
describes the profanation of the Temple in his discourse on the Mount
of Olives. Some prophecy teachers project these teachings into the
future. A Third Temple must be rebuilt, they say, so that these
prophecies can be fulfilled. Others argue that Jesus' prophecy about
the destruction of Jerusalem has already been fulfilled. His prophecy
of full restoration, moreover, will be completely fulfilled at the Second
Coming.

Some Jewish groups believe that the restoration of Temple
worship and sacrifice is needed to fulfil the higher purpose of Israel.
The Temple was rebuilt following the return from Babylonian
captivity. They argue that with today's miraculous ingathering of
Jewish exiles and the restoration of Israeli sovereignty over the
national homeland, the time is right to re-establish the Temple
service. The vast majority of Jews, however, find the idea of reinstat-
ing animal sacrifice repugnant. Many seek a democratic nation which
guarantees freedom of religion for minorities, including Muslims and
Christians. The test of every democratic country, in their view, is how
she treats her minorities. Forcibly taking over a holy site of the

Muslims and rebuilding a Temple violates everything they believe about justice and religious freedom. In their view, it would be wrong to destroy a shrine so sacred to multitudes of devout Muslims in order to build a new Jewish Temple. Their vision of a Jewish state encompasses the values of a free and diverse society with democratic pluralism. Since Jews have suffered brutal oppression as a minority in many countries, and especially in Arab dictatorships of the Middle East, Israelis long to guarantee equality for minorities in their own homeland. The commandment of scripture demands justice for the sojourner in the land, 'for you also were sojourners in Egypt' (Deuteronomy 10: 19).

Prophecies concerning the Temple in Jerusalem have received different interpretations by Bible scholars. All agree, however, that God will be faithful in fulfilling his promises to his people. Israel has been restored in her national homeland according to the divine promise.

The History of the Temple

The Temple was destroyed twice. The first destruction in 587 BCE by the Babylonians is recorded in the Hebrew Bible (2 Kings 25: 1-12; 2 Chronicles 36: 11-21; Jeremiah 39: 1-10). The second destruction in 70 CE by the Romans was predicted by Jesus. According to Josephus, others also spoke about the wrath coming upon the city. Jesus was not the only Jewish prophet who predicted the coming destruction of the Temple. Titus, the Roman general who would later become emperor, led the tenth legion to victory over Jerusalem. The city was burned and the Temple was literally torn apart stone by stone in graphic fulfilment of the words of Jesus, 'not one stone will be left upon another'. The Western Wall, also called the Wailing Wall, is most of what remains. It is only the outer supporting wall. The southern steps of the monumental stairway also survived the Roman devastation.

The First Temple was dedicated during the reign of Solomon (970-930 BCE). His father King David had earnestly desired to build it. But the task was given to his son, wise King Solomon. The glorious edifice was constructed during a period of economic prosperity, territorial expansion and political dominance. The people enjoyed freedom of worship in the Temple ritual. In 587 BCE, the Babylonians completely destroyed the sanctuary and the entire people were exiled.

During the days of Cyrus the Great from the Persian empire, the Jewish people were allowed to return home. After the rebirth of the nation in their homeland, the people longed to restore their place of worship. The old Temple lay in ruins. Under the energetic and visionary leadership of Haggai and Zechariah (*circa* 520 BCE), work began to rebuild the sanctuary. The Second Temple was dedicated in 515 BCE. The restored Temple was far less impressive. At the dedication, the younger generation cried with joy because the Temple had been rebuilt. The older generation, however, cried in deep anguish of spirit because they remembered the glory of the First Temple. They wept in sadness because the new edifice, being built by impoverished exiles, was so inferior in comparison to Solomon's grand Temple. On the occasion of the dedication of the new Temple, one was unable to distinguish between the cries of joy and others of sorrow. This Temple served the people until it was destroyed in 70 CE. During some periods, it was expanded and renovated, as in the time of the Maccabees when national pride and religious fervour as well as freedom from foreign oppression made it possible for massive improvements.

In 167 BCE, the Temple and its Holy Place were desecrated by Antiochus Epiphanes IV. In fact, the consensus of scholarship so identifies the 'abomination of the desolation' mentioned by Daniel with the profaning of the Temple by Antiochus. Some dispensationalists teach that the Antichrist will profane the Third Temple after it is rebuilt. In reality, the Temple was profaned on at least three occasions: by Antiochus in 167 BCE, Pompey in 63 BCE and Titus in 70 CE. The desecration is referred to as the 'abomination of the desolation' in the prophecy of Daniel (11: 31; 12: 11). In 169 BCE, following a two-year-long armed conflict, Judas Maccabee rededicated the restored Temple. They won the battle against Antiochus Epiphanes. Jewish religious freedom was restored. This great miracle of deliverance is celebrated at Hanukkah. In the time of Jesus it was called the Feast of Dedication (John 10: 22).

The most glorious phase of the Temple's history was most probably during the massive expansions by Herod the Great. Herod was a great builder who constructed massive fortifications like

Massada and the Herodian, as well as grand public buildings for the use of the community. His major renovation project was the Temple. He enlarged the entire complex, making significant improvements as he beautified the sanctuary. The Herodian architecture was unsurpassed in beauty and design. Herod invested an immense amount of money in the enormous project. The work of renovation was started about 20 BCE and continued long after Herod's death. In fact, some renovations continued until the Great War which brought the grand edifice of the Temple to the ground. The Temple was destroyed and Jerusalem was burnt. The awesome beauty of the Temple was turned to ashes.

Will a Third Temple be rebuilt? Many Christians believe a new Temple will be built to fulfil prophecy leading up to the return of Jesus. Others strongly maintain that nothing stands in the way of the Second Coming of the Lord. One must always be prepared. The Lord may come at any moment. The rebuilding of the Temple is not necessary. Some Jews have envisioned the rebuilding of another Temple when the Messiah comes. The Temple will be the supernatural work of God. Others believe that the nation should work to accomplish the task on their own. A new Temple would prove Israel's sovereignty. But the vast majority of the Jewish people today do not feel any need for a Temple. There is no urgency to build a Third Temple.

In the book of Revelation, John describes the New Jerusalem. Instead of giving a prophecy about a new sanctuary, his vision describes God living with his people, 'Behold, the dwelling of God is with men. He will dwell with them, and they shall be his people' (Revelation 21: 3). Here the words 'dwelling of God' must refer to the idea of the Temple. In Revelation, however, the New Jerusalem will not have a Temple other than the Almighty and the Lamb with God's people living in the holy city. In rich apocalyptic imagery, John tells what he saw in the heavenly city:

> And I saw no Temple in the city, for its Temple is the Lord God the
> Almighty and the Lamb. And the city has no need of sun or moon to
> shine upon it, for the glory of God is its light, and its lamp is the
> Lamb. By its light shall the nations walk; and the kings of the earth

shall bring their glory into it ... (Revelation 21: 22-24)

In John's vision of the end times, God's dwelling is among his people. There is no need for a physical Temple because the Lord himself will inhabit the people of the holy city:

> *While the vast majority of Jews today share the intense longing of the old Hebrew prophets for justice and compassion, few believe that a Third Temple must be reconstructed. In his highly acclaimed book, 'To Pray as a Jew', Rabbi Hayim Donin explains, 'Others believe that redemption will occur as does a burst of lightning. Amidst awesome miracles, the third Beit Hamikdash [Temple] will appear and come down from the heavens, completely built and finished, conformed to the literal meaning of the verse in Exodus 15: 17: "The sanctuary, O Lord, which Thy hands have established" (Rashi, Sukkah 41a; and Tosaphot, based on Midrash Tanhuma).'[8]*

Donin stresses the diversity of thought among Jewish thinkers and religious teachers. Many believe that the process of redemption will come slowly like the rising of the sun rather than as a burst of lightning. Others stress a suddenness in the divine plan which will be more like a strike of lightning. Prophecy is not clear on such matters. A multiplicity of interpretations exist, yet only the Sovereign of the Universe will determine end time events.

The destruction of Jerusalem is commemorated every year in the liturgy of the synagogue with a day of fasting. The people fast and mourn the fate of their Temple. There is a natural longing for restoration. But prayers and good works make up for the absence of the Temple. The religious faith and pious fervour of the Jewish people has not been diminished. The old rabbis and community leaders encouraged the people to live for God. Prayer is the service of the heart which leads to action, praying to God and helping others have replaced a Temple. After two thousand years of a rich and glorious faith tradition, few Jews view the Temple as a necessity.

No one can predict all the future in detail, on the basis of their Bible interpretation alone. Much depends upon divine sovereignty and the willingness or unwillingness of the people to obey God. A Third Temple may eventually be reconstructed in the future, but such a turn in events does not appear in Bible prophecy predictions. Biblical prophecy speaks God's word to his people, revealing the divine will more than it predicts future events. The inspired words reveal God's purpose. Many times in the sacred writings of the prophets, God has spoken concerning his people returning to the land promised to Abraham. He longs for the people of Israel to experience restoration and rebirth in their national homeland. Prophecy must lead us to awe and wonder at the mystery of God.

The Antichrist and Titus

The Antichrist has been identified with numerous personalities in church history. In modern times, he has been identified with anyone from the Nazi leader of the Third Reich, Adolf Hitler, to the American Secretary of State during the Nixon White House years, Henry Kissinger. While such identifications might be regarded, by many, as highly questionable, often absolute proof for revealing an Antichrist candidate is shown by giving the numerical value of the letters from his name. The name, which equals the number 666, is believed to reveal the Antichrist because of the mark of the beast from Revelation 13: 18. In antiquity, each letter of the alphabet also carried a numerical value which was used in counting. Interestingly, the name Caesar [King] Nero, in Hebrew *Neron Kesar*, just happens to equal 666. At the time of John's writing, the church was experiencing intense persecution from the Roman emperor, Domitian (81-96 CE).

In fact, the term Antichrist in the singular can be very misleading. In reality many Antichrists have appeared (see 1 John 2: 18). The Antichrist spirit opposes God's will. The idea of an Antichrist figure seems to have originated in Jewish apocalyptic thought during the time of the Maccabean rebellion, when the first Antichrist, Antiochus Epiphanes IV, attacked the Jewish people for worshiping the one true God and desecrated the Temple. Antiochus Epiphanes IV is an Antichrist figure. As well as possibly looking for someone with the numerical value for the letters of his or her name adding up to 666, one should be aware of an Antichrist spirit which opposes everything like God. The anointed people of God are called to bring healing, wholeness and salvation to people in need. The force of the Antichrists opposes the high spiritual values and moral principles ordained by God. The Roman General Titus, who later became an emperor and was worshipped as a god, is the perfect figure for the Antichrist in 2 Thessalonians 2: 4.

It is possible that a Third Temple will be reconstructed and yet another Antichrist figure will appear. The danger for sound Christian doctrine concerning the Second Coming of Christ, however, must always be recognised. Jesus taught his disciples that no one knows the day or the hour of the last judgment in which he would appear as the Son of Man. He urged constant preparation. The imminence of Christ's return means that one must always be prepared. In all events, no prophecy in the New Testament predicts the rebuilding of a Third Temple, and there is no legitimate reason for prophecy teachers to proclaim that Jesus cannot return until the Temple is reconstructed in Jerusalem. Paul's writing to the Thessalonians focused on another problem. False teachers had claimed that Jesus had already returned. To correct this erroneous doctrine, Paul made clear allusion to Jesus' teaching (Luke 21) in which Jesus predicted that the Second Temple would be destroyed. This prophecy came true in 70 CE. The apostle Paul wanted the believers at Thessalonica to learn the teachings of Jesus.

The Second Coming

What must believers know about the Second Coming of Christ? Two words are of primary significance, 'Be prepared!' The rest is in the hands of God. No one is able to know the day or the hour. No one will figure out the month or the year. Jesus teaches his disciples that the day of the Lord will come 'as a thief in the night'. However, in the same section Paul challenges that we are 'not of the night' and therefore, whilst we may not know the hour, we should not be surprised when that hour arrives. On one occasion, Rabbi Eliezer told his disciples, 'Repent one day before you die'. His disciples were perplexed. They asked their master, 'How can we know the day we will die so that we can repent?' Rabbi Eliezer wisely warned, 'Spend all your days in repentance'.[9]

So it is with the Second Coming of Jesus. One must seek to be prepared at all times. Two times are unknown to all people. One never knows the day of death or the time appointed for the final judgment. The apocalyptic teachings of Jesus and Paul call upon the listener to heighten his or her spiritual awareness of the times. God is in control. Though the time of death is unknown, the human experience of death is a certainty. In a similar way, the final day of judgment is also a reality. Judgment day will come suddenly and unexpectedly. Jesus stresses what is done in the present in caring for lost and suffering humanity as a way of preparing for the unknown time. Feed the hungry, care for the needs of people at risk and seek first the kingdom. All must be prepared.

Notes

1   See my discussion of the three different meanings of the term Son of Man in the Gospels, **Brad H Young**, *Jesus the Jewish Theologian*, Peabody, Massachusetts: Hendrickson, 1995, pp 243-252.

2   B Sanh 98a. Compare the English translation, ed **I Epstein**, *The Babylonian Talmud* (London: Soncino Press, 1935), p 664.

3   See **M Wise, M Abegg** and **E Cook**, trans and comm *The Dead Sea Scrolls*, San Francisco, Harper, 1996 pp 456-457. See **David Flusser**, *Melchizedek and the Son of Man, in Judaism and the Origins of Christianity*, Jerusalem: Magnes Press, 1989, p 192.

4   **David Flusser**, in collaboration with **R Steven Notley**, *Jesus*, Jerusalem: Magnes Press, 1997, pp 129-130.

5   Paul's two personal letters, 1 and 2 Thessalonians were written close one to the other. Paul was writing from Corinth during his 18 month stay. In 1 Thessalonians, Paul deals with his teachings of the resurrection. The believers feared that their friends who died before the Second Coming of Christ would not be resurrected (1 Thessalonians 4: 13 to 5: 11). Paul assures them that the 'dead in Christ shall rise first' (1 Thessalonians 4: 16). In 2 Thessalonians, Paul addresses his concern pertaining to the false doctrine proclaiming that a clandestine Second Advent of Christ had happened.

6   **Tacitus**, *Histories* 4.81, see also, **D Cartlidge** and **D Dungan**, *Documents for the Study of the Gospels*, p 156.

7   Compare **Josephus**, *War* 1: 23, 4: 491ff. Most probably, the unexpected death of Nero and the sudden elevation of Vespasian to the throne was considered a major sign. See also **Josephus**, *War* 6: 289ff. While identifying Titus with the 'son of perdition' may solve some problems, it also creates new questions. The entire epistle needs further study in light of the history of the Second Temple period.

8   **Hayim Donin**, *To Pray as a Jew*, p 89.

9   See B Shabbat 153a.

Section 2:

The Developing Faith

From Jesus to Paul

John Fieldsend

Abstract

A true understanding of Paul must always be in the context of the life
and teaching of Jesus; one cannot understand him properly in
isolation. From the day of his Damascus Road experience Jesus
dominated his life, and his sole aim was to serve his new master as a
bondservant (though there is a suggestion that *doulos* might also have
an ambassadorial context) and to proclaim, with every fibre of his
being, the good news of salvation that Jesus had inaugurated.

Much of the first part of this essay will therefore be taken up with a
consideration of Jesus. We shall see that where Paul was misunderstood it was because some aspects of the teaching of Jesus were
misunderstood. From the immediate sub-apostolic period Paul's
letters have frequently been used as a basis for the teaching of
Replacement Theology because this has been, and still is, how the
Gospels are frequently interpreted. Paul's teaching on sin and
salvation by faith has been criticised as 'Hellenistic' because it has
been interpreted in relationship with a misunderstanding of Jesus'
attitude to Torah. Most recently of all, the emphasis on the humanity
of Jesus, whilst it has in many ways helped to enrich our understanding of the Gospels, has also, in some cases, tended to lead to an
impoverished Christology, which, at least in part, has led some
scholars to see the origins of Paul's high Christology in a Hellenistic,
rather than a mainstream Palestinian Jewish milieu. Also, a new
interest on the part of Jewish scholars and writers in the person of
Jesus began, from early in this century, an increasingly fruitful co-
operation between Christian and Jewish scholars. However, we need
to understand that this kind of co-operation is not undertaken in a
vacuum, and renewed stresses between the two faith communities
resulting from the Holocaust has brought emotive pressures to

influence not only the understanding of church history, but also on biblical interpretation. All these things have a bearing on our understanding of Paul, and will therefore take up much of the first part of this essay, as they are a necessary prelude to the heart of the subject matter itself.

In the second part of the essay we will look at some of the main criticisms that have been raised regarding Paul's background as a Palestinian Jew of his day, and from the text of his letters seek to respond to them.

Without a doubt Paul has, in every period of church history, been seen by many as the great pioneer of the Gospel. Jesus *was* the Gospel, but Paul has been its interpreter for practically every generation, every culture and every theological system. Through the centuries, from Augustine to the many theologies of today, almost all would lay claim to the teaching of Paul as one of the roots and inspirations of their beliefs.

We may not agree with the totality of Hans Küng's analysis when he writes:

Only through Paul did the Christian mission to the Gentiles ... become a resounding success ...

Only through Paul did this small Jewish 'sect' finally develop into a 'world religion' in which East and West were more closely bound together even than they had been by Alexander the Great.

So, without Paul there would have been no Catholic Church, no Greek or Patristic theology, no Christian-Hellenistic culture ...[1]

But at least this makes us aware of the intensity and breadth of Paul's influence upon the civilisation of the western world and, through the missionary movements of the 18th-20th centuries, upon world civilisation.

Even some respected Jewish theologians recognise Paul's stature. Pinchas Lapide has written, 'For me, Paul is above all a hero of faith, whose tragic failure – like that of his Lord and redeemer – was crowned only after his death with the greatest missionary success in world history. Three times repudiated – by Judaism, by Gnosticism and Gentile cults, and by his own mother church in Jerusalem, this cosmopolitan fought his way through to a global ecumenism by virtue of which he representatively performed for Israel the prophetic task of being 'a light for the nations' (Isa 49: 6).' Lapide continues, 'Franz Rosenzweig rightly observed that it was not Jerusalem but Christianity which brought the Hebrew Bible to the remotest islands, very much in line with the prophecies of Isaiah.'[2]

But despite Paul's undisputed stature and influence, the question has been increasingly asked in recent years as to whether Paul truly understood Jesus, and truly represented his teaching to the world, or whether he so misunderstood and therefore misrepresented Jesus' teaching that, far from being the great apostle of Christ, he became the founder of Christianity. A charge frequently laid against Paul is that he 'falsified the faith *of* Jesus so that it became faith *in* Jesus'. In fact the Jewish writer, Hyam Maccoby, has written a book entitled *The Mythmaker*, which bears the subtitle *Paul and the Invention of Christianity*.

Before we try to understand how such divergent views of Paul have arisen, and especially why, in the past hundred or so years, there has been such a strong challenge to the integrity of Pauline teaching, we have to be reminded of Paul's own self-understanding and his own stated aims and objectives. Only then can we begin to understand and evaluate his life and teaching. We find the fullest summary of his autobiography in Philippians 3: 5-14, and his mission statement in 2 Cor 4: 1-6:

Phil 3: 5-14: Circumcised on the eighth day, of the people of Israel, of the tribe of Benjamin, a Hebrew of Hebrews; in regard to the law, a Pharisee; as for zeal, persecuting the church; as for legalistic right-eousness, faultless. But whatever was to my profit I now consider loss for the sake of Christ. What is more, I consider everything a loss compared to the surpassing greatness of knowing Christ Jesus my Lord, for whose sake I have lost all things. I consider them rubbish, that I may gain Christ and be found in him, not having a righteous-ness of my own that comes from the law, but that which is through faith in Christ – the righteousness that comes from God and is by faith. I want to know Christ and the power of his resurrection and the fellowship of sharing in his sufferings, becoming like him in his death, and so, somehow, to attain to the resurrection from the dead. Not that

I have already obtained all this, or have already been made perfect, but I press on to take hold of that for which Christ Jesus took hold of me. Brothers, I do not consider myself yet to have taken hold of it. But one thing I do: Forgetting what is behind and straining towards what is ahead, I press on towards the goal to win the prize for which God has called me heavenwards in Christ Jesus.

2 Cor 4: 1-6: Therefore, since through God's mercy we have this ministry, we do not lose heart. Rather, we have renounced secret and shameful ways; we do not use deception, nor do we distort the word of God. On the contrary, by setting forth the truth plainly we commend ourselves to every man's conscience in the sight of God. And even if our Gospel is veiled, it is veiled to those who are perishing. The god of this age has blinded the minds of unbelievers, so that they cannot see the light of the Gospel of the glory of Christ, who is the image of God. For we do not preach ourselves, but Jesus Christ as Lord, and ourselves as your servants for Jesus' sake. For God, who said, 'Let light shine out of darkness,' made his light shine in our hearts to give us the light of the knowledge of the glory of God in the face of Christ.

In these passages Paul is making at least two claims, both of which have been deeply challenged by many scholars, both Christian and Jewish, in recent years. The first claim that Paul makes is one regarding his pedigree, as a 'Hebrew of the Hebrews'. The second claim he makes is that his message is not one of his own making, but that he is faithfully and accurately presenting, admittedly mainly for a Gentile audience, the faith that Jesus came to bring. In modern terms, Paul would readily admit to 'contextualising the Gospel for a Gentile audience' (Gal 2: 7-9). However, he would deny any suggestion of adulteration of the pure Gospel message that Jesus not only came to bring but which Jesus incarnated in his own person, in his life, death and resurrection. In order to grasp what hangs on this we have to understand that the Judaism of Paul's day was very diverse, comprising many strands and divisions, and we shall briefly look at these in order more accurately to understand the life of both Jesus and Paul. The main reasons that there has been so much new thinking about the New Testament, and about Jesus and Paul in particular, are twofold. First, the development of biblical archaeology has given us much new information, and therefore a much more detailed background understanding of the times, which in turn has given us new tools for understanding and interpreting New Testament teaching. Secondly, a greater study of the extra-biblical documents of the time has given us a more detailed 'backcloth' for the understanding of the New Testament documents in their social and cultural contexts. These two together led, in the last century, to what became popularly known as the 'Search for the Historical Jesus'. Much of the radical speculation that has arisen from this has to be questioned, but there is much to enhance and deepen our knowledge of Jesus, and of his international apostle and interpreter, Paul.

One of the main challenges to our understanding of Judaism in Jesus' day is our new realisation of its variety. Indeed so varied was the Judaism at this time that some scholars speak of the 'Judaisms' of the period. Another new realisation is that of the rapid and radical changes that took place in Judaism in the first century of our Common Era. So great were these that Louis Feldman, Professor of Classics at Yeshiva University in New York could write 'In this relatively short period of time two great religions developed – rabbinic Judaism and Christianity. For a fuller description the reader should refer to Edersheim's classic work, *The Life and Times of Jesus the Messiah*, or for a more recent treatment, to the introduction and the opening chapters of *Christianity and Rabbinic Judaism – A Parallel History of their Origins and Early Development*.[3]

In understanding the different strands of Judaism of the First Century CE, Lester Grabbe, Head of the Department of Theology at the University of Hull, has described the Judaism of the First Century CE in terms of currents of water flowing in a stream:

Currents refer to smaller fluxes and flows in a broad stream of water. In a stream or river, many different currents can be found. Some will form part of the general movement of the mass of waters, but there will also be currents independent of that flow, perhaps forming eddies or even cross currents, which impede or redirect the main flow. A current may flow separately for a time, then join with another current or currents to form a unity for a while but then branch off once again to go its own way.

Having described the major currents of the *First Century Judaism*
Grabbe summarises:

None of the currents described here constitutes the Judaism of that
time ... Each of the currents formed an important element within first
century Judaism ... they flowed, collided, eddied, and ebbed ... in a
whirling confused mass of constantly changing movement. It is this,
rather than the common image of a static 'orthodoxy' ... which repre-
sents the Judaism of the time of Hillel, Jesus and Herod.[4]

And we may, therefore, add 'the Judaism of the time of Paul'.

Grabbe describes four main currents, namely Textual Judaism –
the priestly and scribal current, Revolutionary Judaism – the political
and 'messianic current, Eschatalogical Judaism – the apocalyptic
current, and Inverted Judaism – the gnostic current'.

Within the Textual current, Grabbe includes the Priests and
Levites, the Scribes, and the Sadducees. He writes:

The priesthood in general, and the high priest in particular,
dominated the Jewish State in the Second Temple period ... the Priests
and the Levites were also transmitters of the written scriptures, the
cultivators of wisdom ... The importance of the Priests has often been
overlooked in favour of other groups ...[5]

Regarding the Pharisees, Grabbe challenges much traditional
thinking. He writes:

Jewish scholars have often seen them as forerunners of Rabbinic
Judaism; second, their frequent mention in the New Testament has
made them a byword in many Christian writings. Neither approach is
helpful because both represent a rather biased point of view.[6]

In his summary he concludes:

They claimed to have traditions from the fathers, which were not
written in the Hebrew Bible. There is no evidence that they claimed
this was 'oral law' (though the rabbis did later develop such a view).[7]

Differing from the traditional emphasis on the difference between
the Pharisees and the Priests, Grabbe suggests:

The best estimate is that (the Pharisees) represented an attempt by a group trying to reproduce the Temple cult in their own home. That is, the laws seemed to turn primarily on eating ordinary food in a state of cultic purity (normally required in the Temple but not necessarily in the home) and thus involved in questions of ritual purity, eating, tithing (since only properly tithed food could be eaten), the Sabbath and festivals ... betrothal, marriage and divorce ... This fits in with a lay movement attempting to imitate the Priests, but it could equally apply to a priestly group trying to extend the Temple regulations outside the Temple to their own homes.[8]

Of the Sadducees, Grabbe writes:

The Sadducees have been everyone's whipping boy. No Jewish group today claims to be heirs of the Sadducees. (Though there are a number of interesting parallels between them and the Qaraites, a medieval 'back-to-the-Bible' movement, which arose in reaction to rabbinic Judaism.)

They accept only written scripture rejecting the 'traditions of the fathers'. This does not mean, of course, that they may not have their own traditional interpretation of the biblical text. People have always had trouble distinguishing between what the text actually says and their interpretation of it.

They are said not to believe in the resurrection or angels ...

The name suggests a connection with the priesthood ... it has often been connected with Zadok, the high priest under David. The Priests in the Qumran texts are also referred to as 'sons of Zadok'.[9]

Of the Essenes, Grabbe writes:

These have been widely associated with Qumran since the discovery of the Dead Sea Scrolls ... No other group is better described in the early sources than the Essenes.

Quoting Pliny the Elder, he continues:

On the west side of the Dead Sea, but out of range of the noxious exhalations of the coast, is the solitary tribe of the Essenes, which is remarkable beyond all other tribes in the whole world, as it has no women and has renounced all sexual desire, has no money, and has

only palm trees for company ... Lying below the Essenes was formerly
the town of Engedi ... Next comes Masada ...
The Priests were given pre-eminence in the Qumran community...as
stated in the Messianic Rule ... The sons of Levi shall hold office ...
under the authority of the sons of Aaron. They shall cause the congre-
gation to go and to come ... under the authority of the sons of Zadok,
the Priests ...[10]

Under the Revolutionary current, Grabbe goes on the describe the
Zealots, the Fourth Philosophy and the Sicarii.

For a further description of the Judaism of the First Century CE
and its main strands, E P Sanders' book *The Historical Figure of Jesus*,
(Penguin, 1993) is helpful.

With this in mind we can understand that the more traditional
division of Judaism into two strands, Palestinian and Hellenistic, has
been both too rigid and, probably, exaggerated. As the latter name
implies, the Jewish communities of the diaspora, which had first been
established after the Babylonian captivity and had developed through
the Persian, Greek and Roman periods, had by now been affected by
the breadth of Hellenistic culture. The Judaism of Palestine, however,
was seen to be a purer form of historical Judaism, less affected by surrounding cultures.

Initially much of the fruit of this research was used, not unnatural-
ly, to help give a new understanding of Jesus, and only then to Paul.
However, in the light of Paul's claims of faithfulness as the interpreter
of Jesus for the Gentiles, we shall first need to concentrate on Jesus.

We are living in days in which there has been a great groundswell
in the Jewish community of re-thinking its traditional understanding
of the person of Jesus. In the place of traditional antagonism and
rejection there is now a new and dynamic restoration of his person as
a good Torah-observant Jew of his day. His character is being
admired and his teaching applauded in both theological and literary
circles. Jewish scholars like Joseph Klausner, Jacob Neusner, and
Pinchas Lapide are almost vying with each other in their admiration
of his teaching. Klausner may have been the first Jew to accept that
Jesus actually made the messianic claims which are attributed to him

in the Gospels, and in this he may remain in the minority among Jewish scholars. However, Lapide has recently written that very controversial (at least in Jewish circles) book entitled *I Believe in the Resurrection of Jesus* (SPCK 1984), though his concept of 'resurrection' is not dissimilar to that of the 'translation' of Elijah in 2 Kings 2.

Added to these affirmations we can quote Martin Buber, Professor of Social Philosphy at the Hebrew University from 1938 to 1951. Buber wrote:

> *It is a peculiar manifestation of our exile-psychology that we permitted, and even aided in, the deletion of New Testament Messianism, that meaningful offshoot of our spiritual history. It was in a Jewish land that this spiritual revolution was kindled; and Jews were those who had spread it all over the land ... We must overcome the superstitious fear which we harbour about the messianic movement of Jesus, and we must place this movement where it belongs, namely in the spiritual history of Judaism.[11]*

Elsewhere he wrote:

> *From my youth onwards I have found in Jesus my great brother. That Christianity has regarded and does regard him as God and Saviour has always appeared to me a fact of highest importance which, for his sake and my own, I must endeavour to understand ... My own fraternally open relationship to him has grown ever stronger and clearer ... I am more than ever certain that a great place belongs to him in Israel's history of faith and this place cannot be described by any of the usual categories.[12]*

Scholem Asch, the well known and highly acclaimed Jewish writer, in one of several novels centring on the person of Jesus of Nazareth, wrote these words:

> *A little less than two thousand years ago, there came into our world among the Jewish people and to it a personage who gave substance to the illusion perceived by our fathers in their dream ... No one before him and no one after him has bound our world with the fetters of law, of justice, and of love, and brought it to the feet of the one living Almighty God as effectively as did this personage who came to an Israelite house in Nazareth in Galilee.[13]*

Elsewhere Asch said:

For Jesus Christ is to me the outstanding personality of all time, all history, both as Son of God and as Son of Man. Everything he ever said or did has value for us today, and that is something you can say of no other man, alive or dead ... He became the Light of the world. Why shouldn't I, a Jew, be proud of it?[14]

Constantin Brunner, a German Jewish philosopher has written:

It is amazing how many Jews write about Jews and Judaism while ignoring the super-Jew and super-Judaism. I refer to Jesus the Messiah and to Christianity ... What happened here? Is it only the Jew who is incapable of seeing and hearing all that others see and hear? Are the Jews stricken with blindness and deafness as regards Messiah Jesus, so that to them alone he has nothing to say? ... Understand, then, what we shall do: We shall bring him back to us. Messiah Jesus is not dead for us – for us he has not yet lived: and he will not slay us, he will make us live again. His profound and holy words, and all that is true and heart-appealing in the New Testament, must from now on be heard in our synagogues and taught to our children, in order that the wrong we have committed may be made good, the curse turned into a blessing, and that he at last may find us who has always been seeking after us.

It is interesting to note that much of this affirmation of Jesus by Jewish academics took place before the rise of Nazism, or immediately after the years of the Holocaust, when the roots of that horrendous event had not yet been investigated or digested. One might also have hoped that the new dialogue, inaugurated by the Council of Christians and Jews (CCJ) since its foundation in 1945, specifically to create a new atmosphere of trust and mutual reconciliation, would have built on the positive writings we have been examining. To an extent some may claim that this has happened, but if it has, it has been at the cost of the integrity of the New Testament ... In the CCJ booklet *Hard Sayings, Difficult New Testament Texts for Jewish-Christian Dialogue* we see the debate continues along the following lines:

But although many Christians are ready to scour patristic texts for

... 'the teaching of contempt', they are reluctant to subject the founda-
tion documents of the Faith to the same critique. While the works of
the Fathers may justly be regarded as the source of much of the perse-
cution endured by the Jews at Gentile hands over the centuries, such a
charge cannot, in their view be levelled at the New Testament. Many
biblical scholars are adamant that there is no connection between the
markedly prejudicial statements against Judaism found in the New
Testament and the barbaric antisemitism of Hitler. ... They refuse to
believe that the so-called 'theological antisemitism' of the Christian
era has any basis in scripture[16].

In response to this the book quotes the Jewish writer Eliezer
Berkovitz:

Christianity's New Testament has been the most dangerous antise-
mitic tract in history. Its hatred-charged diatribes against the
Pharisees and the Jews have poisoned the hearts and minds of millions
and millions of Christians for almost two millenia. No matter what
the deeper theological meaning of the hate passages against the Jews
might be, in the history of the Jewish people the New Testament lent
its support to oppression, persecution and mass murder of an
intensity and duration that were unparalleled in the entire history of
man's degradation. Without Christianity's New Testament, Hitler's
Mein Kampf could never have been written.[17]

In the light of this we have to be cautious at the way we evaluate the
findings of modern scholarship; sensitively to separate the findings of
academic research from that subjective interpretation which the
present highly emotive situation will sometimes understandably lay
upon them.

One of the first fruits to come out of this work is the restoration of
Jesus as a Jew. This may seem an obvious truism, but we shall see
how this fact became so quickly lost to the early church, and how
deep its implications have been on the development of Christianity
through the centuries. Until this work was undertaken Jesus'
humanity was little more than a theological statement, and he was
acknowledged as *ecce homo*, 'the man', that is, he had become univer-
salised for all nations and cultures. In Christian art he could be

presented as blue-eyed and blond for the Aryan races; and equally as middle or far Eastern, Inuit or South American. In one sense that is true and important and, with the emphasis on Jesus' Jewishness, this theological truth may be in danger of being underplayed. At the same time this aspect of the truth can only be properly interpreted if Jesus' life, teaching, and cultural and religious background are first understood in his First Century Palestinian Jewish background; and if the whole Bible, including the New Testament, is read as a Jewish book. One of the basic tenets of the new science of 'contextualisation' is that the subject matter in hand must first be understood in the terms of its natural context and culture.

One of the first fruits of this work was that Jewish scholars began to take a new and sympathetic look at Jesus, and indeed began to reclaim him as one of their most illustrious sons. Today, especially in Israel, as many Jews as Christians are writing about Jesus, and at the Hebrew University in Jerusalem, Jewish and Christian scholars are often co-operating together, as seen in the book, *Christianity and Rabbinic Judaism* previously referred to. This is not without its difficulties, because two millenia of Jewish persecution and mutual antipathy cannot quickly or easily be laid aside. As the Jewish scholar, Samuel Sandmel, has written in his foreword to Pinchas Lapide's groundbreaking book, *Israelis and Jesus* :

'*Contributing to the enigma [of Jesus] have been the inevitable partisanships, some of which have spilled over into scholarship ...*'[18]

He then lists some of the deep misunderstandings and emotions from both sides that have inevitably interfered with the objectivity of true scholarship. It is beyond the scope of this essay to look at these findings in detail. Suffice it is to say that the picture of Jesus that generally emerges is of a faithful observant Jew of his day whose lifestyle was broadly that of a Pharisee of the Hillelite group, and whose ethical teaching was too 'perfectionist' to have been practical and therefore acceptable in his day.

Joseph Klausner, one of the pioneers of this new understanding, wrote in his preface to his book, *From Jesus to Paul*, George, Allen and Unwin, 1946 :

I came to the conclusion, after much research, that Jesus considered

himself to be the Messiah, and that, by means of the repentance and the
morality which he preached in Jewish cities, he expected to bring redemp-
tion to Israel; but it is clear to us now, that Jesus never intended to found
a new religion and spread it among the Gentiles.[19]

In the acceptance of Jesus' self-understanding as Messiah, Klausner is
very much in the minority among Jewish scholars. Most would deny
that Jesus ever thought of himself in messianic terms; contending that
this was something put upon him by the developing church, and in
any case, the Messiah is a human, not a divine, figure.

One of the major limitations for this research is that, other than the
New Testament, there is little surviving Jewish literature available
which broadly covers the period of the life of Jesus, and leading up to
the destruction of the Temple in 70 CE, and the sacking of Jerusalem
in 134. There *is* literature available covering the years leading up to
the birth of Jesus, usually referred to as the inter-testamental period.
There is also a wealth of material available from after 134 CE, the
beginning of the new Jewish diaspora. During this time, we see the
emergence of Rabbinic Judaism as developed by the academy of the
illustrious Rabbi Johanan ben Zakkai at Yavneh, leading up to the
writing of the Mishnah and the Talmud, the foundation of modern
Rabbinic Judaism. But as far as first century writing is concerned, the
New Testament stands almost unique.

At this point it might be helpful to take a slight digression and
look at one or two frequent but typical traditional Christian misunderstandings of the teaching of Jesus. In the story of Zaccheus (Luke
19) Zaccheus' promise of fourfold restitution is usually taken to be a
spontaneous response of deep gratitude for forgiveness. In fact it is a
true 'Torah response' in line with its teaching on restitution, which is
the full amount plus 20% of the amount extorted (Lev 6: 5) or up to
'four or five times' if it involves the person's livelihood (which is the
significance of stealing 'live animals'). Therefore, when Jesus
responds that 'this man too is a son of Abraham', the whole context of
the incident is seen in a totally Judaic milieu. Whether or not
Zaccheus offered the required Temple sacrifice afterwards is not
recorded, but it cannot be argued from silence that he did not.
Further, Jesus' teaching in Mt 5: 23ff, about restitution and reconcilia-

tion before offering the gift on the altar (ie sacrifice) is entirely in keeping with Lev 6: 6. First comes restitution and reconciliation between the human parties, and only then is peace with God to be sought.

When we wish to look at Judaism therefore, both during the lifetime of Jesus and of Paul and the other apostles, we have to place it somewhere between the diverse Judaism at the close of the inter-testamental period and that of the newly emerging Judaism of the post-Yavneh (Jamnia) period. We have already seen that, as well as the obvious continuity which must not be underplayed, there were discontinuities of such magnitude that Louis Feldman could speak of post-Yavneh Judaism as a *new religion*, though we must allow here for a little Jewish hyperbole! When we look for the cause of these discontinuities we see them as arising out of the destruction of the Temple and the sacking of Jerusalem, both of which took place after the life of Jesus and the main ministry of Paul. We can, therefore, reasonably assume that the Judaism that both Jesus and Paul knew was nearer to the Judaisms of the inter-testamental period than the more unified Judaism brought about by the Yavneh academy. However, which of the branches of Judaism gave Paul his background is a moot point which will take much of our attention in the remainder of this essay.

To sum up thus far, if Jesus was a good Jew of his day, and no more, the question that has to be answered is this, 'How has the life and teaching of a Jewish teacher with pharisaic sympathies, who may or may not have understood himself in (human) Messianic terms, turned into a world religion based on one Jesus, Son of God, Messiah of Israel (in divine terms) and Saviour of the world who not only died on a cross as a common criminal, but who, according to his newly emerging followers, claimed to have been born of a virgin, risen from the dead and ascended into the very presence of God whence he had come?'

The radical response from writers like Hyam Maccoby and, more recently, A N Wilson, is that Christianity is the outworking of Paul's fertile imagination based on his largely Hellenistic understanding of Judaism.

The more common and less radical answer has to be necessarily more complex. For those Christian scholars of a more liberal theology who would discount the resurrection as an historical event, and who understand it more as a symbol of a new spiritual awakening, their answer is not radically different from the Jewish answer given above. The same would be true for those Christian scholars who, though they might believe in the resurrection of Jesus as an event acceptable to their personal faith or of Church doctrine, would nevertheless not allow such a belief to dominate their academic findings, which, in their view, must pass the test of scientific and historical verifiability. For this group of scholars the question is not so much, 'How did the Christian faith come into being?' as 'Was Paul's understanding of Jesus as a good Palestinian Jew accurate and therefore, was his presentation of Christianity in accord with its roots in Palestinian Judaism?'

However, even Christians who do not share any of the above reservations cannot simply say to the above groups 'A plague on both your houses! Let's simply go back to the old traditional view of Paul!' The findings of modern scholarship simply will not allow this. The traditional views about Paul that have been handed down in the church through the centuries are now shown to be flawed, and these views, which we shall also need to examine, have been involved with Replacement Theology and Christian antisemitism through much of the church's history. We need to work towards a new understanding of Paul, and also a new understanding of the humanity of Jesus in the context of his late Second Temple Jewishness. We need to integrate all that we know from our Jewish New Testament with the best findings of modern scholarship. We shall now look at some of the developments in the Twentieth Century in our understanding of Paul. Space will only allow us to look at the work of one or two major representative scholars, and for those who would like a summary of a wider field, a good guide would be *Paul, the Law and Justification*, by Colin G Kruse, (Apollos, Leicester, 1996).

Let us now look at some of the specific criticisms that have been laid against Paul, and respond to them.

It has frequently been denied that Paul really knew the heart of Rabbinic Judaism, otherwise he could not have written as he did. Claude Montefiore has argued that Paul's religion was very different from the rich, warm, joyous and optimistic Rabbinic Judaism of CE

300-500. From this he infers that the Judaism of CE 50 was:

> *a better, happier, and more noble religion than one might infer from*
> *the writings of the Apostle.*[20]

Montefiore continues his argument by asserting that:

> *if the Rabbinic Judaism of CE 50 was like that of CE 300-500, then it*
> *is inconceivable that Paul was a Rabbinic Jew before his conversion. If*
> *he was, he could not have developed the theory of the law he elaborates*
> *in Romans, or ignored repentance as he does. He would not have*
> *needed to develop the mystic notions which he did, and would not*
> *have found it necessary to devise the soteriology found in his major*
> *epistles.*[21]

As we have said earlier, this totally ignores the double discontinuity brought about in the second half of the First Century CE. But this anachronistic argument has continued throughout the Pauline debate. As Parkes has written:

> *We have further to admit, on the basis of intellectual honesty, that we*
> *know sufficient of the Pharisees and of Rabbinic Judaism of his*
> *[Paul's] period to be compelled to allow that if it is Rabbinic Judaism*
> *he is attacking, then to a large extent his charges against the law are*
> *unjustified ...much of his argument is irrelevant, his abuse unmerited,*
> *and his conception of that which he is attacking inaccurate.*[22]

Again we have to say that these arguments are not only factually questionable, they are anachronistic in that they are not comparing like with like. Montefiore's assertions are not true, either of the teaching of First Century Judaism before 70 CE, or for the teaching of Jesus. There was a clear and major strand of teaching in the Judaism of those days that all was not well with the nation's relationship with their covenant keeping God and that his hand of judgment was near. Also, secondly, they were looking for God to intervene in a dramatic way to deliver his people. Later rabbinic Judaism might be more accurately reflected by this description, though even here it could be seen to be idealistic rather than realistic.

We shall note later, when we look at the writings of E P Sanders, that he admits that our knowledge of the period of the Pharisees is not suf-

ficient for such confident assertions. We further have to recognise that
the frequently made assertion that Paul's teaching is 'short on repentance' in this context usually means that he does not teach the (later)
Rabbinic concept that repentance is sufficient without the Temple sacrifices. Justification for this teaching, developed after the destruction
of the Temple, is often sought in the teaching of the prophets, but in
context their teaching was not against the Temple sacrifices, but in the
frequent assumption of their automatic efficacy apart from genuine
repentance.

We now come to the work of W D Davies, and let the author
summarise his own thesis:

> '... despite the Hellenistic elements in his thought, Paul of Tarsus
> stood within the main current of First Century Rabbinic Judaism,
> and is best understood as a Pharisee, who had come to accept that
> Jesus of Nazareth was the Messiah. The apostle remained, as far as
> was possible, a practising Jew who agonised over his people, and never
> lost his sense of oneness with Israel (Romans 9), and in his theology it
> was to Judaic concepts that he chiefly turned in wrestling to interpret
> Christ and the Christian life. Pauline Christianity, it is contended, is
> not the antithesis of what became Rabbinic Judaism but its fulfilment
> 'in Christ'.[23]

Davies' work became a classic in its day, until it was challenged by
E P Sanders in his work *Paul and Palestinian Judaism* which has
become for many the benchmark by which all other work is judged.
Before we consider Sanders' views we have to say a word about
nomenclature as it relates to the various divisions within First
Century Judaism as described above. By modern consensus, Rabbinic
Judaism began with Rabbi ben Zakkai and the academy he founded
at Yavneh after the expulsion of Jews from Jerusalem in CE 70, and in
this sense the title of Davies' book is anachronistic. When Davies used
'Rabbinic' he meant 'Palestinian' as a distinction from 'Hellenistic'
Judaism. To that extent Davies and Sanders have given their works
identical titles, but there any similarity ends. At the end of a very long
critique of Davies' work Sanders quotes S Sandmel's opinion of
Davies' work:

> *Davies' book is an admirable book, indeed a great one – and one with*

which I disagree almost one hundred percent. ...' Sanders then concedes that 'his own judgment of Davies's accomplishment would be considerably more positive than that of Sandmel. ...[24]

Of course Sanders had the great advantage over Davies in that the Dead Sea Scrolls had now been discovered and studied, giving a wealth of information about Judaism at the turn of the Common Era. However, it must be said that at the time of his writing, and still to this day, the translating, dating and evaluation of the Scrolls requires much labour, and the results so far have not yet reached anything like a consensus. Sanders' main critique of Davies is in the realm of methodology. Davies had looked at the main themes in Paul's teaching and found these themes also in Rabbinic (ie Palestinian) Judaism. That, says Sanders, is not enough. In his lengthy and detailed introduction he says (p13), 'It is important to look at Palestinian Judaism as a whole and to carry out a comparison of Pauline Christianity and Palestinian Judaism.' Sanders' description of his proposed methodology is lengthy, and the logic of his argument at times tenuous. Indeed, when he proposes to exclude from the overall pattern such 'speculative questions as how the world was created; when the end will come; what will be the nature of the afterlife; *the identity of the Messiah;* and the like', (p17 italics mine) we have to say that this is imposing a methodology on Paul which is bound to lead to failure to understand him, since the identity of the Messiah is not speculative but central to his thesis. It would be valid to take issue with Paul about the identity of the Messiah: it is not valid to look at Pauline religion and yet exclude it!

The value of Sanders' monumental work is his exhaustive study of Jewish sources from 200 BCE to 200 CE, and as a reference book this is of tremendous value. However, in the last analysis Sanders' conclusions are heavily dependent on such works as 4 Esdras, which is usually dated at about 200 CE. Sanders, therefore, does not take seriously enough the double discontinuity of 70 and 134 CE. Towards the end of his book Sanders makes a caveat which is relevant, not only to his own work, but which would apply to every attempt to evaluate Paul's teaching on the basis of comparison with Rabbinic Judaism. He writes:

Our study has not been designed to answer the question of what Judaism was like in Palestine before 70 CE. We have not discussed the Pharisees and the Sadducees as such, for example, but only the surviving literature. It seems to me quite possible that we not only have no Sadducean literature, but also no Pharisaic literature, apart from the fragments embedded in the Rabbinic material. Thus I know a good deal less about Pharisaism than has been 'known' by many investigators. p 426[25]

It would have been helpful if that admission had been made earlier in his argument. And despite Sanders' very detailed investigations, Neusner's assessment is:

In regard to Rabbinic Judaism, Sanders' book is so profoundly flawed as to be hopeless and, I regret to say it, useless in accomplishing its stated goals of systematic description and comparison.[26]

For the next ten or so years Sanders' work, including his later *Paul, the Law, and the Jewish People* (London SCM 1985) became the launch pad for others' thinking to develop. Not until N T Wright entered the fray did we have any really radical new thinking. In his *The Climax of the Covenant: Christ and the Law in Pauline Theology*, (Edinburgh: T and T Clark, 1991), and in his more recent *What St Paul Really Said*, Wright argues that Paul, in the light of his understanding of Jesus of Nazareth, has engaged in a major redefinition of the twin Jewish doctrines of monotheism and election, of God and Israel. Whether or not, and to what degree, we want to agree with Wright in this major redefinition, it is clear that he is bringing the debate about Paul back to the essentials of where it ought to be, namely, 'Did Paul truly understand and faithfully interpret Jesus to the churches he founded and nurtured?' As soon as we ask that question it becomes an inevitable and urgent priority that we take a new look at the person and teaching of Jesus, and his relationship with the Jewish life and society of his day. We cannot just rest on the traditional solutions that have been offered through two thousand years of church history. The many and various findings of modern scholarship that we have sought to apply to Paul must now be applied to Jesus. This is where all attempts at objective, disinterested scholarship almost inevitably become mixed with deeply held community beliefs and our emotional responses not only to centuries, but to two millenia of mutual antagonism and rejection.

Sanders describes Palestinian Judaism in terms of what he calls 'Covenantal Nomism'. We shall spend some time looking at this because this term also covers the ground other scholars cover in different words. He writes:

> 'The 'pattern' or 'structure' of covenantal nomism is this (1) God has chosen Israel and (2) given the law. The law implies both (3) God's promise to maintain the election and (4) the requirement to obey. (5) God rewards obedience and punishes transgression. (6) The law provides for means of atonement, and atonement results in (7) maintenance or re-establishment of the covenantal relationship. (8) All those who are maintained in the covenant by obedience, atonement and God's mercy belong to the group which will be saved. An important interpretation of the first and last points is that election and ultimately salvation are considered to be by God's mercy rather than human achievement.[27]

Sanders then compares this with Paul's teaching in his letters of undisputed authorship, and he concludes that Paul's religion, unlike Palestinian Judaism, cannot be described as covenantal nomism, but is best described as participationist eschatology. He concludes:

> The heart of Paul's thought is not one that ratifies and agrees to a covenant offered by God, becoming a member of a group with a covenantal relationship with God and remaining in it on the condition of proper behaviour; but that one dies with Christ, obtaining a new life and the initial transformation which leads to the resurrection and ultimate transformation, that one is a member of the body of Christ and one Spirit with him, and that one remains so unless one breaks the participationary union by forming another.
>
> Righteousness in Judaism is a term which implies the maintenance of status among the group of the elect; in Paul it is a transfer term. In Judaism, that is, commitment to the covenant puts one 'in'. In Paul's usage, 'be made righteous' ('be justified') is a term indicating getting in, not staying in the body of the saved. Thus when Paul says that one cannot be made righteous by works of the law, he means that one cannot, by works of the law, 'transfer to the body of the saved'. When

*Judaism said that 'one is righteous who obeys the law', the meaning is
that one thereby stays in the covenant. The debate about righteousness by faith or by works of law thus turns out to result from the
different usage of the 'righteous' word-group.[28] PPJ p 514.*

I would make two responses:

First, the whole concept of that aspect of Judaism that can be
described as covenantal nomism, does not clearly arise until the time
of Rabbinic Judaism proper, ie after the destruction of the Second
Temple.

Secondly, ignoring for the moment the finer points of terminology
about 'righteousness', it is clear from Paul's letters to the Ephesians
and Colossians, (though the authenticity of these are questioned by
some scholars) that Paul does make a distinction between the 'path'
by which Jews and Gentiles attain to righteousness, though both arise
out of the atoning work of Christ.

Paul makes a distinction between Jews and Gentiles, saying that
the Gentiles:

*Were separate from Christ, excluded from citizenship in Israel and
foreigners to the covenants of promise, without hope and without God
in the world. But now in Christ Jesus you who once were far away
have been brought near through the blood of Christ. (Eph 2: 11-13).*

Paul then goes on to reveal a 'mystery' that had not previously been
revealed by the Spirit, namely that through the gospel the Gentiles
have become 'heirs together with Israel'. (Eph 3: 6).

The Greek here is not easy to translate. The NIV certainly over-
states the case by adding 'with Israel' without any textual warrant.
However, it does pick up the point that the writer is not saying
simply that the Gentiles and Israel have become heirs together, or
fellow heirs. The fact that the Gentiles are 'to be' or 'to become' fellow
heirs, implies that Israel already is an heir, which agrees with the
statement about the former exclusion of the Gentiles.

In context, the abolition of the enmity, which has to do with the
commandments and ordinances (though different translations have
different nuances as to how this is done) does not necessarily imply
the abolition of Torah, but rather those aspects that exclude the

Gentiles. In any case Greek 'nomos' does not always mean 'Torah' (nomos has a forensic quality, whereas Torah has more the sense of 'teaching' or 'instruction'). Christ has broken down the wall of partition and has made peace between Jew and Gentile. More than that he has reconciled both of them to God. And all this by means of the cross. So the cross is essential for both Jew and Gentile, *but in different ways*. For Jews it is the fulfilment of the Abrahamic Covenant: for the Gentiles it brings them into that Covenant. In that sense we can say that Paul's teaching was not incompatible with the idea of 'covenantal nomism' for Israel and the theme of 'transfer' for the Gentiles.

Having said that, there is a 'transfer' theme in Col 1: 13 in which Paul includes the Jews as well as the Gentiles. But the context here is clearly that of the eschatological Kingdom already made present and real by the resurrection of Christ. Paul's mindset here, as in 1 and 2 Thessalonians, is much nearer that of the writer of 4 Ezra and the writer of Revelation. This is still a part of the 'streams' and 'eddies' which made up the total flow of Jewish thought referred to earlier in this essay. To that extent Sanders and others could be said to be guilty of anachronism in comparing Paul with the covenantal nomism of the Yavneh school of Rabbinic Judaism.

It can be further said that Rabbinic Judaism also knows something of the transfer theme in the Passover ritual. Here there is a strong emphasis of Israel coming out of Egypt and being 'transferred' into the land. And this is not just a 'one off' event. According to the Haggadah, the Seder is a time for each Jew personally to re-enter into that experience:

> In every generation one must see oneself as though having personally come forth from Egypt, as it is written: 'And you shall tell your child on that day, 'This is done because of what the Lord did for me when I came forth from Egypt." It was not our ancestors alone whom the Holy One, blessed be He, redeemed; He redeemed us too, with them, as it is written: 'He brought us out from there that he might lead us to, and give us, the land which He promised to our ancestors.[29]

Jesus' teaching on forgiveness was never based on the redundancy of the Temple sacrifices. On the contrary, he instructed those he healed of leprosy to go to the Priests (Luke 17: 14) where they would be required to fulfil the necessary sacrifices. Jesus taught very clearly that the Temple would be destroyed as an act of God's judgment, a view supported in later Talmudic teaching. There is a passage in the Talmud telling of a scarlet strap in the Temple, which, after the relevant sacrifices, turned white, on the basis of Isaiah 1: 18, to show that God had accepted the sacrifices and forgiven his people. The Talmud relates that for the past forty years the strap had not turned white, indicating God's anger at the lack of true repentance, and therefore of the ineffectiveness of the sacrifices:

> *Our Rabbis taught: During the last forty years before the destruction*
> *of the Temple the lot (for the Lord) did not come up in the right hand;*
> *nor did the crimson coloured strap become white; nor did the western-*
> *most light shine; and the doors of the Hekal (Temple) would open by*
> *themselves, until Rabbi Johanan ben Zakkai rebuked them saying*
> *'Hekal, Hekal, why wilt thou be the alarmer thyself (Footnote:*
> *'Predict thy own destruction'.) I know about thee that thou wilt be*
> *destroyed, for Zechariah ben Iddo has already prophesied concerning*
> *thee: Open thy doors, O Lebanon, that the fire may devour thy*
> *Cedars.'[30]*

There was nothing here in mainstream Palestinian Judaism of which it can be shown that Paul was ignorant. There were two divergent interpretations in Judaism regarding the destruction of the Temple and the cessation of the priesthood and the sacrifices. The (later) rabbinic view that they were no longer necessary, and Jesus' view that he would be their fulfilment. He would be the reconstructed Temple (Mark 14: 58), and he would be the sacrificial lamb (Mark 14: 22). Paul followed Jesus' interpretation, (2 Cor 5: 21), but that cannot be used to divorce him from the mainstream of Palestinian Judaism of his day.

So where should we place Paul in the streams of Judaism we have seen? We shall let Tom Wright, one of the most recent and compelling writers on this subject speak:

> *Saul's persecution of the church, and the word 'zeal' with which he*
> *describes it, puts him firmly on the map of first-century Judaism. It*
> *gives us access to quite a wide database with which to plot the sort of*
> *agendas he must have been following, agendas which make sense of*

> his activity in persecuting the church even beyond the borders of the
> Holy Land itself. It reveals Saul of Tarsus not just as a Jew, but as a
> Pharisee; not just as a Pharisee, but as a Shammaite Pharisee; not
> just, perhaps, as a Shammaite Pharisee, but as one of the strictest of
> the strict.
>
> ...we use the word 'zeal' to indicate warmth of heart and spirit,
> eagerness for a cause – for the modern Christian 'zeal' is something
> you do on your knees, or in evangelism, or works of charity, for the
> first century Jew ...being 'zealous for YHWH', 'zealous for Torah' ...
> comes close to having a holy war ...
>
> A word of contemporary relevance at this point, with due caution
> about the danger of anachronism. If you want to see roughly what
> Shammaite Pharisaism was all about, look at the philosphy which
> inspired Yigal Amir to shoot Yitzhak Rabin in Tel Aviv on 4th
> November 1995. Amir was described as a 'law student'. This didn't
> mean that he was training to be a solicitor or barrister in the Western
> sense, but that he was a student of Torah...
>
> When I saw Amir's face on the front page of the London Times, and
> read the report, I realised with a shock that I was looking at a
> twentieth-century version of Saul of Tarsus.[31]

Even if we feel that Wright is overstating his case, but he may well
not be, one thing comes out clearly. The kind of zeal that Saul was
displaying when he got letters from the Jerusalem leadership to
pursue the followers of Jesus, and when he supported those who
were stoning Stephen, he was expressing the kind of zeal that was
found in the Palestinian Judaism of his day. Those who were
adopting the Hellenism of the diaspora were doing so because they
valued the intellectual breadth of Greek culture. They might not have
been attracted to faith in the Nazarene, because they would have
judged it as narrow as the type of Judaism which they felt they were
growing out of, but zeal, in the terms in which Saul of Tarsus
expressed it, was not a Hellenistic attribute.

Notes

1   **Hans Kung,** *Judaism,* English trans by John Bowden, SCM, 1996, p 363

2   Pinchas Lapide, *Mission ohne Beispiel.* Paulus-Rabbi, Ketzer und Apostel.
     Suddeutsche Zeitubg 6 – 8 June 1987. As translated and quoted by Kung,
     ibid p 363.

3   **Hershel Shanks** Ed, *Christianity and Rabbinic Judaism*, SPCK, 1993

4   **Lester L Grabbe**, *First Century Judaism*, T & T Clark, Edinburgh, 1996
     p 111f.

5   *ibid* p31.

6   *ibid* p39.

7   *ibid* p39.

8   *ibid* p44.

9   *ibid* p44f.

10   *ibid* p46f.

11   Three Talks on Judaism. Translated by **P Levertoff** in *Jewish Opinions
     About Jesus*. Published in Der Weg 7 No 1 (Jan-Feb 1933).

12   *Two Types of Faith*, MacMillan, 1940.

13   **Scholem Asch**, *One Destiny*, Putnams, New York, 1945.

14   **Frank S Mead**, *An Interview with Scholem Asch*, The Christian Herald, Jan
     1944.

16   **Gareth Lloyd Jones**, *Hard Sayings: Difficult New Testament Texts for
     Jewish-Christian Dialogue*, Council of Christians and Jews 1993.

17   *ibid* p3. Quoting *Facing the Truth*. Judaism 27, 1978, p 325.

18   **Pinchas Lapide**, *Israelis and Jesus*, Doubleday & Co, New York 1979.

19   **Joseph Klausner**, *From Jesus to Paul*, George Allen and Unwin, 1946.

20   **C G Montefiore**, *The Genesis of the Religion of St. Paul: Two Essays*, Max
     Goschen, London 1914 p 90.

21   *ibid* pp 59-60, as quoted in *Paul, the Law and Justification*, **C G Cruse**,
     Apollos 1996.

22   **James Parkes**, *Jesus Paul and the Jews*, p 120, London, 1936.

23   **W D Davies**, *Paul and Rabbinic Judaism*, SPCK, 2nd ed 1955.

24   **Sanders**, *Paul and Palestinian Judaism*, SCM Press, 1977, pp 9-10.

25   *ibid* p426.

26   **Neusner**, *Comparing Judaisms*, As quoted by C G Cruse, p 37.

27   **Sanders**, *Paul and Palestinian Judaism*, p 422.

28   *ibid* p 514.

29   *Passover Haggadah*, New English Translation by **Nathan Goldberg**, Ktav
     Publishing House Inc, Hoboken, New Jersey 1993.

30   Babylonian Talmud. Yoma 39b.

31   **Tom Wright**, *What St Paul Really Said*, Lion 1997, pp 26-28.

The Priesthood of James, the Brother of Jesus

Fred Wright

Abstract

A renewed interest in the character of James, the brother of Jesus emerged between 1996 and 1997 commencing with Pierre-Antoine Bernheim's *James, the Brother of Jesus*[1] closely followed by the controversial and highly speculative work *James the Brother of Jesus* vol 1 *The Cup of the Lord*[2] by the eminent but controversial Dead Sea Scrolls scholar, Prof Robert J Eisenman.[3] These works followed a gap of some forty-five years when the eminent German protestant scholar, Oscar Cullman caused a minor outcry by his suggestion that the primacy of Peter and the Church of Rome did not sit comfortably with the pre-eminence of James at the Jerusalem Council as portrayed in Acts 15: 13-21.[4] This essay attempts to examine the priesthood of James, the brother of Yeshua, commencing with a notice in Eusebius reporting the *testimonia* of Hegesippus a Jewish believer and churchman in the second century (c 90-180)[5]. The work of Hegesippus is no longer extant but is received by most scholars as authentic augmented. The notice is augmented with other sources. At the time Hegesippus lived there may have been people alive who knew James, or who knew people who lived at the time of the momentous events surrounding his life and death.

Control of the church passed [from Christ] to the apostles together with the Lord's brother Jakov (James) whom everyone from the Lord's time till our own has called 'the righteous', for there were many James' but this one was 'holy from his mother's womb; he drank no wine or intoxicating liquor and ate no animal food; no razor came to his head; he did not smear himself with oil and took no baths.

He alone was permitted to enter the Holy Place, for his garments were not of wool but of linen'. He used to 'enter the sanctuary alone' and was often found on his knees 'beseeching forgiveness for the people', so his knees grew hard like a camel's from his continual bending them before God and 'beseeching forgiveness for the people'. Because of his 'unsurpassable righteousness' he was called 'the Righteousness and Oblias' in our language 'Bulwark' (fortification or better the protection)[6] of the people and 'Righteousness' – fulfilling the prophets regarding him ... [James was asked] what was meant by the door of Jesus and he replied that Jesus was the Saviour[7] ... there was uproar amongst the Jews, the Pharisees and the Scribes who said that there was a danger that the entire people would expect Jesus to be the Christ. So they collected and said to James: 'Be good enough to restrain this people, for they have gone astray after Jesus in the belief that he is the Christ. Be good enough to make the facts about Jesus clear ...' [James is asked to stand on the parapet or more correctly the top of the staircase.] 'Righteous one', whose 'word we are all obliged to accept', tell us what is meant by the door to Jesus. He replied as loudly as he could ... He is sitting in heaven at the right hand of the great power, and he will come on the clouds of heaven.[8]

In the first section the following considerations will be addressed, from the sources available, what does it mean that he was the brother of Jesus? Was he the first leader of the emergent church and how was he regarded by others? In the second section we address the question, was James a priest and if so what was his role and function? In the third section we will suggest some consequences of the findings in the hope that they will open debate and fuel other studies. Much of the textual material evolves around the death of James as the reason for his death is an underlying tension.

Filial Concerns

The primary concern is, did Jesus in fact have a brother named Jakov (James), and did he become leader of the Nazarenes[9] following the death and resurrection of Yeshua? Despite James being freely acknowledged as the brother of Jesus (Mt 13: 55) along with Judas (Jude) Joses and Simeon, the filial relationship has been the cause of much controversy. The most widely held opinions over the centuries have been those generated by Epiphanius of Salamis who presented him as a son of a former marriage of Joseph, a theory approved of by J B Lightfoot[10] and more recently Richard Bauckham.[11] The second and most pervasive view has been that of Jerome who suggested that James and the other brothers were first cousins[12] probably of the line of Cleopas, assumed brother of Joseph. The overwhelming weight of evidence points towards a natural relationship as there are no suggestions within the New Testament that James is anything other than the natural brother of Yeshua. Tertullian, in the second century held the view that James was the natural brother of Jesus through Mary[13] although he did not accept that Jesus was born through natural generation. As interest in the character of Mary and her virginity grew in the second century, Origin (185-254) appears to have been the first to bring the question of filial relationship to the fore.[14] J P Meir, conducting a review of the word *Adelphos* in the 345 New Testament passages it appears, concludes that the term, when, not used as a metaphor or in a figurative sense, may only be applied to a brother or on occasion half-brother.[15] Even though it does appear, for reasons which will be considered below, that James seems to have been accorded little attention within the Acts or Pauline corpus, it would be highly unlikely, if James were a half-brother, that it would not have been noted particularly by those who wished to downplay his role.

Philological Tensions

James is recognised by two epithets, Zaddik (Heb) Righteous or Just = Dikaios (Gk) = Justus (Lat). And Oblias, which remains obscure. The first is fairly straightforward deriving from the Hebrew word cluster Z-D-K[16] which deals with righteousness or the application of righteousness. The other cognomen *Oblias*, however, is not as straightforward and the best applications are found in the Hebrew words *Oz* or *Maoz* which have the sense of strength, bulwark, or protection, this may be viewed in terms of holding back. This is satisfying in the sense that James is seen as the defender or protector of the messianic community, following Josephus' early testimony, which placed the cause of the downfall of Jerusalem upon the death of James.

Historical and Literary Tensions

The character of James is the subject of an extraordinary amount of non-canonical and extra-biblical literature, much of which may be considered to contain reliable material. There can be little doubt that James enjoyed a massive reputation amongst all of the sectarians. In the non-canonical writings James plays a significant role and is viewed in a positive light. When considering any text or document the nature of the document will be considered both in its literary genre and historical provenance.

New Testament Picture: Acts, The Accepted Paulines and James

It is important that we disregard the traditional picture that James did not accept the claims of Jesus during his lifetime. There is reasonable evidence to point to the conclusion that, along with James, at least two of his brothers were amongst the believers; his mother and brothers spent time together in the early days of his ministry (Jn 2: 12) and were involved with him, giving him encouragement before he went to the feast of Tabernacles (Jn 7: 4). He was witness to the resurrection (1 Cor 15: 7). Was appointed by Jesus to be his successor[17] (cf Acts 12: 17; Gal 1: 19, 2: 9). Presided over the council of Jerusalem concerning the admission of Gentile believers (Acts 15). Insisted that Paul illustrated his adherence to Judaic continuity (Acts 21: 18ff).

Jerome, who we may regard as being in possession of a number of non-extant sources, particularly, The Gospel to the Hebrews,[18] reports that his mother and brothers informed him of the baptism of John and encouraged him, along with themselves, to seek this baptism. Jesus questioned the manner of sin connected with him outside that of ignorance.[19] Jerome further contends that James was present at the Last Supper.[20]

The book of Acts has been the subject of much renewed interest in recent times, particularly its literary genre. The New Testament book of Acts, rather than dealing with the acts of the apostles, as the title implies, really deals with the acts of specific apostles and most particularly Paul who is the dominant figure from chapter 13: 4 to the open-ended completion, with the exception of a notice concerning Apollos (18: 24-28). The ministry of the Holy Spirit, so essential to Paul's theology, features highly in the Acts to the extent that in Pentecostal circles it has sometimes been fondly referred to as the Acts of the Holy Spirit.

The book of Acts suffers from lacunae concerning the election of James and the earliest days of his rule. Eisenman suggests that this is deliberate excision and overwriting to downplay the primacy of James and overplay the role of Paul whose eventual fate is omitted, possibly due to embarrassing circumstances. In a similar manner, Peter, who has played a leading role, vanishes around the same point.[21] Whereas there might be some element of truth in this assertion, it is more likely that Luke's intentions were limited to a particular template.[22] Leaving a piece open-ended with the reader left with an optimistic view is not without biblical precedent *viz* 2 Chronicles. The early Paulines and 1 Peter also give us some minor insights into the relationships between the Jewish believers and the Hellenistic stream which appear to have been tense at times. As data for the emergent believing community and the work of the apostles post-Pentecost we have to use supplementary sources. The Epistle of James has been the subject of much discussion as we will see later. We may best regard it as a summary of James' teaching prepared to be taken to the Diaspora. A review of major sources follows;

Josephus

Anyone wishing to gain an understanding of this period has to rely heavily on the writings of Flavius Josephus. Despite his limitations, his writings, which cover from 400 BCE to almost 100 CE, provide the major sources for gaining knowledge of Jewish history. Josephus provides information that cannot be gained from other sources as well as providing supplementary information to other sources. Josephus' writings, along with other ancient historians, need to be handled carefully as they contain many of the practices common to all historians of the period. Until Eusebius the following cautions apply to most early texts. Following the pattern of the Greco-Roman historians such as Theucydides, early writers were prone to putting contrived speeches in the mouths of real characters that often do not contain any record of what might have been said. Speeches therefore tend to be composed of what the writer thinks should have been said. Wildly exaggerated numbers, particularly casualty lists, obsequious comments towards patrons, self-aggrandisement and personal apologetic run through the works.

Notwithstanding the difficulties, much of what he has to say, in common with other early sources, can be taken at face value when handled properly. As Conrad Gempf has pointed out, in the ancient world rhetoric was power and speech was considered to be a type of action. The ancient world, and particularly the Roman empire, saw persuasion as a potent force that stood alongside coercion.[23] Ancient historians, when giving accounts of speeches in their works, were attempting to give accounts of events rather than transcripts of words. Available documentary sources indicate that they took their task very seriously. Gempf contends that the modern categories of *accurate* versus *invention* are therefore inappropriate conceptual tools. Notices concerning speeches today are expected to be transcripts; a better suggestion is, therefore, to consider documents as being *faithful* or *unfaithful* to the historical event.[24] If the document contains trace elements of the alleged situation that the particular event is presented, as having taken place in, and if the document exhibits traces of the personality of the character, we should then consider the article to be faithful. If it exhibits glaring inconsistencies or incongruities then we should consider the material unfaithful. Gempf's dictum, therefore, should be considered as a useful tool. Josephus shows an interest in James; recording his death[25] and obviously, in common with others, considered him one of outstanding righteousness. A recension of Josephus, quoted by Origin and reported by Eusebius, contains the additional material that the fall of Jerusalem and the misfortunes of the Jewish people were to *avenge James the Just, who was the brother of Jesus, called the Christ, since they killed him who was a very righteous man.*[26]

Eusebius

Eusebius, the great church historian, understood the role of James and in particular his role as Zaddik:

> *And they turned to James, the Lord's brother, to whom the apostles had trusted the throne of the episcopate at Jerusalem ...*[27] *This same James, then, whom the men of old surnamed the Just (another transliteration of Zaddik) on account of his excellent virtue, was the first to be entrusted with the throne of the episcopate at Jerusalem.*[28]

Later Eusebius includes an enigmatic notice that the throne existed in the day of James and was treated with veneration.[29] We may assume that this was something akin to the seat of Moses in the synagogue.

The church historian records extracts from the non-extant writings of Hegesippus, a Jewish believer, whose accounts of James and the early times provide a useful supplement. Eusebius, in the preface to his work, claims originality, indeed that he set out on a *lonely and untrodden path* ... [and] *failed to find any clear footprints of those who have gone this way before him.*[30] A benefit of Eusebius is the departure from classical Greek historiography by extensive use of verbatim citations of documents and letters. The diligence he displayed has served in preserving many extracts from works no longer extant. In terms of reliability, we may cite that two of his quotations have been confirmed by recent discoveries.[31] It is important to note that Eusebius makes no negative comments about the notices of Hegesippus and does not contradict the importance of James or his role as a priest.

Clement of Alexandria (150-215)

Clement's works are preserved in Eusebius:

> Peter, James and John, after the ascension of the saviour, did not claim pre-eminence because the Saviour had honoured them, but chose James the Righteous [Zaddik] as the Bishop of Jerusalem.[32]
>
> To James the Just and John and Peter; the Lord, after the resurrection, committed the knowledge [in turn] they committed it to the other apostles. (James the Righteous who was thrown from the parapet and beaten to death with a fuller's (laundryman's) club.[33]

We observe from Clement that James was elected by the risen Lord and the leadership was committed to him. There have been suggestions that the election was on the grounds that this was because he received the knowledge. The idea owes more to gnosticism than mainline Christianity. In all probability, the Lord spoke to him on the nature of the mission if this incident is not apocryphal or an extension of the notice in 1 Cor 15: 5, 7-8.

The Pseudo-Clementines

The Pseudo-Clementines, consisting of *The Recognitions* and *The*

Homilies, are generally considered to be Hellenistic Romantic novels bearing the pseudepigraphic superscription of Clement of Rome, (Clemens Romanus) considered to hold the third place in succession to Peter as bishop of Rome.[34] Translated by Rufinus, the action caused a tension between him and Jerome. The documents purport to be letters from Clement (Rome) to James, Peter to James and James to Peter. Included are assumed lost materials from documents known as the Teaching of Peter, the Acts of Peter and the ascents or steps of James. The latter focuses upon a large-scale rupture between James and Paul.

The Death of James

In the year 62 CE, shortly after the Roman Procurator Festus died in office, the emperor, Nero, sent Albinus to replace him. As the appointment was being made Agrippa II, king of Galilee and Perea (across the Jordan) made Ananus the younger high priest. (Ananus the elder had five sons who all held this office.) Josephus (not a believer) relates that as Albinus was on the road to his new appointment:

> *Ananus (sometimes Hanan) a bold and insolent man ... thought that he now had a proper opportunity [to exercise his authority] ... so he assembled the sanhedrin of judges, and brought before them the brother of Jesus who was called the Christ, whose name was James (Gk = Jakov Heb) and some others. And when he had formed an accusation against them as breakers of the law, he delivered them to be stoned. But those who seemed the most equitable of the citizens, and accurate in legal matters, disliked what was done. They also sent to king Agrippa, desiring him to send to Ananus that he should act so no more; for what he had done was not to be justified, some of them also went to meet Albinus, as he was on his journey from Alexandria, informing him that it was not legal to assemble a sanhedrin without his consent.*

Albinus was furious and made threats to punish Ananus for what he had done and instructed king Agrippa to dismiss him from his position.[35] Ananus continued to play a leading role subsequently and gets mixed reports from Josephus.

Clement simply records that James was thrown down from a

parapet and beaten to death with a fuller's club.[36]

Hegesippus gives an extended version of the events which Eusebius faithfully reproduces following on from our opening text where James was invited to stand on the parapet, and to the consternation of the opposition, gave testimony to Jesus:

> *Many were convinced and gloried in James' testimony crying: Hosanna to the son of David. Then the scribes and the Pharisees said to each other: We made a bad mistake in affording such testimony to Jesus. We had better go up and throw him down, so that they will be frightened and not believe him. Ho Ho! they called out even the righteous one has gone astray! – fulfilling the prophecy of Isaiah:*
>> *Let us remove the righteous one, for he is unprofitable to us.*
>> *Therefore they shall eat the fruit of their works. (Isa 3: 10)*
> *So they went up and threw down the righteous one. Then they said to each other let us stone James the Righteous, and began to stone him, as in spite of his fall he was still alive. But he turned and knelt, uttering the words: I beseech Thee Lord God and Father, forgive them; they do not know what they are doing.[37] While they pelted him with stones, one of the descendants of Rechab, the son of Rechabim – the priestly family to which Jeremiah the prophet bore witness [Jer 35] called out; Stop! what are you doing? The righteous one is praying for you. Then one of them, a fuller, took the club and brought it down on the head of the Righteous one. Such was his martyrdom. He was buried on the spot, by the sanctuary, and his headstone is still there by the sanctuary.[38]*

Was James a Priest and if so What Manner of Priest?

Before we proceed to offer a series of models for the priesthood of James we should first ascertain if this is a legitimate question. Secondly, we must consider the works of Epiphanius and his younger contemporary, Jerome, as they increase the role and status of James.

Epiphanius of Salamis

Epiphanius, the bishop of Constantia, is ranked among the leading contenders against heresy, particularly the teachings of Origen[39] in which he co-operated with Jerome from 382. His main work, the *Panarion* (the medicine box – refutation of all heresies) contains valuable materials that would otherwise have been lost, but his use of sources are somewhat self-limiting relying mostly on the previous works of Hippolytus and Irenaeus. It is to Epiphanius that we are indebted for information concerning the survival and knowledge of the Nazarenes.[40] Epiphanius repeats the notice in Hegesippus concerning James' priesthood but after a definitive piece of displacement theology, where the throne and royal seat of David are transferred to the church, he adds the following curious passage:

> The priestly honour that it holds, because he who is high priest and chief of high priests afterwards was installed as the first bishop: James called apostle and brother of the Lord[41] ... he became a Nazarite. Wherefore he was also allowed to enter the holy of holies, just as the law commanded the high priests according to the scriptures on the other hand he was even allowed to wear the high priest's mitre[42] on his head. So relate many who came before us concerning him, Eusebius, Clement and others.[43]

This notice could be taken to mean that James was perhaps regarded by the believers as the high priest of the Israel that was renewed and sanctified by the blood of the Messiah. Epiphanius, after contending that James was the son of Joseph only, immediately repeats material from Hegesippus but with the addition of material relating to a possibility of high priesthood. The full implications are included in the eschatological model offered below.

The High Priestly Imagery

Let us recall the words of our major sources:

> Eusebius quoting Hegesippus, 'He alone was permitted to enter the Holy Place, for his garments were not of wool but of linen. He used to enter the sanctuary alone.'[44]
>
> Epiphanius and Jerome concur, Wherefore he was allowed to enter into the holy of holies, just as the law commanded the high priest.[45]

The first consideration is the expression 'just as the law commanded the high priest'. Is it to be understood as a parallel, or does it simply underline the convention that James was acting in a high priestly capacity, either officially or unofficially? We must disregard the notion of unofficial activity, as the text clearly demonstrates that he was permitted. The information that he was beeseeching mercy for the people, or nation reflects Yom Kippur activities, underlining the question 'was James at one time functioning in a high priestly capacity' and if so how could this be? The notion is reinforced by the request made to him by his opposition as the righteous one **to whom we all must listen.** One to whom all must listen is obviously a person carrying the ultimate authority.

Jerome, who studied Hebrew and spent time in Palestine, particularly Bethlehem, gives a similar notice to Eusebius quoting Hegesippus. Jerome adds that his person was considered to be so holy that they earnestly sought to touch the hem[46] of his garment.[47]

Some Suggested Models for the Priesthood of James

Following are some suggested models concerning the priesthood or high priesthood of James:

1   The Hellenistic Romance Model

The literary model suggested above would disregard any of the information in the notices above as mere imagination and myth, particularly as James features so highly in the Pseudo-Clementines and Pseudepigraphical works. The tendency in the modern age is to dismiss the mythos of any particular social group as mere invention. Such an attitude disregards Schelling's dictum that a nation [and for this we may substitute any social group] comes into existence with its mythology.[48] That is to say, that the content of the segment of the mythos may well reflect an event, or folkway, that is essential to the understanding of the material that is under consideration. The general, self-definition and attitudes of any social unit can often be formed by the mythos, albeit in literature, music or art. An outstanding example would be in the First Crusade (1096-99) where the attitudes of the French armies were coloured more by the *chansons de Geste*.[49]

We must dismiss this model immediately, as our analysis is not concerned with mythos but with solid tangible material contained in Josephus. The said material is contained in both the extant recension and, what we may safely assume, was the recension viewed by

Origen and Eusebius. To add to the validity of these notices, we might add that as heresy hunters, Epiphanius and Jerome would have been some of the first to point out that the data contained in the said notices were flawed, particularly in their fight against Origenism. We should point out that writers of the major sources all spent time in the holy land, and the areas of culture in the region, and are therefore more likely to have access to no longer extant documents and possibly oral traditions. Oral history, particularly cast in the form of the epic or the saga, often repeated by rote, contains material that changes little over the centuries.[50] In addition, the notices in most cases are too compact to properly be considered within this genre.

2   Priestly Succession Model – Could James have been a member   of the Mishmarot?

In the Second Temple period the priesthood contained 24 mishmarot (courses)[51] which were composed of several families in each course who served for a week, twice a year.[52] The priesthood was passed down through the male line of the tribe of Levi. The priesthood had been divided into the twenty-four courses by David (1 Chron 24: 1-6), the divisions being re-affirmed by Solomon (2 Chron 8: 14). Assuming that James was the son of Joseph of the tribe of Judah, we can dismiss the male line of descent to account for a role as a hereditary priest. There is, however, a second line to follow in that from the female line there was a priestly connection with Elizabeth, Mary's undefined kinswoman referred to by Luke (1: 5) as a daughter of Aaron, who was married to Zechariah, a priest of the mishmar of Abijah[53] (Luke 1: 5-8 cf Neh 12: 4). We are informed that Mary hurried to visit her, implying that she lived not too far away. Whether the family of Jesus lived in Nazareth (Luke), of which there is little evidence of its existence in this time, or in Bethlehem is open to question. The small town of Nazareth is not mentioned by Josephus, who was a military commander in the area. Nazareth receives its first notices in Hebrew literature of the early medieval period as a place occupied by priestly families after the destruction of the Second Temple.[54]

We are in possession of information that the priests lived not only in Jerusalem, but that some lived in the Galilee, only attending Jerusalem when it was their time of service.[55] In the genealogy of

Mary we find two ancestors bearing the then unlikely name of Levi. In studies of biblical characters it is sometimes difficult to ascertain if people's names, cognomens, titles or offices are being used. Without reading too much into it, could it be possible that there was a priestly line attached to Mary's family? The difficulty of names, cognomens and titles feature highly in the gospels. The person known as Thomas called Didymus (both mean twin) does not designate the person by a familial name. Likewise, Thaddeus (Heb = *shad* = breast) and Lebbeus (= *leb* = heart) obviously the same person, cause us to look further for the identity of the person. A further problem with names is the abundance of Miriams (Marys) we are faced with, including data that points towards Mary having a sister of the same name.

3   Nazarite-Rechabite Model

We have observed in the notices above that James was a Nazarite (Num 6: 1-21) from birth, holy from his mother's womb. The Hebrew word 'cluster' associated with the term, has the sense of one separated. Nazarite vows could be taken by men, women[56] and slaves but not gentiles.[57] The vows could be for a period of time, or in perpetuity, until such a time as the person wished to be released by a payment to the Temple. In the person of the Nazarite the layman is given the status akin to the priest as he is holy to the Lord.[58] His uncut hair being the outward symbol of his dedication. A further notice worthy of attention is that of Hegesippus concerning the cry of the Rechabite at the stoning of James above. Epiphanius identifies this particular individual as Simeon bar Clopas, cousin of Jesus and successor of James.[59] Both Hegesippus and rabbinic tradition associate the Rechabites with the priesthood. There are three suggestions concerning the Rechabites: (i) that they were foreigners who had married into the tribe of Levi and thus the priestly orders;[60] (ii) that as descendants of the Kenites, thus they were associated with Moses by marriage and *ipso facto* included into the priesthood by this initial marriage, and (iii) they were the descendants of Jonadab B Rechab who was involved in the overthrow of the Omriad dynasty and his descendants were extreme Nazarites (Jer 35)[61] and as such were accorded priestly status due to their advanced state of purity and *de rigor* lifestyle. The objection that James could not have been a priest,

because he did not smear himself with oil and took no baths, points
that he could not enter the sanctuary as the priests had to wash both
their hands and feet before entering, may be disregarded. The notice
refers to the Hellenised practice of attending the public baths, often
places of iniquity, and the Greco-Roman practice of smearing oil on
the body to supposedly cleanse and beautify.[62] As a rigourist such
practices would have been abhorrent to James. The objection that the
priests ate the parts of the sacrifices and therefore this speaks against
vegetarianism should be overlooked and placed into the frame of
nazaritism. During the late Second Temple period there were several
groups who were seeking purity and freedom from all pollution.
Some such groups practised daily bathing and ate only wild plants
considering all meat to be polluted as being the fruit of animal forni-
cation. A striking example is the case of Judas the Maccabee who was
of the priestly line. In 167 BCE, along with nine others, he withdrew
into the wilderness and ate nothing but wild plants to avoid defile-
ment (2 Macc 5: 27).

4   Eschatological Model

The model starts with the assumption that there is no substance in the
notice and the notion belongs to an eschatological model. A suggestion of how the early church, particularly the Jewish stream, may
have appropriated the idea is suggested below:

John the Baptist	=	Elijah redivivous
Yeshua	=	King of Kings
Yakov	=	Priest of Priests
The three	=	The priestly Triumvirate
12 apostles	=	Heads of the twelve tribes of Israel[63]
The 70	=	Sanhedrin[64]
The believers	=	Subjects of the Kingdom

An apposite question is; was there a place in the eschaton for a Third
Temple in the thought of the Second Temple? The expectation was for
the restoration of the people and a purified faith.[65] Various passages
used widely in the first century imply that this might include a Third
Temple. From the canonical scriptures; Isa 44: 28; 56: 1-8; 60: 3-7,10-14;

66: 18-24; Ezek 40-43; Micah 4. From the Pseudepigraphia; Tobit 14: 5;
1 Enoch 90: 28f; Test Benj : 2; Ps Sol 17: 34.

The immediate problem with the eschatological model is that the
notices concerning both the priesthood and assumed high priesthood
of James are set in the Second Temple and James' death preceded the
destruction of the physical building.

5   Revolutionary Model

Both Eisenman,[66] and Schonfield[67] before him, connect Early Jewish
Christianity with revolutionary movements. When one looks at the
causes of the great revolt it becomes obvious that it was not simply a
desire to be free of the Roman yoke but a desire for restoration of the
nation and a removal of corruption and pollution in the cultus.
Should we simply dismiss the death of James as merely a preventative execution. Both the New Testament and Josephus attest the
impact of John the Baptist and his campaign against corruption and
pollution. There can be little doubt that despite romanticised stories,
John's execution was a preventative measure against a popular
uprising against the Herods.[68] Preventative executions featured
throughout the reign of the Herods, examples being the extermination
of Herod the Great's immediate family,[69] Messianic pretenders and
their offspring, *ie* James and Simon, the sons of Judas the Galilean.[70]
The execution of Jesus may also be presented as a preventative
measure, remembering that Jesus was condemned to death by the
Romans as a suspected revolutionary, the cleansing of the Temple
being the causal event (Mark 11: 17 and parr).[71] The setting of James'
execution in the time of the uprising against Rome, therefore, could
reasonably be placed into such a category. The pro-Roman leadership
were anxious not to bring large-scale reprisals upon their heads if
another revolutionary group arose led by the brother of one already
executed on similar (although trumped up) charges. There is little
doubt the main concentration of zealot fervour was in the Galilee,
particularly in Gaulonitis and Sepphoris. The family of James and
Yeshua are conveniently situated in this locale.

Such a line of reasoning may seem satisfying but it flies in the face
of the events, even as recorded by Josephus. If we recall, the tensions
between the believers and their opposition in the twenty-five years or

so recorded in Acts were chiefly centred on rights concerning the temple and its environs. The notices concerning James' priesthood show a line of causal continuity possibly reaching its highest tensions between the rigorists and accommodationists in the early days of the great revolt. It could be considered that James was the spiritual leader of the Zealot movement and opposition high priest on their behalf. If this were the case, one would assume that, despite his deficiencies, Josephus would have included a notice to this effect in his writings. A difficulty in dealing with ancient documents is the many recensions. In the case of Josephus, we may assume, as noted above, that there was a recension known to both Origen and Eusebius (also possibly Epiphanius and Jerome). The non-extant recension, if it contained a notice concerning a direct link between James and the Zealot/Sicarii movements, would surely have been commented on, particularly by the later writers who considered Jewish Christians neither Jews nor Christians as exampled in his correspondence with Augustine.

6   The Priestly Conflict Model

In the early first century, after the despotic reign of Herod and the weak reign of Archelaus, the high priests became the *de facto* leaders of the nation.[72] It should be noted that the Temple contained the treasury and those who controlled the Temple wielded enormous power. By the year 59 CE the general accommodationism and corruption of the high priests caused bitter enmity to arise from the ordinary priests who were suffering both spiritual and physical deprivation. The tensions erupted into violence and, against this background, the stopping of sacrifices on behalf of foreigners initiated by the priest. Josephus considered this to be the causation of the fall of Jerusalem.

The wearing of linen was apparently a privilege of the upper echelons of the priesthood. Josephus offers an undated notice that the Levites and, from the sentence construction, possibly the lower ranks of the priesthood only gained the right to wear linen in the time period immediately preceding the revolt of the 60s[73] around the time of the death of James. These were tumultuous times. The priesthood itself was in a state of corruption and struggles for power. The last legitimate Hasmonean high priest, Aristobulus, was murdered by drowning on order of Herod, his father, shortly after his investiture at the age of seventeen.[74] From this point the priestly office, dominated by the Sadducees, was the subject of appointment by either the kings, or the Romans by purchase, or according to how the wind blew. The high priesthood was dominated in this period by the powerful families of Boethus, Phani and Annus.[75] Each high priest served for one year but at the end of his tenure of office he retained the honours and most of the privileges accorded to the office. The effect was to create something akin to a power elite who jealously guarded the office and the Temple environs. The upper levels of the priesthood plundered the poorer priests to the extent that many died of starvation or disease, caused by deprivation.[76] The last high priest, according to Josephus,[77] was a stonecutter named Phanni (or Phanasus) B Samuel (67-68 CE) of the village of Aphtha, a relative by marriage to Hillel, who was not of a high priestly family. Josephus, who was disgusted by his elevation in *Ant,* states that he was elected by the people, but in the expanded version in *War* the notice reports the mishmarot of priests named Eniachim, 'were responsible for his election by the casting of lots'.[78] The priesthood was generally considered to be either open only to the Levites or more generally the sons of Aaron, the high priests being from the descendants of his eldest son (Lev 21: 10). Phineas and his house were accorded a perpetual priesthood on account of his zeal (Lev 25: 10, 13). In the time of David, the high priesthood was a joint position held by Abiathar and Zadok (2 Sam 15: 35, 20: 25; 1 Kings 4: 4; 1 Chron 15: 11). Solomon deposed Abiathar (1 Kings 2: 27). From this point the priesthood descended from Zadok. Ezekiel teaches that only descendants of the family of Zadok had the right to hold the hereditary position (Ezek 40: 46; 44: 15 etc).

The battle for purity in the priesthood was attended by extreme measures. In the latter days of the Temple the sacrifices for, or[79] on behalf of, foreigners were suspended, even though throughout the history of the Temple this had been a general practice.[80] If a priest served in a state of uncleanliness at the altar, the young priests would take him outside and split open his head with a club.[81] It may be here that we can develop a scenario for the death of James that fulfils the requirements of the available data. James, for reasons that may only be speculated upon, assumed the role of at least a member of the priesthood on either hereditary, eschatological or revolutionary grounds. It may be better to think of this action as a prophetic action in line with the cleansing of the Temple by his elder brother Yeshua (Mk 11: 15 and parrs). On a specific or particular occasion, he assumed the role of the high priest in offering atonement for the people. The immediate difficulty here is that the atonement of James was in prayer, not with the blood of bulls and calves (Heb 9: 12) which would entirely be in line with one who was the successor of Yeshua whose teaching pointed to the end of animal sacrifice. The action may have been authorised or a reaction against the impure and therefore considered to be unacceptable sacrifices of the official priesthood. Hegesippus in his notice, may have preserved the underlying tensions which offer an answer in part to the question; Did James enter the Holy place or Holy of Holies in a state of uncleanliness? The state of uncleanliness does not mean that he did not follow the regulations of ritual purity, rather that he did not qualify to enter the inner sanctum by liege or purchase. Was James something akin to a people's high priest? If this indeed were the case can we attribute his death to a reactionary move by the establishment against (a) the popularity of the individual or (b) the movement he represented? The notice concerning the stoning of James would fit well into this scenario as it was the standard punishment for blasphemy. One entering the Holy of Holies without the benefit of election by the ruling body would have been considered guilty of blasphemy. Hegisippus' record of the events may be a composite of several strands of the truth relating the events that point to James' death being attributable to a power struggle concerning the priesthood. If this is the most persuasive model then we must assume that Christianity was a far more potent force in the late 50s and 60s than was assumed. If James was the leader of such an important movement, to the extent that he was in a position to be considered the people's high priest, further research is essential.

Conclusion
There can be little doubt the earliest and most reliable of the early church fathers accepted the notices concerning the priesthood of James as authentic, to the extent that they needed to pass little or no

comment upon them. The absence of testimonia concerning James in the canonical writings poses an enigma. Were the records of his discipleship and election to the leadership of the emergent church deliberately ignored, overwritten, omitted, excised, or redacted out deliberately as they were considered to stand in stark contrast to the Hellenised stream of Christianity presented by the Pauline circle? We might also ask; was James' insistence on keeping the traditions of Judaism considered an embarrassment? The priestly conflict model appears to sit most comfortably within our limited sources. Alternatively, we are left with the eschatological model as a comfortable but weak second choice. It may be that we will never know the exact role and status of James' priesthood although we can be content with his role as the accepted leader in the emergent community. There is little doubt that he was of enormous influence and that the rigourist stream of faith in Yeshua the Messiah had a strong following in Jerusalem, possibly to a much greater extent than has been appreciated. James' relationship with Paul and the Hellenised stream is a question that is usually happily fudged over; or Jewish Christianity dismissed as an aberration that was short-lived. As Dr Ray Pritz has illustrated, Nazarean Jewish Christianity had a clear self-definition and lasted well into the fourth century as recorded by Epiphanius and Jerome.[82]

Abbreviations

Acts	**Winter B W** *The Book of Acts in its First Century Setting* Vol 1, Eerdemans, and **Clarke AD** (eds), Grand Rapids, 1993 and Paternoster Press, Carlisle 1993 6 vols
Ant	**Flavius Josephus** *Antiquities of the Jews*
HE	**Eusebius** *Ecclesiastical History*
Pan	*Epiphanius Panarion* (refutation of all Heresies)
PARDES	Journal of *The Centre for Biblical and Hebraic Studies*
M San	*Mishna Sanhendrin*
T San	*Tosefta Sanhedrin*
Vir Ill	**Jerome** *Praise of Illustrious Men*
War	**Flavius Josephus** *Jewish War*

Notes

1 **Bernheim Pierre-Antonine Jaques**, *Ferèr de Jésus*, Éditions Noêsis, Paris 1996. English version tr **Bowden J**, SCM, London, 1997

2 **Eisenman R**, *James the Brother of Jesus vol I The Cup of the Lord*, Faber, London, 1997.

3 Both books were reviewed by the writer in the Journal of PARDES, The Centre for Biblical and Hebraic Studies, Vol 1 No 4, Sept 1997

4 **Cullman O**, *Peter, Disciple – Apostle – Martyr*, SCM, London, 1953

5 Hegesippus visited Jerusalem, known at the time as Aelia Capitolina during the reign of Antoninus Pius (138-161).

6 For those not conversant with Greek there is no indefinite article therefore the use of the definite article is important – otherwise it would be in the sense of one of many.

7 According to Jerome, Ananus publicly attempted to get James to recant that Christ was the son of God.

8 HE 2: 23;4 quoting the 5th book of Hegesippus Hypomnemata.

9 The accepted first name for the early believers possibly based on Isa 11: Acts 24: 5, Pan 29: 1: 3; 6: 2: Tertullian Adv marc 4: 8. For a full discussion see **Pritz R**, *Nazarene Jewish Christianity*, Magnes Press, Jerusalem, 1988, groundbreaking work on the subject.

10 Lightfoot was particularly interested in the family of Jesus see **Lightfoot J B**, *Saint Paul's Epistle to the Ephesians and Galatians*, Macmillan, London 1890.

11 **Bauckham R**, *The Brothers and Sisters of Jesus: an Epiphanian Response to J P Meier*, Catholic Bible Quarterly 56, 1994, p 686-700

12 **Jerome**, *Contra Helvidius* (c 383 CE)

13 Adv Marcion 4: 19; de Verig vel 6

14 Comm in Mt 10: 7 Hom in Luke 7

15 **Meir J P**, *A Marginal Jew*, NY Doubleday, Vol 1 1991, p 328 n 7

16 ie at Qumran, the Teacher of Righteousness is referred to as Moreh Yoreh ha-Zedek

17 HE 7: 19

18. A few fragments remain. Collected by Klostermann Apocrypha II (Kliene Text 8) 1929

19 Contra Peleg, 3: 2

20 Vir Ill 2

21 **Eisenman R**, *op cit*

22 A term I have borrowed from Dr Loveday Alexander, *Acts and Ancient Intellectual Biography in Acts* p 37 who in turn borrowed it from Susie Orbach writing in *The Guardian* 27 March 1993. Possible templates are the life of Socrates and a continuation of Old Testament salvation history.

23 **Mellor R**, *Tacitus*, Routledge, London 1993, p 113-114

24 **Gempf Conrad**, *Public Speaking and Published Accounts in Acts*, p 300-303

25 Ant 20: 1 (197-203)

26 **Origen**, *Contra Celsus* 1: 47 tr **Chadwick H**, Cambridge University Press, 1953, p 43, cf 2: 13, See also **Origens** *Commentary on Matthew* 10: 17

27 HE 2: 23: 1

28   HE 2: 1: 2

29   HE 18: 2: 19

30   HE 1: 1: 3

31   **Nobbs A** , *Acts and Subsequent Ecclesiastical Histories in Acts,* p 159

32   **Clement,** *Outlines Book 6*

33   *ibid* Book 8

34   Peter 62-67, Linus 67-68, Cletus 78-90, Clement 90-100 CE

35   **Clement,** *Homilies book 8 in HE*

36   HE 2: 23

37   Luke 23: 34. Steven also alluded to these words that almost became a standard for martyrs

38   HE 2: 23: 4-17

39   (i) The Pre-existence of souls as taught by Plato (ii) The human nature of Christ existed before the incarnation (iii) All men and evil devils including satan will be saved at the last (iv) That at the resurrection our bodies will be transformed into absolutely ethereal bodies.

40   Epiphanius lists twenty pre-Christian heresies and sixty from the Christian era, working on scheme of increasing wickedness. For a good translation of Panarion 29 and the definitive study of the Nazarenes see **Pritz R**, *Nazarene Jewish Christianity*, Magnes Press, Jerusalem, 1988, translation of Pan pp 30-35

41   Pan 3: 8-9

42   For the linen mitre (*misnephet*) see Ex 28: 36-39 for the plate (*nezer*) see Ex 29: 6, 39: 30, Lev 8: 9

43   Pan 4: 4

44   HE 2: 23;4

45   Pan 29: 4: 3; 78: 13: 5-8

46   Tzit Tzit see Nu 15: 38-39 cf Luke 8: 44-47

47   **Jerome,** *Comm on Gal 1: 19*

48   Alluded to in **Schirer W**, *The Rise and The Fall of the Third Reich*, Secker and Warburg, London, 1959 and 1960, p 102

49   Le Chanson d'Roland, Aliscans etc for a full discussion see **Wright F**, *The Cross Became a Sword, the Soldiers of Christ and the First Crusade*, RW Publishing, Harpenden 1995, p 23

50   The Serbian and Icelandic Bards are good examples along with Chanson de Geste. African tribal genealogical lists where there was no literacy were transmitted by rote.

51   Ant 7: 14: 7 (365)

52   **Tosef,** Taan 4: 2 ; 22 et al

53   After the exile only four of the courses returned (Ezra 2: 36-39) They were reconstituted under their old names, Abijah being the eighth course.

54   **Flusser D**, (tr) **Glucker J,** *Jewish Sources in Early Christianity*, MOD Books, Tel-Aviv 1989, p 15

55   *ibid*

56   The most famous female Nazarite was Queen Helena of Adiabene, Nazir 19b

57   Nazir 61b

58   Philo I L A 249

59   Pan 78,14: 2-6

60   So Williamson GA HE 2: 23: 17 n 1

61   Eisenman sees the Rechabites as extreme Nazarites and proto-Zealots in
      James Brother Jesus *ibid*.

62   If no water was available for bathing sometimes the body would be
      smeared with oil and the oil scraped off.

63   Lk 22: 30 and parr

64   The Sanhedrin had jurisdiction in tribal affairs, false prophets, false
      priests (Mishna San 1: 5) declare a scholar rebellious, and elect a king or
      a high priest (Tosefta San 3: 4)

65   ie Ben Sirah 48: 10 Ps Sol 11 along with the traditional canonical
      passages concerning the return: for a full discussion of the latter see
      Wright F, *Words From The Scroll of Fire*, Jerusalem, 1994, Ch 14. The
      Return in its Biblical Context.

66   *op cit*

67   **Schonfield H**, *The Jesus Party*, Macmillan, NY 1974

68   Ant 18: 5: 2 (116-119)

69   Ant 16: 11: 7 (392-393)

70   Ant 20: 5: 2 (102)

71   **Sanders E P**, *Jesus and Judaism*, London, SCM, 1985, p 57

72   Ant 20: 10 (251)

73   Ant 20: 9: 6 (216-18)

74   War 1: 22: 2 (437)

75   Yoma 18a, Yev 61a

76   Ant 20: 8: 8 (179-182): 20: 9: 2 (204)

77   Ant 20: 101 (227)

78   War 4: 3: 8: (155)

79   War 2: 17: 2 (408)

80   War 2: 17: 2 (411f)

81   M San 9: 6

82   **Pritz R**, *op cit*

The Kingdom of Heaven

By Joseph Frankovic

In a thoughtful essay entitled *Christ's Lordship and Religious Pluralism*,
Krister Stendahl, wrote the following:

> But it remains a fact worth pondering that Jesus had preached the
> kingdom, while the church preached Jesus. And thus we are faced
> with a danger: we may so preach Jesus that we lose the vision of the
> kingdom, the mended creation.[1]

Stendahl has brought into sharp focus the fact that Jesus' preaching
centred on the Kingdom of Heaven. Christian preaching, however,
may often centre on the *person* of Jesus without adequate attention
being given to his *message*. This emphasis risks down-playing the significance of the Kingdom of Heaven and blurring the challenges,
responsibilities, demands, and privileges of being a disciple of Jesus. A
key verse in the quest for attaining an accurate understanding of the
Kingdom is Matthew 6: 33: *'But seek first his Kingdom and his righteousness and all these things shall be added to you.'* This verse serves as an
excellent example of what Bible scholars call a *parallelism*. The ancient
Jewish mind enjoyed repeating the same idea in a parallel structure.
For instance, Proverbs 20: 1 says, *'Wine is a mocker, and strong drink a
brawler.'* Here 'wine' is paired with 'strong drink,' and 'mocker' with
'brawler'. Hebraic parallelisms also appear in the Greek of the New
Testament. Matthew 6: 33 is a synonymous parallelism which has been
preserved in the Greek. Thus, if one can unlock what 'his Kingdom'
means, one can use that information to unlock what 'his righteousness'
means. Likewise, if one can unlock what 'his righteousness' means,
one can unlock what 'his kingdom' means. The approach taken here
will be to start by unlocking the meaning of 'his righteousness.'

From the Greek of Matthew 6: 33, *dikaiosunae* has been translated
into English as 'righteousness'. If one operates on the premise that
Jesus was not teaching in Greek, but in Hebrew (or perhaps in

Aramaic), then an effort to identify what he said in Hebrew may prove helpful.

Underneath the Greek *dikaiosunae* is some form of the Semitic root *tsadak*. From that same root, the noun *tsedakah* in Hebrew carries a range of meanings. During the first century CE, when Jews spoke a type of Hebrew known as Mishnaic Hebrew, *tsedakah* had come to mean almsgiving. For example, in Matthew 6: 1 the Greek *dikaiosunae* means charitable deed. This is a good indication that underneath *dikaiosunae* lurks the Hebrew word *tsedakah*, because *dikaiosunae* in classical Greek does not mean almsgiving. *Dikaiosunae* only takes on this meaning when Hebrew (or Aramaic) has influenced the Greek.

When modern Bible translators have encountered the Old Testament Hebrew word *tsedakah*, too often they have woodenly translated it into English as righteousness. For example, examine the context of Micah 6: 3-5. English translations of the passage read something like:

> *My people, what have I done to you? How have I made you weary? Answer me! I have brought you up from the land of Egypt. I have redeemed you from the house of slavery. I sent before you Moses, Aaron and Miriam. My people, remember what Balak, King of Moab, counselled, and what Balaam, son of Beor, answered him! From Shittim to Gilgal, in order that you may know the tsidkot Adonai.*

Nearly all English translations have rendered *tsidkot Adonai* as 'the righteous acts of the Lord'. The Revised Standard Version, however, reads differently. What is the context of this passage? Speaking on behalf of God, the prophet reminded the people that God had brought them up from the land of Egypt and had sent before them Moses, Aaron and Miriam. Micah was speaking about Israel's departure from Egypt. He was reminding the people how God had redeemed their ancestors. In fact, Micah 6: 4 explicitly says, '*I have redeemed you from the house of slavery.*' Note that 'house of slavery' is paired with 'the land of Egypt'. God had liberated the Israelites from the bondage of Egypt.

The exodus event stands out as the most spectacular saving act of God on behalf of the Jewish people recorded in the Hebrew Bible. It was the superlative redemptive act of the Old Testament. God brought his people out of slavery; he went before them; he defeated their enemies; he provided water and food for them in the wilderness. This was an awesome display of God's redemptive power on behalf of his people.

Reconsider Micah 6: 5, *'In order that you may know the tsidkot Adonai.'* *Tsidkot* is the plural of *tsedakah,* and *Adonai* simply means 'Lord'. In light of the context, how should this phrase be translated? The RSV translators rendered this phrase, 'the saving acts of the Lord.' These translators recognised something very important, namely that *tsedakah* in Hebrew often, but not always, means righteousness. In Jesus' day, as mentioned above, it could mean almsgiving. Already in the biblical period, *tsedakah* could also mean a redemptive or saving act.

Surveying the nuances which are listed for the word *tsedakah* in *The New Brown-Driver-Briggs-Gesenius Hebrew and English Lexicon,* which is the standard Hebrew to English lexicon of the Old Testament, one discovers that mentioned under the sixth and seventh nuances are the adjectives 'redemptive' and 'saving'.[2] The RSV's translation of Micah 6: 5 reflects a greater degree of sensitivity to the context of the passage. The other English translations have failed to capture the essence of the phrase *tsidkot Adonai.* Israel is to remember how God had acted redemptively on their behalf.

Enough data has been assembled from Micah 6: 3-5 to unlock the second part of the parallelism in Matthew 6: 33. The Hebrew noun *tsedakah* can refer to God's redemptive activity as in the phrase *tsidkot Adonai.* Moreover, the ancient Jewish scholars who translated the Hebrew Bible into Greek rendered *tsidkot Adonai* as *dikaiosunae tou kuriou* (literally, 'righteousness of the Lord').[3] Thus, applying this information to Matthew 6: 33, one could say that a more dynamic rendering of 'seek first his righteousness' would be 'seek first his redemptive activity or plan'. Capitalising on the parallel structure of Matthew 6: 33, one now knows something about the Kingdom of Heaven, too. A link exists between God's redemptive activity and the Kingdom of Heaven. A principal feature of the Kingdom of Heaven is God's redemptive power at work in the affairs of humanity.

Is the expression 'Kingdom of Heaven' found in the Old Testament? The phrase 'Kingdom of Heaven' does not appear in the Old Testament. There are only two bodies of literature where the expression 'Kingdom of Heaven' appears repeatedly as a sort of technical term.[4] They are rabbinic literature and the New Testament, especially the Synoptic Gospels of the latter. Throughout their gospels, the first three evangelists described Jesus as speaking frequently about the Kingdom of Heaven (or Kingdom of God). Yet the term 'Kingdom of Heaven' does not appear in the Old Testament. A master of pedagogics, would Jesus have invented a technical term and expected his audiences to grasp it? One would be more correct to assume that Jesus borrowed a term, which was common in his day among the Jewish sages, and tailored it for his purposes. The way in which Jesus spoke of the Kingdom of Heaven was similar to the way the sages, and those who came after them, the rabbis, used the expression. It was not identical, but similar. Much can be learnt about how Jesus understood the Kingdom of Heaven by examining first how the ancient sages of Israel understood it. Once familiar with their ideas on the subject, one can then compare and contrast their teachings to what Jesus taught about it.

If a Christian were to ask a Hebrew-speaking rabbi where the Kingdom of Heaven first appeared in history, he would answer: *Adonai yimloch leolam vaed.* In dynamic English that means, 'The Lord reigns forever' (Exodus 15: 18). This was the response of Israel in the song of thanksgiving, which they sang at the Red Sea. They sang this song because they had been redeemed. God had delivered them in a most dramatic way from their enemies. They had seen it with their own eyes. They had walked through the parted waters. Thus, the sages concluded that the Kingdom of Heaven was first manifested at the parting of the Red Sea.[5]

Now someone might argue that God remains in total control all the time. How then could the sages have claimed that this was the first time that God had exercised his sovereignty in creation? A distinction needs to be made. The sages of Israel clearly recognised the sovereign rule of God over the entire universe. They were, however, more inclined to speak about God's sovereignty in a more qualified sense. There is a verb in Hebrew, which they were fond of using in reference to the Kingdom of Heaven. That verb is *lehamleech*, and it comes from the same three-letter root as the word *melek* which is 'king' in Hebrew. *Lehamleech* means to enthrone somebody as king. The sages and rabbis were fond of talking about God in terms of his people enthroning him as king. There is a distinction to be made between God's absolute sovereignty over the universe and those who have chosen to recognise that sovereignty and obey his will. The rabbis enjoyed talking about people of faith, who had submitted their wills to God and were allowing him to reign in their lives. Although many people maintain a belief in an omniscient and omnipotent divine being, fewer people undertake the next step and respond in a radical way to God's absolute sovereignty. The Kingdom of Heaven is established upon people who have submitted to the will of their heavenly Father. They have made God king, and he reigns in their lives.

The Septuagintal translation of Exodus 15: 18 is rather interesting. The translators of the Septuagint dynamically translated this verse in a way that may reflect their understanding of the Kingdom of Heaven. Anybody who has worked seriously with biblical texts knows that a pure translation exists only in theory. As soon as one translates from one language to another, one has entered the realm of interpretation. The Septuagint translators did not render Exodus 15: 18 as literally as they could have. The Hebrew says: *'The Lord will reign forever and ever.'* The verb is in the imperfect form, which roughly corresponds to the future tense in English. The ancient translators, however, rendered this imperfect Hebrew form as a present participle in Greek: *'The Lord is reigning forever and ever.'* God's redemptive power was a reality in the lives of the Israelites. They had just passed through the parted waters. God was reigning in their midst.

From the prophet Micah one learns that a basic characteristic of God's righteous acts is redemption or salvation. Thus, *'Seek first his righteousness'* is more clearly paraphrased as *'Seek first his redemptive activity'*, which is in parallel with *'his kingdom'*. From Exodus 15: 18 one learns that the Kingdom of Heaven, according to Jewish thought, first became manifest in history at the Red Sea.[6] Moreover, the ancient Jewish scholars, who translated this verse from Hebrew to Greek sometime around 200 BCE, allowed their perception of God's redemptive activity as a present reality to find expression in the translation. The Septuagintal translation of Exodus 15: 18 indicates that the Lord reigns forever ... in the present.[7]

A parable from an early rabbinic commentary on Exodus sheds additional light on the Kingdom of Heaven. This parable is a midrashic comment on Exodus 20: 2, *'God spoke all of these words, saying, "I am the Lord your God, who brought you forth from the land of Egypt, from the house of slavery."'* The parabolic comment on the verse follows:

I AM THE LORD, THY GOD: Why were the Ten Commandments not mentioned at the beginning of the Torah?... This can be compared to a king who entered a province and said to the people, 'I will reign over you.' But the people answered him, 'You have done nothing beneficial for us that you should merit reigning over us.' What did the king do? He built for them a wall, he built for them a water system to bring water inside of that wall, and he went out and made war on their behalf [against their enemies]. Then he said to them, 'I will reign over you.' They answered him, 'Yes, please reign over us!' Thus, God brought forth Israel from Egypt, he divided the Sea for them, he caused the manna to fall for them, he raised up a well in the wilderness for them, he brought the quail for them, he made war against Amalek for them, and then he said to them, 'I will reign over you.' And they answered him, 'Yes, please reign over us!'[8]

Did God first give the Israelites the Torah or did he first redeem them? He redeemed them. Notice that the Ten Commandments begin, *'I am the Lord your God, who brought you forth from the land of Egypt, from the house of slavery.'* They open with an affirmation of the great redemptive act, which God had done on behalf of his people. A pattern is emerging: first, an individual experiences the redemptive power of God, and then, he or she responds to that redemptive encounter. The normal response of an individual after he or she has been redeemed, saved or set free by God is, 'Yes, please reign over me.'[9]

The Kingdom of Heaven is about redemption. It is a present reality. The Kingdom of Heaven is God's redemptive power impacting humanity. The natural response of a person who has experienced that power is obedience to God.

In the Synoptic Gospels one meets difficulties in trying to understand precisely what Jesus meant when he spoke about the Kingdom of Heaven.[10] The reason is that in Christian tradition two cases of an early conflation of ideas occurred. Apparently, these ideas were not originally linked together in Jesus' teachings. In other words, in each of the two cases there were originally two separate motifs, and somehow elements from each of the motifs became mixed with the other.

In Jewish thought, eternal life and the Kingdom of Heaven stand out as two distinct concepts. In Hebrew, *Olam habah* basically corresponds to what Christians talk about as eternal life. The Kingdom of Heaven is a separate term that has to do with God's redemptive activity and obedience to his will. If one takes a concordance and examines the phrases 'Kingdom of Heaven' and 'Kingdom of God,' which are synonyms, one discovers that in the synoptic tradition, the terms 'Kingdom of Heaven' and 'Kingdom of God' appear about fifteen times in Mark and over thirty times both in Matthew and in Luke. If one examines the expression 'eternal life,' one will see that it appears in each of the synoptic Gospels about three times.

What happens when the same exercise is repeated with John's Gospel, which is not part of the synoptic tradition? The expression 'eternal life' appears in John about ten times, whereas the phrase 'Kingdom of God' occurs twice in Jesus' conversation with Nicodemus. This feature of the Gospels has unwittingly caused Christians to conflate these two concepts. If the main proclamation of Jesus is the Kingdom of Heaven in the synoptic tradition, one can easily assume wrongly that the main proclamation of Jesus in John is also the Kingdom of Heaven and, therefore, eternal life must correspond with the Kingdom of Heaven. A simple, but facile solution to this difficulty in the text is to treat the Kingdom of Heaven and eternal life as equivalent expressions. If a reader of the gospels chooses this common, simple solution, then he or she will struggle with attaining an accurate understanding of the Kingdom of Heaven. Happily, through comparative study with ancient Jewish sources, one is able to see that in the synoptic tradition, the Kingdom of Heaven is a concept distinct from eternal life. Moreover, in the synoptic tradition the weight of Jesus' teachings is clearly on the Kingdom of Heaven. A theological shift in Christian thinking was already underway by the time that John began writing his gospel.[11]

A second conflation of ideas that occurred early in Christian tradition, was that the expression Kingdom of Heaven became identified and interchangeable with the *parousia*.[12] (This Greek word means 'coming' or 'arrival' and is used in theological literature with reference to Jesus' second coming). When preaching sermons,

Christian preachers will sometimes identify the Kingdom of Heaven with the *parousia* or describe it as appearing at the Lord's return. In academic literature, too, this idea finds expression.

A famous scholar named C H Dodd wrestled with trying to understand Jesus' teachings on the Kingdom of Heaven. He recognised in the synoptic tradition that there was a present sense to the concept,[13] but he was also aware of verses that seem to describe the appearing of the Kingdom of Heaven at the *parousia*.[14] He developed an idea that he called, 'realised eschatology'. This is what Dodd wrote:

> Here then is the fixed point from which our interpretation of the teaching regarding the Kingdom of God must start. It represents the ministry of Jesus as 'realised eschatology,' that is to say, as the impact upon this world of the 'powers of the world to come' in a series of events, unprecedented and unrepeatable, now in actual process.[15]

Dodd's conclusion represents a serious attempt to wrestle with certain difficulties resident in the synoptic tradition. From the perspective of one who has spent considerable time reading rabbinic literature and the synoptic gospels, however, he may have misinformed much Protestant Evangelical theology. C H Dodd wrote that, 'It represents the ministry of Jesus as ... the impact upon this world of the powers of the world to come in a series of events, unprecedented and unrepeatable, now and in actual process.' Was Dodd saying that the redemptive power, which had been demonstrated in Jesus' ministry was unrepeatable and will not happen in our day? What would Smith Wigglesworth have thought about that? Dodd's words are elusive to interpret. The lack of clarity in his explanation has been generated by the synoptic Gospels themselves, because their language on this subject, in places, can be inconsistent. Was Dodd suggesting that when believers are obedient to the will of their heavenly Father that there will not be a breaking forth of the miraculous in terms of healing and deliverance from the bondage of sins, *ie* manifestations of God's redemptive power in force? Exactly what Dodd intended to communicate is not easily ascertained, but he wrote 'unrepeatable' in reference to the miraculous. Dodd's writings have pointed a lot of Protestant evangelical thinking on a path which has a tendency to emphasise the future aspect of the kingdom, while at the same time, giving lip service to its present aspect.[16] If one takes seriously comparative study with rabbinic literature, the emphasis of the Kingdom of Heaven is in the present. It is a present reality in full force among those who have made Jesus Lord.

Consider the parables of the mustard seed and the leaven, which talk about the expansion of the Kingdom of Heaven. In the parables of the mustard seed and the leaven, does the Kingdom of Heaven appear suddenly at the end of this age? The Kingdom of Heaven is already here. It continues to expand steadily. These two parables do not fit into the model of the Kingdom of Heaven appearing suddenly with the return of the Lord. Nor is the process of a seed growing steadily described suitably as a series of 'unrepeatable' events.

The parable of the mustard seed warrants special attention because it is repeated by Matthew, Mark and Luke, and all three of the synoptic evangelists agreed that the parable describes the Kingdom of Heaven. Apparently some parables, which carry introductions as being about the Kingdom of Heaven in the first three gospels, were originally told by Jesus in regard to other subjects. Consider for example the parable of the net (Mt 13: 47). In Matthew 13: 31 one finds the parable of the mustard seed, which is followed by the parable of the leaven (Mt 13: 33). Eleven verses after the parable of the leaven, following an explanation of the parable of the tares (which is introduced as a Kingdom parable), the parables of the hidden treasure and the pearl appear (Mt 13: 44-46). Although the parables of the tares, mustard seed, leaven, hidden treasure, pearl and net have been clumped together one after the other in Matthew and are introduced as Kingdom parables, only the parables of the mustard seed, leaven, hidden treasure, and pearl are authentically about the Kingdom of Heaven. Jesus originally told the parables of the tares and net not to teach about the Kingdom of Heaven, but the final judgment. Matthew's decision to clump these two parables together with four Kingdom parables influenced the manner in which he chose to introduce them.[17] Being caught off-guard suddenly and separating the good from the bad are motifs belonging to the terrible day of the Lord, the coming of the Son of Man or *parousia* and the final judgment (See also, Matthew 25: 31-46 and 2 Peter 3: 10).[18]

Jesus' eschatological views regarding the end of the age, which culminates with the *parousia*, stress the need to be ready at all times.

Unlike the Kingdom of Heaven, which has been slowly growing, the return of the Son of Man will be sudden. Consequently, Christians must be living in obedience to the divine will now, lest they be found delinquent when the terrifying eschatological judge suddenly comes. Rabbi Eliezer ben Hyrcanus made the same point this way: 'Repent one day before death!' And, of course, his disciples asked, 'How does one know the day one will die?' To that Rabbi Eliezer replied, 'That is good reason to repent today.'[19]

Modern scholarship has achieved a consensus of opinion that the Kingdom of Heaven stood at the forefront of Jesus' preaching.[20] Yet, if one enters a bookstore specialising in charismatic and/or evangelical materials, one will find a prominent section promoting books about end-time prophecy. Sadly, one generally finds a less prominent section dedicated to books on the Kingdom of Heaven. In regard to the Kingdom of Heaven, the Catholic Church may be more accurately educating its laity on this subject than clerics from other denominations. The following quotation comes from the literature being disseminated among Catholic parishioners in the United States:

> It *[the Kingdom of God] exists wherever God's will is at work. And God's will is at work wherever people are faithful to the command that we love one another ... We can define the Kingdom of God* as the redemptive presence of God. *This redemptive (or saving) presence of God can be found in everyday personal experiences ... When we pray, 'Thy Kingdom come', we are hoping also for the inbreaking of God's power – right now – in our daily lives. Our God is a living God. God's power is a present power.*[21]

This description of the Kingdom of Heaven offers a refreshing perspective because it accentuates the present reality of God's redemptive activity in peoples' lives. Moreover, this short article begins by stating, 'The Kingdom of God is at the heart and centre of Jesus' preaching.'[22] The *parousia*, although a significant feature of Jesus' preaching, was not the centrepiece of his proclamation. Ideally, contemporary Christian writing, preaching and teaching should echo the same emphases that were resident in Jesus' preaching and teaching. If they do not, then the laity runs the risk of losing sight of the vision of the Kingdom of Heaven.

The Kingdom of Heaven resembles a concept in the mystical tradition of rabbinic Judaism called *tikkun ha'olam*, which literally means 'mending the world'. When one becomes a member of the Kingdom of Heaven, one becomes a partner with God in spreading redemption throughout a broken world. That person goes out and feeds the hungry; clothes the naked; visits those who are in hospital and prison; prays for the sick and defends the rights of the orphan and widow. A person who has entered the Kingdom of Heaven gets involved in people's lives. He or she pursues a lifestyle characterised by mending our broken world: where there is hatred, he or she sows love; where there is injury, pardon; where there is doubt, faith; where there is despair, hope; where there is darkness, light; and where there is sadness, joy.

As Christians get involved in people's lives, God backs their efforts with his redemptive power. Most Christians can remember times when they have seen God move redemptively in a subtle or remarkable way – both are miraculous. Jesus' disciples have entered into a unique relationship with God. Empowered by his Holy Spirit, they selflessly dedicate themselves to involvement in the ongoing task of feeding, clothing, sheltering, educating, befriending, comforting, defending, redeeming and healing hurting humanity.[23]

Psychologically, that can be hard to accept, because as Rabbi Tarfon once explained, 'The day is short, the task is great, the workers are sluggish, the reward is generous and the Master of the house is urgent.' He went on to add, 'It is not your responsibility to complete the task, but you are not at liberty to desist from it.'[24]

For a Christian, the proposition that Jesus' disciples have been assigned to a task, of which they will likely see only limited results in their lifetime, is not alluring. To accept that the task at hand resembles bailing water out of a leaking boat challenges both psychologically and emotionally. As Christians bail, the boat takes on water. Yet that is what God has instructed Jesus' disciples to do. Being obedient does not require understanding God's reasoning.

On television and radio, from the pulpit and in Sunday school, an immature theological approach to God and man reverberates through much popular Evangelically oriented preaching and teaching. As a result, too many Christians never get around to disciplining themselves to sit down and start bailing. Instead, they happily devote themselves to some more enticing church sanctioned activity or simply jump ship altogether by becoming consumed with eschatological speculation about end-time scenarios, hidden numerical codes embedded in the biblical text, and self-gratifying thoughts about the vindication of the righteous and punishment of the wicked at the coming great and final judgment. Nevertheless, Jesus wants his followers to be wholeheartedly bailing a listing vessel.

Hopefully, this paper has brought certain aspects of the Kingdom of Heaven into sharper focus. The Kingdom of Heaven is the present reality of God's redemptive power in the world today. Upon experiencing God's redemptive power, one's natural response is 'Lord, what may I do for you?' which then translates into a life of good works. The Bible indicates that God is always active among two groups of people: (1) among those who have made him King, and (2) among the poor, the captive and the down-trodden. A principal objective of the first group is to emulate God, and to emulate our heavenly father means extending a hand of friendship, assistance, redemption, and love to the second group. This constitutes the major thrust of the work of the Kingdom of Heaven. To those who submit themselves to his redemptive agenda and commit to mending a broken world, God gives his Holy Spirit for empowerment and the ongoing expansion of his Kingdom (cf Luke 4: 18-19; Acts 2: 38 and 5: 32).

Appendix: Proposed cause of the ambiguity concerning the Kingdom of Heaven in the synoptic Tradition

Although not the primary concern of this essay, the writer will outline briefly what he thinks has contributed to the ambiguity concerning the Kingdom of Heaven in the synoptic tradition. Jesus, like other sages of his day, connected ideas by means of web-like logic. He linked together imagery, motifs and verses of scripture into complexes or clusters of ideas. The analogy of a grape-like cluster serves as a helpful didactic aid.

As already mentioned, there were apparently two distinct idea-clusters that became conflated early in Christian tradition. One cluster may be called the Kingdom of Heaven (or Kingdom of God) cluster. The following grapes belong to this cluster:

1   The present reality of God's redemptive power exercised on behalf
    of his people (Exodus 15: 18).
2   The finger of God (Exodus 8: 19 and Luke 11: 20).
3   The motif of steady, consistent expansion (Matthew 13: 31-33).
4   The phrase 'entering the Kingdom of Heaven' (Matthew 5: 20 and
    21: 31).
5   The motif of the VIP status of participating in the Kingdom of
    Heaven (a rabbinic comment on Exodus 15: 2; Matthew 11: 11 and
    13: 17).
6   The motif of the captives being set free, the blind seeing, the deaf
    hearing, and the lame walking (Isaiah 61: 1-2; Matthew 11: 5 and
    Luke 4: 18).

The other cluster may be called the Coming Kingdom cluster. The
following 'grapes' belong to this cluster:
1   The Son of Man (Daniel 7: 13 and Matthew 25: 31).
2   The verb 'coming' in conjunction with imagery of judgment
    (Malachi 3: 1-3; Daniel 7: 13 and Matthew 25: 31-46).
3   The motif of separating (Malachi 3: 1-3; Matthew 13: 24-30; 13: 47-
    49 and 25: 31-46).
4   The motif of judgment (Malachi 3: 1-3; Matthew 25: 31-46 and John
    5: 27).
5   The motif of suddenness, like a thief in the night (Zechariah
    9: 14 *LXX*; Malachi 3: 1; Matthew 24: 43, 25: 1-13 and 2 Peter 3: 10).
6   The motif of the day being known only to God (Zechariah 14: 7;
    Matthew 24: 36, 24: 42-44, and Acts 1: 7).

The data that has been supplied above merely outlines these two
complexes or clusters of ideas. Additional motifs and verses could be
added to the list.

The concept of the Kingdom of Heaven deals more with the
limited, but expanding reign of God among people. In a strict sense,
the Kingdom of Heaven is limited to those people who have made
Jesus Lord, but grows with each new person who says 'yes' to Jesus.
The Coming of the Kingdom deals more with a future event referred
to in the Hebrew Bible as the terrible Day of the Lord. In Jesus'
teachings, the terrible Day of the Lord seems to be synonymous with

the coming of the Son of Man or *parousia*. On that day, God's absolute
sovereignty will be manifested universally. Thus, in a certain sense,
the Kingdom of Heaven climaxes in the *parousia*, but this remark in no
way blurs viewing the Kingdom of Heaven as being in full force
today among those who have made Jesus Lord.

Early in the transmission process of the synoptic tradition, 'grapes'
from the first cluster got mixed with 'grapes' from the second cluster.
This transposition of 'grapes' can be readily seen in some of the introductions of the parables, which claim to speak of the Kingdom of
Heaven.[25] Moreover, the Kingdom of Heaven (*malchut shamaim* in
Hebrew) could easily have been conflated with the Coming Kingdom.
Daniel 7: 13-14 played a lead role in spawning the Coming Kingdom
cluster. In this Aramaic passage, the words 'sovereign power'
(*malchu*) and 'his kingdom' (*malchutay*) appear. It is not difficult to
imagine how the Kingdom of Heaven and the Coming Kingdom
could have been conflated on a literary level, particularly as apocalyptic ideas became more influential in nascent Christianity.

A simple fundamentalist approach, which is embraced by many
Christians, both clergy and laity, fails to do justice to the complexities
generated by the text. Conclusions about the Kingdom of Heaven
based on such an approach will be askew. The Kingdom of Heaven
does not appear suddenly; it grows steadily. It does not appear when
Jesus returns; it is fully operative today among those who have
pledged allegiance to God's radical redemptive agenda and have
been empowered by his spirit. The Kingdom of Heaven is not about
separating the good from the bad nor is it about judgment. Rather, it
is a special period in redemptive history that is characterised by hope,
healing, restoration, grace and forgiveness.

From a Kingdom of Heaven perspective, things are getting better
in the world today. The Kingdom of Heaven is always doing one
thing – growing! Moreover, the days of the Kingdom of Heaven constitute a unique time in God's redemptive activity, which will end
with the coming of the Son of Man. This will be the terrible Day of the
Lord. As Rabbi Abahu once said, 'Greater is the day of rain than the
day of resurrection (judgment), for the day of resurrection (judgment)
benefits only the just, whereas the day of rain benefits both the just

and the unjust' (Ta'anit 7a; cf Matthew 5: 45).

Notes

1   **Krister Stendahl**, *Meanings: The Bible as Document and as Guide*, Philadelphia, Fortress Press, 1984, p 236.

2   **Francis Brown, S R Driver, and Charles A Briggs**, *The New Brown-Driver-Briggs-Gesenius Hebrew and English Lexicon*, Peabody, MA: Hendrickson, 1979, p 842, no 6666. See also **William L Holladay, ed.**, *A Concise Hebrew and Aramaic Lexicon of the Old Testament*, Grand Rapids: Eerdmans, 1983, p 303. Definition 7c) reads, 'what God gives = salvation, deliverance'.

3   In ancient Jewish texts, both translated from Hebrew or originally composed in Greek, *dikaiosunae* assumed the role of a technical term that mechanically translated or represented the Hebrew *tsedakah*.

4   The eminent scholar R H Charles wrote, '... the expression hardly ever occurs in apocalyptic ...'. **R H Charles**, *Religious Development Between the Old and the New Testament*, London: Williams and Norgate, 1914, p 48. In reference to the Qumran Scrolls, Brad Young has written, 'However the technical term 'Kingdom of heaven' never appears.' **Brad H Young**, *Jesus and His Jewish Parables*, Mahwah, New Jersey: Paulist Press, 1989, p 225.

5   See **Joseph Hertz**, *The Authorised Daily Prayer Book*, rev ed, New York: Bloch Publishing, 1985, p 371.

6   When Jesus spoke of the Kingdom of Heaven, he drew from the imagery of the narratives in Exodus. For example, by using the phrase 'finger of God,' Jesus directed a provocative statement toward those criticizing him. The force of Jesus' reply comes from the allusion to Exodus 8: 19. In addition to Jesus' teachings on the Kingdom of Heaven, two old descriptions of messianic pretenders also reflect a similar linking of messianic expectations with imagery from the Exodus narratives. In Jewish Antiquities 20: 97, Josephus wrote about Theudas: '...[he] persuaded the majority of the masses to take up their possessions and to follow him to the Jordan River. He stated that he was a prophet and that at his command the river would be parted and would provide them an easy passage'. (Note the linking of the miracles at the Red Sea and the Jordan River in Psalm 114: 3.), *Jewish Antiquities, in The Loeb Classical Library*, trans Louis Feldman, Cambridge, MA: Harvard University Press, 1965, p 441. Describing a similar tragic event which occurred in the middle of the fifth century CE on the isle of Crete, Socrates wrote, 'A certain Jewish imposter pretended that he was Moses, and had been sent from heaven to lead out the Jews inhabiting that island, and conduct them through the sea.' *The Ecclesiastical History of Socrates Scholasticus in The Nicene and Post-Nicene Fathers, v 2*, eds Philip Schaff and Henry Wace, Second Series, Grand Rapids: Eerdmans, 1983, p 174.

7   The Greek Orthodox Church accepts the Septuagint as canonical. Greek Orthodox Christians read a different canonical text from Protestants. They have a nice benefit from reading the Greek of Exodus 15: 18. The Septuagint's translation brings the present reality of God's reign into sharper focus.

8   Author's translation of Mekilta de-Rabbi Ishmael on Exodus 20: 2. For a Hebrew text of this parable, see **H S Horovitz** and **I A Rabin**, eds. *Mechilta D'Rabbi Ismael*, Jerusalem: Wahrmann Books, 1970, p 219.

9   Compare carefully Matthew 10: 7, 8 and Luke 10: 9. The present writer

views the Lukan wording to be closer to the original instructions of Jesus.

10 Jesus employed the term 'Kingdom of Heaven' with two principal nuances. The first, which is the subject of this paper, refers to wherever God has taken charge of a situation, the Kingdom of Heaven is at hand (Luke 11: 20). The second refers to those people who have made Jesus Lord, ie, the people who constitute the redemptive movement that Jesus is leading (Matthew 11: 11). Thus, a person can participate in this redemptive movement by entering the Kingdom of Heaven (Luke 18: 25). The common denominator between these two nuances is God's taking charge. Whenever a supernatural manifestation of God's power occurs, he has taken charge. Likewise, he has also taken charge of the lives of those who have decided to follow Jesus.

11 For further discussion on the synoptic tradition and the Gospel of John, see **J Frankovic**, *Reading the Book: A Popular Essay on Christian Biblical Hermeneutics*, Tulsa, Oklahoma: HaKesher, 1997, pp 24-28.

12 For further discussion of this subject, see the appendix of this essay.

13 See Matthew 11: 12 (NIV) and Luke 11: 20.

14 See Mark 15: 43 and Luke 19: 11. Note also Matthew 16: 28 and its parallels in Mark 9: 1 and Luke 9: 27.

15 **C H Dodd**, *The Parables of the Kingdom*, rev ed, New York, Charles Scribner's Sons, 1961, p 35.

16 In the past, scholars have criticised Dodd's views for minimising the futuristic aspect of the Kingdom of Heaven. Ironically, here the present writer challenges Dodd's conclusions for not maximising the present aspect. **George Eldon Ladd**, *A Theology of the New Testament*, Grand Rapids: Eerdmans, 1987, p 59. Dodd's influence on this subject throughout New Testament accademic literature has been widespread. For example, one commentator wrote, 'Jesus preached the coming of God's Kingdom in the future and the inauguration of it in his own life and ministry.' **Daniel J Harrington**, S J, *Interpreting the New Testament: A Practical Guide*, Collegeville, MN: Liturgical Press, 1990, p 89.

17 **Brad H Young**, *Jesus and His Jewish Parables*, Mahwah, New York: Paulist Press, 1989, pp 219-221, 235.

18 Ibid, p 192.

19 Avot de-Rabbi Natan, chapter 15. For the Hebrew text of this saying, see Salomon Schechter, ed Aboth De Rabbi Nathan, Israel: np, nd, p. 62.

20 Ladd, p 57.

21 **Richard P McBrien**, *'What is 'The Kingdom of God'? A Theologian Explains the Key Image of the Gospel,'* Catholic Update (1980), p 2.

22 Ibid, p 1.

23 Compare Matthew 9: 35, where Jesus is described as being about the work of the Kingdom, with Matthew 10: 1, where the responsibility for the work of the Kingdom is shifted to the disciples.

24 M Avot 2: 15, 16. For a Hebrew text of Rabbi Tarfon's saying, see Hanoch Albeck, ed. The Mishnah (Seder Nezikin) (Jerusalem/Tel Aviv: Bialik Institute/Dvir Publishing, 1988), p 362.

25 See Young, p 192.

Section 3:

The Growing Tree

Three in the Holy One of Israel:

Towards a Hebraic Expression of the Concept of Trinity

Simon Hawthorne

Abstract

This essay explores the thesis that the Church emerged from a Hebraic milieu and Semitic mind-set and yet was swept away by the current of Hellenistic thought by the time it came to formulate its Christology and pneumatology into credal statements. We begin with reference to the most recent attempts to rediscover alternative approaches to understanding the Trinitarian nature of God in the work of Moltmann and Heschel. Then we consider the general Semitic approach as opposed to the Hellenistic and post-enlightenment Western methods. Finally, we will examine such possible alternatives to the traditional methods of explaining Trinity such as *panav, K'vod, Shekinah, Adonai Tzidkeinu, Memra/Davar, Shem, Reshith, Malach YHWH and Metatron.* Having weighed the merits of each in turn, we will close with a consideration of the several heresies which beset the Church in its formative years and see whether the Hebraic concepts would have managed to resist the heretical teachings as successfully as the Hellenistic concepts managed to do.

Modern Trinitarian doctrine has emerged from within the world of Hellenistic philosophy. Yet the writers of the scriptures were all Jewish and approached such questions with a Semitic mind-set. My purpose here is to explore the possibility of the development of Trinitarian definitions within a Church which had resisted the advances of Hellenistic philosophy. It is not my intention purely to translate the Jewish concepts into the Hellenistic mind-frame, but to bring the Semitic mind-set to bear.

The Hellenistic approach to discussion of the doctrine of the Trinity has been the hallmark of western Christianity since the Fourth Century CE. The presumptions of the Cappadocian Fathers, such as the need to defend the impassibility of God, has only recently been challenged by Jurgen Moltmann. He notes that the selection of characteristics 'appropriate' to the divine nature as propounded by Greek philosophy would lead to the exclusion of 'difference, diversity, movement and suffering from the divine nature'.[1] The logical conclusion which he deduces from this is that 'If God were incapable of suffering in every respect, then he would also be incapable of love',[2] which is palpably risible.

In his quest away from the impassible, apathetic God, Moltmann writes of the work of Abraham Heschel.[3] Unlike Philo, Judah Halevi, Maimonides and Spinoza, Heschel had espoused a theology of the divine *pathos*. In this, God was moving out of himself and into his people. This approach owed less to the world of abstract concepts and more to the sphere of the relational. God was not controlled by passions as the Greek gods on Olympus, but was freed by virtue of their existence to enter into a meaningful relationship with the people whom he had chosen and whom he loved.

It was the Semitic approach which first led Heschel to his bipolar theology of the covenant. This was couched in terms of the dichotomy of God's freedom and involvement. In himself God is free. He is not in subjection to any external pressure, control or destiny. He is unaffected in himself by any events. Yet he is committed on account of his *pathos* to his covenant as to his creation. This suggests some attempt to comprehend the vast gulf between the transcendence and immanence within God's dealings to which the term *Shekinah* is applied. (This will be discussed in much greater depth below.) Having determined this primary bipolarity, Heschel explored a second bipolarity by which the sympathetic response of man comes before the Lord. Since God also controls this response, the prophet comes to have the name *ish-ha-ruach* (a man filled with God's Spirit). God's Spirit is responding to God's *pathos*, so a second self-differentiation in God becomes perceptible.

What is the quality of the Semitic approach to the Trinity which makes it unique? The principal difference is that the Hebraic mind is not prone to unsubstantial or abstract vagaries. It is always keen to relate belief to practice. Worship shapes belief, practice reinforces theology. Action is equally paramount. It is not enough to believe the right things in Judaism, it is essential to practise them – this evokes the Epistle of James and the teaching of Jesus, much of whose Jewishness is lost to the Church. Finally, there is the aspect of relationship. It is almost stereo-typical to represent the Jewish mother fussing over her son, or the pride of the Jewish father at the Bar Mitzvah, but these are integral parts of the Jewish nature. Within this concept of relationships it will be possible to explore some of the types and symbols which were applied to God. These may then be weighed against the difficulties which are inherent within them before any conclusions may be drawn. The backdrop for this study is that of early Jewish Christianity, the Old Testament and the later Jewish writings such as Cabbalah, Midrash, Talmud and Pesharim.

The nature of relationship within Semitic culture is essential for this discussion. The understanding of covenant is that it is principally relational. God has revealed himself as one who desires to be in relationship with his creation. This is the basic premise for any Semitic approach to knowing God, but most pronounced in the understanding of the incarnation and its effect upon any discussion of the Trinity. While the Greeks spoke in terms of perichoreisis or Tillich of the 'dialectic of the Trinity'[4], Hebrew thought expects this kind of activity and does not seek to rationalise it. There must be activity within God, for God is not static but dynamic and active within creation and beyond. The best approach to this dialectic from a Semitic view-point is that of Herschel previously discussed. The dual bipolarity of God's activity naturally presupposes some plurality within God Himself, but this could not have been known unless it had been revealed. In Hebrew thought the key to knowing a person was knowing their name. This begins with God's revelation of himself as YHWH. 'By extension from the Old Testament theological connection of the Name as the manifestation of YHWH, the expression came to mean the power by which God accomplishes his works.'[5] There were other names available to the earliest Jewish Christians. Ab, Ben and Ruach HaKodesh (Father, Son and Holy Spirit) were all biblical names which conveyed some truth of the Trinity, but there were obvious problems with these names as Trinitarian definitions. For one thing they connoted a hierarchical structure within the Godhead, for another they gave the impression of there being three individuals rather than three hypostasis and led to a charge of Tritheism. Jesus also describes himself in 'more characteristically Semitic and unphilosophical language'[6] (Rev 1: 8) as 'He who is and was and is to come.' These names were the starting point for discussion, but there were other names or titles applied to God by Jewish writers which merit discussion. These include *Panav, K'vod, Shekinah, Adonai Tzidkeinu, Memra (Dabar, Logos), Shem, Reshith (Arche) and Metatron*.

Panav (Face) and *K'vod* (Glory) had both been used consistently in the Old Testament to speak about the presence of God. Eichrodt writes of these being used as a result of 'a sense of the tension between the immanence and the transcendence of God and from a desire for its resolution.'[7] The glory of God was that which was unapproachable, the face was the image of God (in the sense of the Greek *eikon*) which could be approached and, paradoxically, could not be seen. (Ex 33: 11,20). Most intriguing, perhaps, is the setting of *panav* beside *ruach* in Psalm 139: 7[8] suggesting not so much a Trinitarian approach as a lack of concern for the respective definitions within Greek thought. This is crucial for our investigation. The Jewish approach is far less concerned with precise details or pedantic definitions. As the language itself is not precise and follows few rules, so also is Hebraic thought in general. *K'vod* has connotations of majesty and splendour, reminiscent of Isaiah's vision (Ch 6), as with appearances at Sinai, but *K'vod* alone was not sufficient to sum up God's presence so the rabbis coined another word: *Shekinah*.

Shekinah is one of those words which is difficult to translate. It is usually rendered presence, but contains much more than this. Cloud, thunder, voice, smoke, fire, light; each of these are contained within the concept of *Shekinah*. Perhaps 'awesome presence' would be a better rendition. Much could be said about these individual aspects, Fire (Esh ha'*Elohim*) fills the Temple at the dedication; and the Apostles at Shavuot (Pentecost) [2 Chron 7: 1; Acts 2: 3]. The multiplicity of results and actions within the composite unity which is *Shekinah* might seem to be sufficiently helpful in itself – even if some of the individual symbols do need further exposition – but Franz

Rosenzweig has some additional, useful insights from the writings of Jewish mysticism:

> *The Shekinah, the descent of God to man and his dwelling among them, is thought of as a divorce which takes place in God himself. God himself cuts himself off from himself, he gives himself away to his people.'[9]*

It is not simply the case that God reveals some part of himself, like the corner of his robe, in smoke, light and sound-effects. This is God tearing himself from himself to communicate, almost to touch his creation. This is the immanence of God at work, close to his creatures, and God himself is paying the price for that intimacy. This glance at the internal separation or divorce within the Godhead is a helpful introduction to the concept of Immanuel, perhaps the most precious name for Jesus: God with us, incarnated to human form yet still, by his own admission, one with the Father. (John 10: 30)

As incarnate Man, Jesus also fulfils the role of YHWH *Tzidkeinu* according to the Rabbinic expectations of Jeremiah's (23: 6) prophecy: 'Though he shall be a perfect man, yet he is YHWH *Tzidkeinu*, the Lord our Righteousness.'[10]

The title Logos had seemed promising and its Hebrew forms (*Memra* and *Dabar*) might have been much more fully developed had Greek thought not subsequently predominated. Philo was the first to speak of the Logos in terms of Creation and John's prologue exalted the Logos to divine status. Yet there had been a tradition within Judaism whereby the *Memra* of God acted as God and was worshipped as such. This is equally true of the *Shem* (Name) of God. While it has currently passed into everyday orthodox speech as a circumlocution of YHWH, its history has endued it with more reverence than the English translation might suggest. Saint Ephrem, the Syrian, helpfully explores the Semitic usage of names within his own culture. He wrote,[11] 'that God has many names that are perfect and exact,/and he has names that are borrowed and transient;/these latter he quickly puts on and quickly takes off.' By way of example, Ephrem refers to the names such as 'Being' or 'Creator'. These are considered perfect since they are applicable at all times. Some, which are held in common with mankind (eg Father) are still perfect 'since they are terms which are eternally applicable to him, whereas when applied to human beings this is only a temporal matter: no one is born already a father.'[12]

When Paul wrote of Jesus as the *arche* (Beginning) [Col 1: 18] it is not clear whether he intended it to be taken as a title. Were it so, it would add much to the confusion of John 1: 1.[13] It is all-encompassing, since it is not only *Logos* which is called *arche*, but the Hebrew equivalent *Reshith* is applied to *Hokmah* (wisdom) in Proverbs 8: 23. Danielou observes, 'The Jerusalem Targum similarly relates *Reshith* to Hokmah, pre-existent Wisdom.'[14] So there is a title which is applied to the Word (the Son within the Johannine tradition) and the Wisdom (traditionally Spirit – and feminine – within the Hebraic tradition). This is intriguingly advanced by the Latin writing of Aristo of Pella where, according to Saint Jerome, he writes in his Dialogue of Jason and Papiscos: *In filio deus fecit coelum et terram.*[15] Thus we have *Logos* and *Hokmah* linked to the beginning and active in creation, traditionally the preserve of God alone.

Of all the names which may be used for a Hebraic understanding of the Trinity, one of the finest is that of *Metatron*. Rabbi Simeon ben Jochai stated, 'The Middle Pillar (in the Godhead) is the *Metatron*.'[16] This in itself was surprisingly close to a Trinitarian understanding of God, but was complemented by the work of Rabbi Bechai:

> God said to Moses 'Come up into the Lord'; this is Metatron. He is called by this name Metatron, because in this name are implied two significations, which indicate his character. He is Lord and Messenger. There is also a third idea implied in the name Metatron: it signifies a Keeper.[17]

The impact of three concepts within the one image is not therefore strange to Judaism, but it is vital that we do not fall into the Hellenistic trap of asserting or inferring from this that the Father, Son or Holy Spirit have specific roles within *Metatron*. In Semitic thought it is the synthesis which is important. The fact that there is an example of three images within a single concept is of primary interest here. It may be added that Rabbi Bechai also described *Metatron* as 'The eldest of his (God's) house, who is the first-begotten of the creatures of God, who is the ruler of all he has.'[18] Quite apart from the obvious parallel with Hokmah in Proverbs 8, this pre-Christian teaching also foreshadows the language of Paul, and subsequently Nicaea and Chalcedon, where Prototokos is applied to the pre-existent Christ. In the century after Christ, Rabbi Akiba added to the debate by lavishly describing *Metatron* as 'The Angel, the Prince of God's countenance ... the Angel, the Prince of glory ... the Angel, the Prince of lords ... '[19] Thus the *Metatron* comes to have qualities which are divine, but this is more than an alternative form of description for God. For *Metatron* is also 'The Mediator of all that cometh from heaven down to the earth, or from the earth up to heaven.'[20] Here we have an echo of the work of mediation which is performed by Christ and described in the Epistle to the Hebrews (8: 6, 9: 15, 12: 24).

Rabbi Akiba's emphatic description brings us to an area which might not be expected within Christian theology but which was crucial to early Jewish Christian theology – namely angelology. With the exhortations of the first chapter of Hebrews and the supremacy of Christ above the angels, it seems almost blasphemous to suggest that Christ was 'an angel' *per se* and it was because of misunderstanding that this term was later discarded by the church. Yet there is much within Jewish angelology, particularly with reference to the *Malach YHWH* (The Angel of the Lord) or the *Malach Habb'rit* (The Angel of the Covenant) within the context of Old Testament theophanies to require a deeper consideration of this image. While the notion of Angel was discarded by the Greeks, it may well have had considerably more force if the Church had remained primarily Jewish:

> *The Semitic categories which underlie this expression are not Hellenistic concepts. In fact the word Angel has an essentially concrete force; it connotes a supernatural being manifesting itself. The nature of this supernatural being is not determined by the expression but by the context. The word represents the Semitic form of the designation of the Word and the Spirit as spiritual substances, as 'persons', though the latter terminology was not to be introduced into theology until a good deal later. 'Angel' is its old-fashioned equivalent.*[21]

In the theophanies, the Angel did not merely speak for God, he spoke as God. The Cabbalah makes much of this in its commentary on Genesis 22: 'If this Angel had been one of the (created) intelligences, Abraham would not have obeyed his voice, when restraining him to do what God had commanded him.'[22] There is a certain, irrepressible logic about this argument, but the understanding of the Angel as a divine person is heightened by *Malachi* 3: 1, where we have *Malachi* (My Angel/My Messenger) Adon (The Lord) suddenly coming to his temple and the *Malach Habb'rit* (Angel of the Covenant) whom you delight in. The implication of the Vav consecutive before the *Malach Habb'rit* has the force of 'even' which makes the Angel 'The Lord whom you seek' and who is coming to his Temple. This is in accord with Origen who, much to the consternation of Jerome, claimed to have received from a Hebrew that the two Cherubim of Isaiah 6 were the Son and Holy Spirit while Irenaeus wrote of the Cherubim and Seraphim as representative of the Son and the Spirit in their action in the world.[23] There was no confusion within early Jewish Christianity between divinity and the Angel of God/the Covenant. However, with the rise of Arianism a more concrete proof was requisite and, faced with the possibility of Ebionism, this branch of angelology seemed to offer an inadequate solution. It is clear, however, that the nature of the Angel of God within the divine theophanies was perceived by Jewish Christians to be examples of divine activity and could ultimately have led to a fuller discussion of plurality within the Godhead.

As regards the principle that God is understood in terms of his action, it is not necessary to add much to what has already been said by Herschel and Rosenzweig. God must necessarily be active within himself and the outworking of this action may be perceived in concepts such as *Shekinah*, the dual bipolarity and even the Divine love later espoused by Richard of Saint Victor. Although the latter is not definitively a Jewish work, the concept owes more to a practical approach to the Trinity than many of the theoretical attempts postulated before and since.

The greatest action of God, and therefore the greatest revelation of his nature, is the incarnation and the dual work of salvation and sanctification. It is helpful in the study of a person's identity to have some idea of how they work. In his manifestation in human flesh, Jesus showed the nature of the Father, but infinitely more so in his work of salvation. For the Hebrew, God is the source and effector of all deliverance. In bringing the ultimate deliverance from the power of evil and from the bondage of sin from which no amount of devotion to a holy Law could provide, Jesus was enacting the character and desire of the Father and this work is brought to perfection, as we might expect from a perfect God, by the continuing work of the Holy Spirit. Much more needs to be said on this matter, but the principle has been established. God is not passively spectating. That is not the God who has revealed himself in covenant with his people. He is intimately concerned and, in the person of Christ, incarnationally concerned to the point of suffering the rage of creation at its most brutal in order to prove that supreme love is even stronger and that God's life is the desired and attainable target.

The key to understanding the Trinity from within the Jewish Christian mind-set is worship. This is the essence of a belief put into practice. It is one thing to rationally prove that Jesus is God, it is something quite different to worship him as such. Yet this is clearly what has always happened within orthodox Jewish Christianity. Jesus as the *Shem* (Name) or *Memra* (Word) was worshipped. We have seen how, 'The Name is used to designate YHWH in his ineffable reality, and is therefore a Semitic equivalent of what the divine ousia was to be for the Greeks.'[24] Nassi has shown that by placing a capital 'W' before Word (*Memra*) as it appears in the Jerusalem Targumim, it is possible to see that the Word was involved with the giving of the Law (Exod 20: 1), the provision of the ram (Gen 22: 13). It also allows for prayer (Gen 22: 14) and worship (Num 10: 35f) of the Word and Name respectively.[25] Whether or not this was the original intention of the passage is not clear, but it does create space for the precedent whereby the Word of God and his Name are afforded the same veneration as himself.

A significant change to Hebrew worship, apart from the recognition of the divinity of the Son and Holy Spirit, was the manner in which Jesus addressed God. It had been acceptable in penitential prayer to address *Avinu Malcheinu* (Our Father and our King), but was inconceivable that God might be addressed as 'Abba'. The thought that our hearts might also cry 'Abba, Father' (Rom 8: 15) introduced a new facet of speaking of God which, through practice, came to be an essential part of regular worship. The possibility of such an intimate relationship with the Divine Majesty spoke volumes into the debate about the person and nature of God.

The most important single prayer of Judaism, the central credal statement and joy of every Jewish person is the *Sh'ma*. (Deut 6: 4). Its significance to this debate cannot be overstated since it represents the classic statement of the unity of God and appears to be the key-text of monotheism. Yet this is not the closed door which it at first appears. Even here Jewish people throughout the ages have noticed plurality within the God-head. Nassi writes: 'In these words we hear first the singular, YHWH, Jehovah, then the plural Eloheinu, Our God (strictly gods), and then once again the singular, Jehovah, concluding with *echad*, one, meaning to say 'These Three substantive Beings are the One God.'[26] Rabbi Menachem gives the reason for this three-fold repetition as being that 'the word *Sh'ma* does not here signify Hear; but to gather together, to unite ... The meaning implied is, the Inherent-Ones are so united together, one in the other without end, they being the exalted God.'[27]

Following his revelations regarding *Shekinah*, Franz Rosenzweig has something to say of the *Sh'ma* also, 'To pray the *Sh'ma Israel* in the historical experience of God, in the experience of the exile, means: To acknowledge God's unity – the Jew calls it *uniting* God. For this unity is in that it becomes; it is a Becoming Unity.'[28] This brings us back round to the concept of separation and re-unification within the dialectical relationship of the Trinity. This, as we have observed, means a continuously active God whose nature is revealed through the inter-action with his creation.

There is an etymological quirk which supports R Menachem's unusual translation of the *Sh'ma* and that concerns the last word: *Echad*. In the Hebrew language there are two words for 'One'. The first, *yachid*, speaks of an isolated one, single and separate. There is only one as in the sun in the sky. The other form is the word in this context, *echad*. This speaks of a composite unity, many parts making one, complete whole. I have one body, but it is made up of many parts, blood, skin, bone etc, the one body would be rendered *echad*. It should be noted also that both *Adonai* (My Lord) and *Elohim* (God) are plural in form. Part of the revelation of God from the earliest time seems to have been preparing a monotheistic people for the doctrine of the Trinity. Nassi makes much of the use of the third person plural as God speaks to himself (eg Gen 1: 26; 11: 7 Isa 6: 8) but I remain unconvinced that this was not merely idiomatic Hebrew.

The question remains whether or not these images, names and definitions would have succeeded in the face of Ebionism, Arianism and Monophysitism. Some images are clearly flawed. Rays from light or day, while compatible with the Cappadocian Fathers stumble before Arius since both are created in Genesis 1. *Malach* YHWH, *Metatron* and Reshith, while helpful as images, do not fully convey the force of Trinity. Even *Shekinah*, or *Memra/Hokmah* fail to encapsulate the *huyot* (Divine subsistencies). Faced with the onslaught of Arianism and Monophysitism from without, and Ebionism and Elkesaism from within, Jewish Christianity could not provide the philosophical definitions which would have satisfied the rational debates of the Fourth Century. Where the words failed, the concepts and approach may have succeeded. Recognition of the actions of God, couched in the context of a worshipping community committed to practice rather than theoretical analysis of the minutiae of Trinitarian faith may well have prevented the stifling of a faith which has become burdened with over-intellectualism and rationality to the point where, as a living faith it can scarcely breathe. Perhaps here is the place for a freshness of doctrine in the face of stifled Christianity and it may be that the Semitic mind-set remains Christianity's best hope of receiving from God; Father, Son and Holy Spirit, that breath of life.

A Brief Guide to some Beliefs and Heresies of the First Four Centuries CE

Arianism: Fear that the elevation of the Son and the Holy Spirit to divine status might create a polytheistic religion. Many in the Early Church, led by Arius (c 250-336) pressed for a return to the affirmation that there is one God alone. The Son they saw as an angelic or supernatural Being, the First-born (*Prototokos*) of all Creation but not eternal and not of the same substance (*ousia*) as the Father. The Spirit was the manifestation of the Father. Anti-Arian doctrine was promulgated at the councils of Nicaea (325) and Chalcedon (451).

Response: As we have seen, the Jewish Christian position was not that acceptance of the divinity of the Son and the Spirit would lead to a polytheistic faith, but that the Trinity was in fact inherent within received Jewish teaching. Principally, Jesus was being worshipped as God and that was the key to Jewish Christian doctrine. As regards angelology, we have also seen that the *Malach* Ha'brit was a divine figure and the *Malach* YHWH was the divine element within Old Testament theophanies. Had this argument been more forcibly articulated, we might today be speaking of Jesus as an angelic figure without in any way diminishing his deity.

Semi-Arianism: The Semi-Arians believed that the Son was of like substance with the Father (*Homoi-ousios*) but they could not accept that he was of the same substance (*Homo-ousios*). They were therefore classed as heretics by orthodoxy at the same councils as the Arians.

Response: The Jewish Christian position is that there is no differentiation to be made between the several parts which constitute *Echad*. They would not state that the smoke within *Shekinah* is different from the fire which is different from the voice etc. All are parts of the same whole and emanate from the same source. Within the example of the *Metatron*, there would be no distinction made between Keeper and Lord, or between Messenger (*Malach*) and Keeper. Each part is equally God. For all of the sphere of angelology, only God can effect his purposes in salvation history and these actions of salvation and sanctification may only be the work of the One (*Echad*) God.

Ebionism: The Ebionites (Or 'Poor Ones' from the Hebrew *Ebion* = Poor) held that poverty was an ideal. They observed the Jewish Law (*Torah*) meticulously and repudiated Paul as being antinomian. Their conceptual frame of reference was similar to that of the Jewish Christians (as many of their number considered themselves to be) but they refused to acknowledge the deity of Christ.

Response: There is much evidence within the New Testament that some Jewish Christians saw no tension between observing the Law (*Torah*) and worshipping Jesus as God. He was seen as the one who had given the Law (whether this is taken as coming from God (the scriptural view) or from the Word of God or from the *Malach* YHWH (the Zoharian view). The tendency to dismiss all Jewish Christians as (even potential) Ebionites does a great disservice to a faithful group of devout believers within the orthodox parameters of received Christian faith.

Elkesaism: Like the Ebionites, they remained faithful to Jewish customs, with circumcision and obedience to *Torah* expected. In regard to Jesus, the Elkesaites saw him as just another man whose virgin birth was a recurrent event. Elkesai received his book of wisdom from an angel 96 miles high accompanied by a feminine being; the former being the Son and the latter the Spirit. From this group came Mani who was to introduce his own form of heresy: Manichaeism.

Response: While the representation of the Son and Spirit as colossal angels is concordant with some Jewish Christian thinking, the assertion that Jesus was an ordinary man is clearly antipathetic to Jewish Christian teaching. If Jesus is merely a man, yet effecting some form of salvation, then God has not fully entered into relationship with his own and we cannot know him any more fully than through the former covenants. This invalidates the promise that, 'they shall all know me, from the least of them to the greatest' (Jer 31: 34), and makes the God of Israel to be a liar. The work of salvation and sanctification would also be rendered ineffective as shown above.

Manichaeism: Mani (216-276) rebelled from Elkesaism to teach one of the last gnostic heresies. His understanding was that there was a cosmic upheaval of primordial chaos. A great battle ensued, between darkness and light, and humanity emerged as a damaged product of the conflict in need of salvation. Jesus was one of many saviour figures who appeared through history.

Response: The Jewish Christian teaching from the first sermon of the Christian era is that there is only one Saviour. The pre-historical narrative of Mani owes more to Babylonian legend than to Jewish tradition and, as such, is based on such premises to be clearly heretical and heterodox. Jewish Christianity affirms that God is sovereign over his creation. He is the only one who effects salvation and this is done in the person of his son, Jesus.

Marcionism: Marcion (c 80-160) wished to disengage the New Testament from the Old which he saw as being superseded. In his canon of scripture even the New Testament was radically doctored to remove all Jewish connections.

Response: The Marcionite heresy is the antithesis of Jewish Christianity which seeks to promote the continuing faithfulness of God's activity in salvation history. His work was antisemitic in its character and the Jewish Christians would gladly have joined with the Church Fathers in denouncing Marcion for separating the event of salvation from creation and God's purpose as revealed through scripture in its entirety.

Monophysitism: Nestorius (fl 428-451) propounded the view that Christ was the conjunction (*synapheia*) of two distinct natures. The two remained distinct throughout however closely connected they became. Eutyches, the monk of Constantinople (c 378-454), argued that the two natures came together and became one. This was in turn refuted by the *Tome* of Pope Leo (c 400-461) at the Council of Chalcedon. His teaching, still accepted as orthodox, was that the two natures (physis) were perfectly united yet remained two within the union.

Response: The Semitic interest had long since declined by the fifth century CE. Where precision and exact definition were required Hebrew, a language notorious for its inexact nature, and Hebraic thought – similarly unconcerned with precise details would not have been helpful. Where insights may have been found were within the concepts of union within *Shekinah*, *Metatron* and *Elohim* within the *Sh'ma*. It is far beyond the scope of this essay to explore this possibility but it remains a field ripe for investigation and further study.

Monotheism: Strictly the belief that there is only one God. Its modern development has been in opposition to animism, polytheism and monolatry as a definition of Christianity as a religion. It should be stressed that, however, the three Persons of the Trinity are expressed, they are one (*Echad*) and not three Gods. In its earliest forms, Monotheism was the orthodox position as opposed to non-Christian beliefs but an over-reliance upon the 'One' within Monotheism has hindered the development of the doctrine of the Trinity.

Response: Judaism is a Monotheistic faith; Jewish Christianity is Trinitarian. The fact that there is only one God remains primary, but the truth that the One God has revealed himself in three *huyot* (Divine subsistencies) or *hypostases* (Persons) is integral to doctrinal belief. This is reinforced by the practice of worshipping Jesus and the Holy Spirit as God and by the direction of prayer to the Father through the Son by the power of the Holy Spirit.

Tritheism: The belief that there are three Gods. Usually an argument made against the Church from outside (particularly from Judaism). This is not, nor has it ever been, orthodox Christian doctrine.

Response: Jewish Christians are as keen to affirm that God is One as they are to affirm that there is only one God. The accusation of tritheism can only be refuted by clear demonstration that the concept of composite unity (*Echad*) is not unique to Jewish Christians but is central to Judaism itself, whether within the *T'nakh* or the *Zohar*.

Bibliography

Brock Sebastian, *The Luminous Eye; The Spiritual World Vision of Saint Ephrem the Syrian*, Cistercian Publications, Kalamazoo, Michigan 1992

Danielou Jean, *A History of Early Christian Doctrine Vol 1: The Theology of Jewish Christianity*, Darton, Longman & Todd, London 1964

Eichrodt Walther, *The Theology of the Old Testament; Vol 1*: SCM, London, 1987

Hanson R P C, *The Transformation of Images in the Trinitarian Theology of the Fourth Century in 'Studia Patristica' Vol XVII Part 1*, Pergamon Press, Oxford 1982

G W H Lampe, *Athens and Jerusalem: Joint Witnesses to Christ*, in *The Philosophical Frontiers of Christian Theology*, Ed Hebblethwaite and Sutherland, Cambridge University Press, Cambridge, 1982

Moltmann Jurgen, *The Trinity and the Kingdom of God*, SCM, London, 1983

Moule C F D, *The Borderlands of Ontology in the New Testament*, in *The Philosophical Frontiers of Christian Theology*, Ed Hebblethwaite and Sutherland, Cambridge University Press, Cambridge, 1982

Nassi Rabbi Tzvi, *The Great Mystery* or *How can Three be One?* Yanetz, Jerusalem, 1974

Riggans Walter, *Image and Reality; The Use of Jewish Symbolism by Messianic Jews*, Mishkan, Jerusalem, 1993

Williams Jane, *Trinity and Unity*, Darton, Longman & Todd, London, 1995

Wilson Marvin, *Our Father Abraham*, Eerdmans, Grand Rapids, 1994

Notes

1   **Moltmann**, SCM, p 21
2   Op Cit p 23
3   See **Moltmann**, Op Cit pp 25-27
4   'The doctrine of the Trinity does not affirm the logical nonsense that three is one and one is three; it describes in dialectic terms the inner movement of the divine life as an eternal separation from itself and return to itself.'- **Paul Tillich**; *Systematic Theology* Vol 1 p 56
5   **Danielou** 1964 p 148
6   **C F D Moule** 1982 p 5
7   Eichrodt 1987 p 214
8   (Ana eleicha mirucheicha/v'ana mipaneicha evrach?) Lit: 'Where [can] I go from your Spirit/and where [can] I flee from your face?
9   **Rosenzweig**; Quoted in **Moltmann** Op Cit p 29
10   **Takuni HaZohar** Cap 67, p 130 Quoted in *The Great Mystery* 1974 p 70
11   Faith 44: 2 Quoted in **Brock** 1992 p 63
12   **Brock** Op Cit p 64
13   En arche ain ho Logos. [In the Beginning was the Word – In God was God!]
14   Op Cit p 167 The personification of Hokmah while considered by some to have been a good example of hypostatisation does not seem to have been much in evidence within early Jewish Christian writings.
15   'In the Son God made the heavens and the earth.' Quoted by **Danielou** Op Cit p 167. This is compounded by the assertion of Origen that Aristo was a Jewish Christian anyway!
16   Quoted in **Nassi** 1974 p 61
17   Quoted in **Nassi** 1974 p 61
18   *Ze Metatron avdo shel makom; Tsakon beito sha'ho t'chilat b'riyotiv shel makom; Hamashal b'col asher lo.* **Nassi** 1974 p 63
19   **Nassi** 1974 p 64
20   **Zohar** Vol 2 Exod p 51 Amsterdam Edition; Quoted in Nassi 1974 p 66
21   **Danielou** 1964 p 118
22   **Nassi** 1974 p 52
23   See **Nassi** pp 134-9
24   **Danielou** 1964 p 148
25   Op Cit pp 32-35
26   Op Cit p 17
27   **R Menachem** of Recanati; *Commentary on the Pentateuch* (Venice Edition) p 267 Quoted in Nassi Op Cit p 21
28   Quoted in **Moltmann** Op Cit p 2

Settlement, Expulsion and Restoration

The Jews of England: 1066-1656

John C P Smith

Introduction

Jewish life in medieval England was nasty, brutish and short-lived; an episode which left a scar on Jewish history as a whole. The Jews, being royal property, were continually milked by the Crown, despised by the Church, the victims of ritual murder accusations and associated riots, and eventually completely expelled. As the renowned Anglo-Jewish historian, Cecil Roth observes, 'England had played an important and unenviable role in the martyrdom of the Jewish people'.[1]

Not that the tale is all bad. Life under Henry II, for example, was so 'good' as to cause considerable resentment among the general population. More than a few financiers managed to retain enormous wealth despite losing so much of their income to the Crown. Even amongst the poorer Jews, there would have been those who lived a relatively untroubled life, but with an uneasy peace with their Christian neighbours.[2]

Yet, taken as a whole, the story of Jewish life in medieval England is indeed a tragedy. Perhaps less apparent, however, is the extent to which this dark period of English and Church history has deeply engrained its mark upon English, and more specifically English Christian, attitudes to the Jewish people, and hence also to Israel.[3] For out of the medieval demonisation of the Jews of England came a number of hideous caricatures which have remained down the centuries. This is an issue the English Church ignores at its peril. It is a subject worthy of detailed study and an appropriate response.

In contrast to the medieval period, the seventeenth century saw a more encouraging approach by many professing Christians to the Jewish people. The Reformation had opened up the Bible to the laity, leading to an increased interest in Hebrew, prophecy – especially that which referred to the Second Coming of Jesus – and hence the prophetic people of Israel, the Jews.

It is often true that life is more than meets the eye. Reading between the lines of historical events in order to try and gauge the quality of life of a particular person or group, is an interesting challenge which confronts everyone wishing to understand history in some depth. This essay will outline Anglo-Jewish history in the Middle Ages and beyond, and in so doing, will try to shed some light on what life was like for the Jews of England.

Servi Camerae

The Jews of mainland Europe knew very little of the land across the sea, until William, Duke of Normandy, won his historic victory at Hastings in 1066 to become king of England. Jews under his domain, particularly from the town of Rouen, followed him across the channel and settled in London. The community was considerably boosted by those fleeing the early Crusades on the Continent.[4]

From its inception to its expulsion in 1290, the medieval Jewish community of England was the property of the Crown: the Jews were *servi camerae* ('servants of the chamber'). Successive kings, with greater or lesser degrees of rapacity, enjoyed the financial support of the Jews, who in turn benefited from the Crown's protection. Henry I (1100-35) introduced a charter for the Jews which became the model for this relationship for nearly two centuries. It guaranteed them liberty of movement throughout the country, protection from misusage, free recourse to royal justice and responsibility to no other, and a special provision to ensure a fair trial. These aspects of the Charter comprised the oxygen of the community's life, without which its existence was endangered.[5] The idea was to give the Jews enough freedom to carry out their allotted task: usury.[6] As Jews (at least, the wealthy financiers) made money on the interest of loans to members of the public, so the king was able to profit from them. As Cecil Roth puts it, the Jewish community was 'The Royal Milch-Cow'.[7] Other provisions of the Charter specifically relate to this financial aspect: Jews were to have relief from ordinary tolls, and were permitted to retain land taken in pledge as security for a loan.

Thus, while medieval Jews were not subjects as were other Englishmen, they nevertheless held a special, almost privileged, position.[8] Artificial though these conditions may have been, they enabled not a few Jews to flourish. The Pipe Roll of the 31st year of Henry I (1130-1), the earliest extant record of the Exchequer, mentions Jewish financial activities. The picture that emerges is of a relatively strong community, centred in London and headed by a few wealthy magnates, foremost of which was Rabbi Joseph (Rubi Gotsce), a man with a considerable reputation in the intellectual world.

Seeds of Disaster

At the same time, however, we see the seeds of disaster begin to take root as the Crusading spirit slowly began to pervade England. In 1130 the Jews of London were accused of killing a sick man, the result of which was a fine of £2,000 imposed by the Exchequer. This sum was more than sufficient to cancel the Crown's debt to Jewish financiers (which was perhaps the very reason behind the accusation). Such debilitating fines were to increase both in severity and frequency.

Whereas this special relationship between Crown and Jewry had begun with the former borrowing, or receiving in the form of gifts, large sums from Jewish financiers, it was now entering a new stage: Jews were arbitrarily fined, either because of a special need on the part of the Exchequer[9], or as a punishment for a purported crime of the Jewish community, or a member thereof. Such accusations, though generally highly disputable and often quite ridiculous, became a regular occurrence and were utilised not only by the Crown to replenish the Royal Exchequer, but also by debtors of the Jews as an excuse for violence and ultimately evasion of their debts. The first recorded instance of the notorious ritual murder accusation – the idea that Jews used Christian blood in their religious rites, especially in connection with Passover – was in England. In Norwich, in 1144, a young boy, William, was found dead in a wood near his home. The Jews were accused of enticing him away and crucifying him in mockery of the Passion of Jesus. In the ensuing uproar, a leader of the

Jewish community was murdered by a lawless knight who had been in his debt.[10]

Peace

The reign of Henry II (1154-89) marked a time of relative peace both for England and its Jewish community. The Crusading spirit was gaining momentum, and whilst the king mulcted the Jews, he nevertheless protected, even encouraged, them. He confirmed and extended his grandfather's charter, formally granting them the privilege of internal jurisdiction in accordance with Talmudic Law.[11] This undoubtedly engendered a certain amount of bitterness amongst the populous:

> *By an absurd arrangement they were happy and renowned far more than the Christians, and, swelling very impudently against Christ through their good fortune, did much injury to the Christians.*[12]

However, as H G Richardson argues[13], there was not the kind of 'universal dislike' of which some historians speak. Indeed, Jews even had close ties with Christian institutions and clergy.[14]

The intention of the Assize of Arms in 1181 was simply to usefully employ all available weapons, rather than a specific ploy against the Jewish community. However, the fact that it left Jews defenceless bode ill for the future and less halcyon days.

An outstanding Jewish figure of this period was Aaron of Lincoln, one of the leading European financiers of the twelfth century. He made large advances both to the Crown and private individuals, having important interests in twenty-five counties. His loans even helped build two cathedrals![15] In terms of liquid assets he was probably the wealthiest person in England when he died in 1185. His outstanding credits, owed by 430 people throughout the country, totalled £15,000 which amounted to three quarters of the annual royal income. A special branch of the Exchequer, the *Scaccarium Aaronis*, was set up to deal with these debts.

Towards the end of Henry's reign, the financial strain placed on the Jewish community by the Crown intensified. In 1188, in order to finance his proposed Crusade, the king imposed the first English tax on personal property, the Saladin Tithe. The Jewish contribution, fixed at one quarter of their property, was expected to raise £60,000.

In comparison, the population at large was to raise £70,000, each individual being taxed just a tenth of their property. The collection was not fully completed when, in 1189, Henry died 'leaving the throne to his worst-hated son'[16], Richard Lion-Heart.

Dark Days

For the Jewish community of England, the new king's reign began disastrously. A contingent of Jews had made their way to Westminster Hall on Sunday 3 September 1189, bearing gifts for the king on the day of his coronation. They were refused entry, as the king had forbidden Jews (and women) to attend, but a few managed to slip by. The doorkeeper threw them back out in a great commotion, which was enough to spark the onlookers to violence. False rumours spread throughout London that the king had given an order to kill the Jews. The Jewry was set on fire and thirty Jews lost their lives, including the eminent Rabbi Jacob of Orleans.

Though the king made a token attempt to quell the disorder, matters worsened when he left for France at the end of the year to spend six months gathering crusading forces. In England, detachments assembled in readiness for the coming Crusade. In early February, 1190, a series of violent attacks began against the Jews.[17] In Lynn, Norfolk, the Jewish community was almost wiped out. Houses were pillaged and Jews butchered or burned in the flames which destroyed a good part of the city. The example was followed in Norwich, but most Jews managed to take refuge in the royal castle. In Stamford, at the Lent fair, there was a large gathering of Crusaders. A riot ensued and only those Jews who reached the castle in time escaped with their lives. In Lincoln, amidst much havoc, royal officers largely succeeded in protecting the Jews and their property. In Dunstable, the entire Jewish community chose baptism to avert a massacre.

York

The most tragic occurrence was at York.[18] The local baronage was heavily indebted to the Jews, and one Richard Malebysse (wild beast) and his associates determined to wipe out their debts. In March they broke into the house of Benedict of York.[19] They murdered everyone in the house, looted the place and then burnt it down. Terrified, most of the rest of the Jews in York took refuge in the castle – those who did not were baptised or murdered. The warden, apparently genuinely wishing to protect the Jews in the castle, allowed them to shelter in Clifford's Tower, while he applied to the sheriff for help. However, the Jews felt unable to trust the warden. Fearing their imminent doom – whether it be baptism or slaughter – Rabbi Yomtob of Joingy urged the community to mass suicide. Burning their belongings, they set fire to the whole building. Over 150 died including the learned Rabbi Elijah of York. The very next day, Palm Sunday, 1190, fifty-seven Jews were murdered at Bury St Edmunds. The survivors were expelled.

King Richard was angry at the maltreatment of his Jews. Apart from anything, the Royal Exchequer stood to lose from the Jews' impoverishment. An inquiry was set up and punishment exacted.[20] Also a new system was introduced for governing Jewish affairs, particularly those of a financial nature. This eventually developed into the Exchequer of the Jews, or *Scaccarium Judaeorum*. In connection with this was the office of *Presbyter Judaeorum*, generally filled by wealthy Jewish magnates who were to advise on Jewish affairs and activities.

Drastic Decline

Despite the new structures, the reign of John saw a drastic decline in the economic situation of the Jews. He began his reign with a semblance of grace[21], but ended by thoroughly extorting the Jews. After his fateful campaign in Ireland in 1210, the king returned to Bristol where he issued instructions for the arrest of all Jews (at least, men of substance). He then imposed a tax of unprecedented magnitude, the Bristol Tallage. The property of those unable to pay was confiscated, and in some cases was demolished to make use of the building materials. Even the poorest Jews were made to pay, or else leave the country.[22] Some, who were accused of concealing assets, were hanged.

Many left England at this time. Further trouble was to follow as the country plunged into civil war. In 1215 the London Jewry was sacked and the houses demolished. The death of John in 1216 brought a respite from the violence.

Religious Fervour

The reign of Henry III (1216-72) saw a marked increase in *religious* anti-

Jewish sentiment. The IV Lateran Council of 1215 found the Jews responsible for the alarming spread of heresy in Europe. Stephen Langton, the Archbishop of Canterbury, was determined to put the Jews in their place. They were made to pay a tithe to the Church. Then, in 1218, a royal decree enforcing the distinctive clothing act, (also of the IV Lateran Council) demanded that Jews wear a distinguishing badge, ostensibly to prevent unwitting intercourse.[23] At the Council of the Province of Canterbury, at Oxford in 1222, a convert to Judaism was tried and subsequently burned. The Council made further harsh rulings to humiliate the Jews and restrict their activities.

The Crown continued to exact a heavy toll on the community. In 1236, ten of the wealthiest Jews were arrested, their ransom being set at 10,000 marks. In 1239, after an alleged murder in London, one third of the community's property was confiscated. In 1244, the Jews were fined 60,000 marks following a ritual crime accusation. It took six years to collect the money. By mid-century the Jews were destitute. In 1255, in order to meet his enormous debts, Henry mortgaged the entire Jewish community of England to his wealthy brother, Richard of Cornwall, as security for a loan of just 5,000 marks. It was a sorry end to the king's misguided policy concerning the Jews, as Roth explains:

> *The consequences of such rapacity should have been obvious to any intelligent being. The king was like a spendthrift with a cheque-book, drawing one amount after the other in utter indifference to the dwindling of his resources. Even as regards his personal interests, the policy was foolish. It progressively impoverished the English Jewries, rendering them less and less remunerative to the Exchequer as time went on. Moreover, in order to support these constant calls upon their purse, they were compelled to exercise still greater acquisitiveness in their business affairs, grinding desperately out of their clients the amounts that they would be compelled so inexorably to surrender to the Crown. Never was it more true that the Jews were like a sponge, sucking up the floating capital of the country, to be squeezed from time to time into the Treasury; while the king, high above them and sublimely contemptuous of their transactions, was in fact the arch-usurer of the realm.*[24]

The same year, the diabolical case of 'Little' St Hugh of Lincoln brought further suffering to the Jews. The boy Hugh had been missing for over three weeks when he was found dead in a cesspool, most likely having fallen in while playing. It so happened that Jews from all over the country had gathered in the city for a wedding. A Jew by the name of Copin was tortured until he confessed to killing the boy for ritual purposes. In the presence of the king, who had rushed to Lincoln, Copin was tied to a horse's tail, dragged up and down the streets and then hung. Nearly one hundred other Jews were implicated. Eighteen of them, whose demand for a mixed jury comprising both Jews and Christians was seen as an admittance of guilt, were hanged immediately. All but three of the rest were also convicted and sentenced.

Local Expulsions

Throughout Henry's reign there were a number of local expulsions. In 1231, Simon de Montfort expelled the Jews from his city, Leicester. In 1234 there were expulsions from Newcastle, Wycombe, the entire county of Warwick and parts of East Anglia. Further such occurrences followed at Southampton in 1236, Northamptonshire (excluding the county town) in 1237, Berkhampsted in 1242 and Newbury in 1243. In 1253, Jewish settlement was forbidden except by special licence. The result of all this was an influx of Jews to the few major centres, which produced great resentment among the general population of those areas.[25]

During the turbulent years of the Civil War (1260s) the Baronial party took every opportunity to get at the Jews, whom they saw as supporters of the Crown. In every town they entered they destroyed Jewish business records, often to their personal benefit. Many Jews lost their lives and a large number fled to the Continent.

Edward's 'Reforms'

When Edward came to the throne in 1272, he realised that reform was vital if he was to strengthen the monarchy and curb the power of the great magnates. A new approach to the Jews was particularly necessary. Although the king's father had inherited a prosperous Jewry, he had left a Jewish community in ruins. In 1275, the Common Council of the Realm met at Westminster and issued the *Statutum*

Judeismo: Jews were henceforth forbidden to lend money at interest (currently the only occupation open to them), but rather were permitted, for the first time in English history, to become merchants and artisans. For this reason only, they were now allowed to have contact with Christians, and even to lease lands for a period of ten years for the purpose of tillage and farming.[26] However, these provisions were accompanied by restrictions: Jews could only live in certain appointed towns; the wearing of a distinguishing badge was now to begin at the even earlier age of seven[27]; and an annual Eastertide poll tax was introduced for all Jews over twelve years old. But it was the spirit of the *Statutum Judeismo* rather than its details, that made it impracticable. Roth writes:

> *Under medieval no less than under modern conditions, economic emancipation was impossible without social emancipation. Men cannot transact business unless they meet as equals; merchants cannot make a living if there is a lack of understanding with their customers; artisans need a friendly environment in which to serve their apprenticeship, to practise their craft, and to dispose of their productions. All this was expressly excluded by the terms of the Statute, which affirmed and extended (instead of modifying) the former discrimination, and forbade the Jews to be 'levant and couchant' (have social intercourse) amongst the general population.[28]*

The farming option was also unworkable as the Jews were confined to a few cities, and in any case, the farming provision was only a temporary one. Roth concludes that 'to change ... the Jew's manner of life while he remained subject to the same insecurity, the same prejudices, and the same differentiation as before was an impossible task'.[29]

Plea for Mercy

The Jews drew up a petition imploring the king and council to modify the Statute, and ending with a pathetic plea for mercy. But Edward pressed on with his reforms, while amazingly continuing to fine the Jews. The very same year he ordered a tallage of £1,000. Those who could not pay were imprisoned, their chattels sold for the Treasury, and their wives and children deported. Only a handful of wealthy Jews managed to accommodate themselves to the Statute's requirements, trading in corn (in Bristol, Canterbury, Exeter and Hereford) or wool (in Lincoln, Norwich and Oxford). For the poor, faced with starvation, there were few alternatives. Some converted; others turned to criminal activity such as highway robbery, clandestine usury, and coin 'clipping'.[30] Numerous Jews were arrested on the latter charge, often on little or no evidence[31], and many were subsequently hung.

His reforms having failed, the king faced few options in dealing with the Jewish problem. Giving the Jews social emancipation was unthinkable in the thirteenth century (even to the Jews!), besides which, the English Church was experiencing a period of extremism. Another alternative was to return to the former practice of allowing the Jews to engage in usury. While this option was certainly considered, it was never realised. The only remaining alternative open to Edward was to expel the Jews from England. It was, after all, not a new concept. In 1182, for example, Philip Augustus had expelled the Jews from the kingdom in France. There were also, as discussed earlier, many instances of local expulsions in recent English history. The king had nothing to lose: the Jewish contribution to the Exchequer had shrunk from one seventh of the royal yearly income a century before, to around one per cent. With anti-Jewish religious sentiment running so high, Edward could only gain from the Jews' banishment.

Expulsion from England

In 1290, on the 9th day of the Jewish month of Ab[32] – a day of mourning on which both the First and the Second Temples had been destroyed[33] – the expulsion of the Jews of England was decreed by an act of the king in his council. Writs were issued to the sheriffs of the various English counties ordering the Jews' expulsion by 1 November. Those remaining after this date were to be executed. The king ordered that no person should 'injure, harm, damage, or grieve'[34] the Jews, and most made safe passage to the Continent, mainly France. However, there were instances of murder and robbery[35], and others died when their ships sank. Roth sums up the experience of medieval life for the Jews of England, thus:

> England had played an important and unenviable role in the
> martyrdom of the Jewish people. It was here that the Ritual Murder

Accusation, which subsequently proved responsible for such wide-spread misery, first reared its head. At no other time in the blood-stained record of the Middle Ages were the English horrors of 1189-90 surpassed ... The final tragedy of 1290 was the first general expulsion of the Jews from any country in the medieval period.[36]

For three-and-a-half centuries there was no formal Jewish community in England.

Restoration

The re-admission of the Jews to England – or, more accurately, 'the public recognition of a Jewish community in this country'[37] – is generally dated at 1656. Thereafter the Jewish community grew steadily, though slowly and with great caution, from around 160 people (thirty-five families, of whom 90% were Sephardi) to approximately 800 by the end of the century. The latter half of the 1700s saw a population explosion such that by the close of that century there were 15-20,000 Jews living in England, two-thirds of whom resided in London. But let us step back and examine what factors were involved in the re-establish-ment of a Jewish community in England. To do this we will look at the social, religious, political and financial climate which had led to the Expulsion of 1290 and see to what extent these conditions had been reversed, or negated. Other factors will also be examined.

Perhaps the most important element in the re-establishment of a Jewish community was the religious climate. England, at the start of the seventeenth century was the centre of what amounted to a religious revolution, the so-called Reformation. For the first time since the formation of the institutionalised Church in the fourth century, Christians were beginning to challenge established doctrines and practices as they began to read the Bible for themselves.[38] The Pope was no longer thought of as infallible; on the contrary, many in England came to view him as that hated figure in Christianity, the Antichrist. This is in total contrast to the religious climate in the country just prior to the expulsion. At that time the strong anti-Jewish decrees of the Church authorities found their harshest expression in England. Jews were equated with the Devil and there were routine accusations against them of blasphemy, magic and cheating. Now, three-and-a-half centuries later, there were many voices speaking out against these medieval prejudices. Robert Maton, in his book *Israel's Redemption* (1642), advised Christians not to 'contemne (holding contempt) or revile the Jewes, a fault too common in the Christian world'.[39]

But far more significant than this negation of the past was a widespread active interest in the Jewish roots of Christianity, the Hebrew language, the role of the Jewish people in the fulfilment of 'end-time' prophecies, and other related topics:

> *The religious developments of the seventeenth century brought to its climax an unmistakable philo-Semitic tendency in certain English circles. Puritanism represented above all a return to the Bible, and this automatically fostered a more favourable frame of mind towards the people of the Old Testament.*[40]

For most ordinary folk, it was a revelation to discover, for example, that Jesus was in fact himself a Jew. In 1617, John Traske was imprisoned for being an active 'Judaiser' – a promoter of Jewish feasts and practices amongst Christians, such as the celebration of Passover. Movements such as Seventh Day Adventism sprang up at this time.

Enlightenment

The Enlightenment had also sparked a quest for the universal philosophical language. In the minds of those at the forefront of this quest 'the supernatural qualities of the Hebrew language, the search for the original *lingua humana*, and the development of a philosophical language were linked'.[41] In fact, 'by the mid seventeenth century, after much discussion, most Englishmen agreed that God spoke Hebrew'.[42] The interest in Hebrew inevitably had its effects on people's attitudes to Jews, as Katz explains:

> *On a popular level, the continuous glorification of Hebrew, not only as a sacred language like Greek, but as a unique divinely infused, supernatural method of communication, helped to turn men's minds towards Jews and to erode the medieval conception of the obscurantist, Pharisaic Jew.*[43]

Associated with this belief in the supernatural qualities of Hebrew, was Christian scholars' fascination with Jewish Kabbalah, a form of mysticism in which ordinary words are given a much greater signifi-

cance than their literal meanings. Lurianic Kabbalism, which placed
particular emphasis on the process of redemption, 'was the one well-
articulated and generally accepted form of Jewish theology [in the
mid-seventeenth century]'.[44] This was of profound interest to
Christians, especially those who perceived the approaching return of
Christ, the Millenarianists. The theologian Thomas Brightman (1562-
1607) predicted that Jesus would return to inaugurate his thousand
year rule in 1650. Although the jurist and Member of Parliament,
Serjeant Sir Henry Finch (1558-1625), was imprisoned by King James
for his book, *The World's Great Restauration, or the Calling of the Jews*
(1621), he was by no means isolated in his beliefs. Not a few other
churchmen believed that the redemption of the Jews was near, many
predicting it would start in the 1650s (including several who believed
1656 to be the year!). Most agreed that the Jews had to be 'called to
Christ', or converted, before the Redemption and the fall of Rome.
There existed 'the hope that the Jews, so long deaf to popish or
episcopal blandishments, would be unable to withstand a pure form of
Christianity, once they had the opportunity of becoming acquainted
with it at close quarters'.[45] Furthermore, citing the biblical passages
which speak of the Jews being gathered to Israel from every corner of
the world, some were convinced that the Jews must first be living in
England before these prophecies could be fulfilled.[46] But while seventy
per cent of the prolific ministers who published their works between
1640 and 1653 can be identified as millenarians, it was the likes of the
extremists such as Thomas Tany and John Robins who kept the Jewish
issue in public view[47]: the Jews were a modern living nation.

Menasseh ben Israel

Millenarianists certainly helped to influence the public's attitude to the
Jews, yet they had little idea of how the Jews were to be readmitted to
England – in fact, many were far more interested in seeing the Jews
return to Israel than to England. It was the seemingly obscure debate
over the Lost Ten Tribes of Israel[48] which helped, indirectly, to take the
issue into the political dimension by gripping the attention of the
charismatic Dutch rabbi and scholar, Menasseh ben Israel, probably as
a result of his interest in mysticism.[49] Menasseh was a popular preacher
to whom thronged both Gentiles and Jews. Many at home and abroad

(including England) 'were in the habit of consulting him on matters of Jewish scholarship. He had thus become a representative figure in Gentile eyes, and considered himself qualified to speak to those in authority on behalf of his people as a whole.'[50] In 1651, John Thurloe, Cromwell's Chief of Staff (and Secretary of State from 1652) who believed that Cromwell's regime heralded the millennium, advised the Rabbi on a visit to Amsterdam to make formal application to the English government, which he did. However, owing to the outbreak of war between England and Holland, and Menasseh's subsequent sickness, Manuel Martinez Dormido (otherwise David Abrabanel) went in his stead. When the Council of State eventually decided, in Cromwell's absence, not to act upon Dormido's petitions, the Protector seemingly 'intimated to Dormido that he was completely in favour of his project; but considered it desirable for Menasseh to come over and treat of the matter in person'.[51] Although the Rabbi had not meanwhile fully recovered from his illness, he was nevertheless determined to go to England, and did so. On 12 November, 1655, Cromwell presented Menasseh's petition at a meeting of the Council of State. This *Humble Address* outlined 'the case for Readmission [and was] argued almost exclusively on grounds of political expediency'.[52] It began as follows:

> *Three things, if it please your Highnesse, there are that make a strange Nation well-beloved amongst the Natives of a land where they dwell: (as the defect of those three things make them hateful) viz. Profit, they may receive from them; Fidelity they hold towards their Princes; and the Noblenes and purity of their blood. Now when I shall have made good, that all these three things are found in the Jewish Nation, I shall certainly persuade your Highnesse, that with a favorable eye (Monarchy being changed into a Republicq), you shall be pleased to receive again the Nation of the Jews, who in time past lived in that Island: but, I know not by what false informations, were cruelly handled and banished.[53]*

The Rabbi then elaborated on his three points in some detail.

Whitehall Conference

Reaction to the debate over the proposed readmission of the Jews to England was mixed. Cromwell decided to convene a conference at

Whitehall in December, 1655, to resolve the issue. He invited politicians, lawyers, businessmen and clergy. Although the Expulsion of
1290 was deemed legally no longer binding, the delegates could not
agree on the conditions of a future Jewish presence in the country: how
worship was to be conducted; whether synagogues could be erected
and, if so, where; whether the Jews were likely to proselytise; where
they would live; in what professions they would engage; etc. The latter
was a particular sticking point with the merchants of the City, who
claimed they would suffer great financial loss if Jews were allowed to
compete on an equal par. While the average English businessman of
the seventeenth century would have been quite aware that Jews were
not all stingy money-grabbers, he would still have regarded Jewish
merchants with some suspicion both as a result of such portrayals as
Shakespeare's Shylock, and more recently in the light of the success of
international Jewish trade. Despite Cromwell's lengthy efforts on
behalf of the petition[54], he was forced to dissolve the conference.

However, Menasseh ben Israel was not the only Jew to have made
contact with Cromwell. Antonio Fernandez (otherwise Abraham
Israel) Carvajal, a man of considerable wealth and widespread commercial connections, was naturalised along with his two sons as an
English subject in 1655[55]. However, his most notable achievement in
generating political sympathies for the Jews was his involvement in
the national secret service. With the help of his associates he was able
to provide Cromwell with invaluable information regarding the
Spanish enemy.[56] Another Jewish businessman, the Dutch-born
Simon (otherwise Jacob) de Caceres, also gave valuable service to
England. His advice and information concerning Jamaica helped
greatly in its settlement after it had been conquered from Spain.[57]

If Cromwell was aware that the likes of Carvajal and de Caceres
were in fact Jews,[58] then it must undoubtedly have been another factor
in giving him a positive disposition towards the Jewish cause.[59]
Nevertheless, the legal recognition of the Jewish settlement came not
from any decision of Cromwell himself, but as Hyamson relates, 'it
came almost incidentally from a decision of the courts'.[60] He continues:

> The outbreak of war with Spain endangered the position of most if not
> all the Jewish merchants of England, who were at least nominally
> Spanish subjects. Antonio Rodrigues Robles, the first to be threat-

ened, had not been prominent in the efforts to obtain formal recognition for the community, but in the crisis his cause was that of all the Jews of London. Within a few days of the opening of the proceedings against Robles, the Jews, in a body, petitioned Cromwell for permission to conduct, without molestation, religious services in accordance with the Jewish ritual ... and to acquire land for a cemetery.[61] Simultaneously Robles defended himself against the threatened confiscation of his property by the public announcement that he was a Jew, reciting in a brief autobiographical note his sufferings on that account. His petition was supported by affidavits of fellow Jews.

A Synagogue and a Cemetery

The reply of the Council of State to the petition of Robles' fellow Jews is unknown since the pages of the Council Book with the records for that day have been torn out. However, the charges against Robles were withdrawn. 'As a Spanish Catholic his position had been open to question. As a refugee Jew he was safe.'[62] (Despite this, Menasseh ben Israel returned to Amsterdam, despondent. Pollins argues that 'behind all the millenarianism and his economic argument for admission, Menasseh was really looking only for a home for Jewish refugees'.[63] It was not until well into the next century that England could be described as such.) In August the Jews of London sent to the community in Amsterdam for a Torah Scroll, and by the end of the year they felt confident enough of their position for Antonio Carvajal to take out a 21 year lease on a house in Cree Church Lane, for the purpose of converting it for use as a public synagogue. Work began on the property and the synagogue opened shortly after. The following February, Carvajal and de Caceres leased land in Mile End for use as a cemetery. 'Jewish settlement and rights had been re-established in England without any formal legislation.'[64]

From Expulsion to Re-settlement

The Expulsion of 1290 had been the result of a combination of factors: First, owing to the Crown's repeated and devastating levies on the Jews, they had been sucked financially dry and could no longer be of any direct benefit to the king.[65] Secondly, religious anti-Jewish sentiment in England was at its zenith, and this, coupled with general resentment and ill-feeling towards the Jews, meant that Expulsion would be a popular move for the king both amongst the clergy and the populace.

England in the mid-seventeenth century 'was a very different world from the middle ages'.[66] First, the medieval social hierarchy which had squeezed the Jews into the singular role of usury no longer existed – the re-established community comprised merchants, gem importers, financiers, bullion dealers, and physicians. Secondly, apart from those in the City who didn't want new competition, Cromwell and others must have been attracted to the financial benefits of allowing Jewish businessmen to settle in England [see note 56], and in fact had already experienced this in the likes of Carvajal [see note 55]. Thirdly, with the Reformation, some of the sting of medieval religious anti-Semitism had been removed from the general population, and, to a certain extent, there were the beginnings of philo-Semitism. Also, and related to this, having broken with Rome, England was no longer under the spell of long-established Catholic anti-Semitism and could do as it wished.

Furthermore, with the advent of all types of separatist sects Jews were no longer alone as a minority. This worked in their favour in several ways. First, 'attention was now diverted from the Jews ... by such minorities as the Roman Catholics, who, besides being unpopular were, at this stage, politically dangerous'.[67] Secondly, reason argued – and the age of Enlightenment had made logical reasoning fashionable – that tolerance of one group demanded the same of another.[68] Another factor aiding the re-settlement drive was due to the corollary of this sectarianism – the weakness of the national Church, 'the only body which hitherto had sufficient strength to persecute those who held minority views in the matter of religion'.[69]

Surely another important element in creating a climate favourable to the re-establishment of a Jewish community was the discreet manner in which the Jews concerned conducted themselves in public. Great pains were taken to ensure that they would be thought of as nothing other than quiet, upright, trustworthy and loyal.[70] (In fact they even succeeded in giving the impression to some, if not many, that most Jews were intelligent, successful businessmen.)

In the final analysis it was the incident with Antonio Rodrigues

Robles which precipitated the recognition of Jews in England – 'as is not unusual in British history, developments [towards re-admission] had their source in *ad hoc* responses to immediate problems rather than in profound ideological theorising'.[71] However, this must not be taken in isolation, for it was a combination of all the above factors which created the right climate for this new beginning. This is illustrated in H N Brailsford's analysis of why Cromwell favoured the admission of the Jews:

> *Was this because the Old Testament had taught him to think of them as God's chosen people, or was it for commercial reasons and because they worked for his intelligence service? His mind worked to and fro between the City, Whitehall and the Holy Land without a sense of incongruity; the probability is that all three considerations influenced him.[72]*

The time was right – in the minds of the commissioners at Robles' proceedings; in the mind of Cromwell; in the minds of increasing numbers of politicians and theologians; in the minds of those with commercial enterprises, business partnerships and other contacts with the Jews; even if not in the minds of many others, including certain elements in the City – for a recognition of the legitimacy of the residence, work and worship of the Jews in England.

Bibliography

Harold Pollins, *Economic History of the Jews in England*, Oxford University Publications, 1982/4, 0-19-710048-1

H G Richardson, *The English Jewry Under Angevin Kings*, Greenwood Press, 1960/83, 0-313-24247-X

Cecil Roth, *A History of the Jews in England*, John Trotter Publishers, 1964/89, 1-871840-00-7

Jonathan A Romain, *The Jews of England – A Portrait of Anglo-Jewry through Original Sources and Illustrations*, Michael Goulston Educational Foundation, 1985/8, 0-907372-04-X

David S Katz, *Philo-Semitism and the Readmission of the Jews to England, 1603-1655*, Clarendon Press, 1982/3, 0-19-821885-0

Albert M Hyamson, *The Sephardim of England*, Methuen, 1951

Notes

1   **Roth**, *A History of the Jews in England*, p 90.

2   Indeed, some church leaders felt it their duty to prevent what they saw as an unhealthy amount of social intercourse between Christians and Jews. Neither did this friendliness go unnoticed by Jews on the Continent: Elhanan ben Israel, a medieval Jewish writer, expresses surprise 'that in the land of the Isle [England] they are lenient in the matter of drinking strong drinks of the Gentiles and along with them' (Tosaphot [cited in *The Jews of England*, **Romain**, p 16]).

3   Under the guidance of Prof R Wistrich, the author of this essay conducted 'A Survey of Christians Attitudes to Israel and the Jewish People' amongst 67 Christians in Reigate (Surrey, England) in 1993. The results were submitted as a final-year degree dissertation. They revealed a striking ambivalence in Christian attitudes. Many, it seems, would say that they are in favour of the Jewish State, yet their remarks on specific issues betray at best an indifference towards the Jews and at worst a barely veiled resentment.

4   Indeed, Rouen was itself the site of a great Crusading massacre in 1096.

5   On not a few occasions the provisions of the Charter were broken, either by the populous taking the law into their own hands and attacking the Jews, or, as with the York tragedy of 1190, by the Jews no longer feeling able to trust the Crown's protection.

6   In this they had no choice. '[In western Europe,] trade was everywhere organised on a co-operative basis, and impregnated with a feeling of religious solidarity which left few loopholes for the unbeliever. Accordingly, the Jew was driven to employ his capital in the only manner that remained open. Unable to engage in personal enterprise, he had to finance that of others – to lend out his capital, that is, at interest. This tendency became all the more marked since an impossible idealism backed by faulty exegesis was causing the Church – oblivious of the fact that credit is a necessity in any society which has progressed beyond its most rudimentary stage – to oppose the lending of money at interest in any circumstances whatsoever.' [*A History of the Jews in England*, **Roth**, p 3.] However, poorer Jews inevitably did of necessity engage in work other than usury, illegally if need be. (The poor constituted approximately one third of the Jewish population according to Lipman's analysis of the Norwich community, 1220-40 [*The Jews of Medieval Norwich*, **V D Lipman**, p 65, cited in *Economic History of the Jews in England*, **Pollins**, p 18]. Of 150 Jews, ten were wealthy, thirty upper-middle-class, sixty ordinary middle-class, and fifty were poor.

7   **Roth**, *A History of the Jews in England*, ch III.

8   In fact, the notion of a 'normal subject' is out of place in the Middle Ages. This was the era of feudalism, in which each person had a definite place in a neat social structure, from king to sheriff, from landlord to serf. Thus the position of the Jews is not so strange as it might at first appear.

9   The first example of the Exchequer's new financial policy was in 1159 when a tallage was imposed on the towns of the country and on the Jews in order to raise money for the king's expedition against rebellious Toulouse.

10   Later examples of the ritual murder accusation include the notorious

cases of Harold of Gloucester (1168), Robert of Bury St Edmunds (1181), and 'Little' St Hugh of Lincoln (1255).

11   Except in the case of offences against public order.

12   William of Newburgh, Historia rerum anglicarum, ed Howlett, i 280 [cited in *A History of the Jews in England*, **Roth**, p 10].

13   *The English Jewry Under Angevin Kings*, **Richardson**, pp vii,viii.

14   Despite laws forbidding it, abbeys and minsters used plate, vessels used in worship and even relics of saints to secure loans from Jewish financiers. Jews could place women and children in monasteries for safety in times of disturbance. Jewish financiers kept their business deeds in cathedral treasuries. Jews even participated in monastic politics, supporting their favoured abbot.

15   At Lincoln and Peterborough.

16   **Roth**, *A History of the Jews in England*, p 17.

17   There were three primary reasons for these outbreaks: (i) Crusaders were angry at the wealth of the Jews when they, poor Christians, were about to risk their lives to redeem the Holy Land from the infidel. William of Newburgh writes that the Crusaders were 'indignant that the enemies of the cross of Christ ... should possess so much when they had not enough for the expenses of so great a journey' (i 310 [cited in *A History of the Jews in England*, **Roth**, p 21]). (ii) There was a popular notion that even a hardened sinner would be welcomed to Paradise for killing a paynim. (iii) It was Lent, when deep-rooted religious passions ran high. (Compare today's outbreaks of violence by Moslem Arabs in Israel during the month of fasting of Ramadan, when intense religious devotion often finds physical expression.)

18   A Jewish community had been in existence here since at least 1130.

19   He had died as a result of wounds received during the coronation riot, but his wife and a few others continued to live in the house.

20   However, the ring-leaders escaped to Scotland. Also, those who were punished (fined) most severely were relatives and allies of the Bishop of Durham, who just happened to be the rival of William Longchamp, the official responsible for dealing with the episode.

21   As anti-Jewish feeling in London became a serious threat, the king intervened to protect the Jews. In 1203 he wrote to the mayor, 'If I give my peace even to a dog it must be kept inviolate' [cited in **Roth**, *A History of the Jews in England*, p 33].

22   In fact the king's declared policy on the Jews, as laid out in the Mandate to the Justices assigned to the Custody of the Jews in 1253, was that if they could not be of benefit to the Crown they should not remain in England.

23   However, only after 1253 was the badge consistently enforced.

24   **Roth**, *A History of the Jews in England*, pp 51-2.

25   In an attempt to prevent the situation from worsening, Jews in Canterbury even took measures themselves to put a halt to the Jewish influx.

26   However, this provision would expire after fifteen years.

27   On the Continent, the usual age at which Jews had to begin wearing the badge was twelve for girls, and thirteen for boys.

28   **Roth**, *A History of the Jews in England*, pp 71-2.

29   **Roth**, *A History of the Jews in England*, p 72.

30   This involved filing the edges of coins and then putting them back into circulation while melting the clippings into bullion.

31   Accusations against the Jews came from even the most disreputable characters. Debtors of the Jews were obviously trying to use the judicial system to have the Jews done away with, thus writing off their debts. Such accusations eventually became so widespread that the king had to intervene.

32   18 July, 1290.

33   Later, in 1492, the Jews were expelled from Spain, also on the 9th of Ab.

34   Cited in *A History of the Jews in England*, **Roth**, p 86.

35   At Queenborough, on the mouth of the Thames, the master of a ship carrying Jews suggested they all disembark in order to stretch their legs, after running aground on a sandbank. When the tide rose, he ran back to the ship and prevented the Jews from re-boarding, telling them to call on Moses to save them. The entire party drowned and the sailors made off with the property, though they were eventually brought to justice and hanged. Other cases similar to this one also occurred.

36   **Roth**, *A History of the Jews in England*, p 90.

37   **Hyamson**, *The Sephardim of England*, p 13. Hyamson explains that while 'the existence of a Jewish community in London was openly admitted and accepted only at the beginning of 1656, ... there can be no doubt that this Community had then been in existence, in secret, for some years' (p 12). In fact, individuals and families of Sephardi Jews, mainly from Portugal and Spain, are known to have been resident in England on and off since just a matter of decades after the Expulsion of 1290. These were marranos, or conversos (secret or crypto-Jews), fleeing the Inquisition, most of whom were merchants.

38   The Bible was translated into English under James I (*The King James Authorized Version*) in 1611.

39   **R Maton**, *Israels Redemption* (1642), pp 68-9 (cited in **Katz**, *Philo-Semitism and the Readmission of the Jews to England, 1603-1655*, p.101).

40   **Roth**, *A History of the Jews in England*, p 149.

41   **Katz**, *Philo-Semitism and the Readmission of the Jews to England, 1603-1655*, p 45.

42   Ibid, p 44.

43   Ibid, p 88.

44   **Scholem**, *Sabbatai Sevi*, p 25 (cited in **Katz**, *Philo-Semitism and the Readmission of the Jews to England, 1603-1655*, p 75).

45   **Roth**, *A History of the Jews in England*, p 149.

46   The key prophesies are found in the following passages of the Bible: Deuteronomy 30: 3-5; Isaiah 11: 11-12, 43: 5-6; Jeremiah 16: 14-15, 23: 3,7-8, 30: 3, 31: 8; Ezekiel 36: 24, 39: 25,27-28. The passage in Isaiah chapter eleven is particularly relevant as it makes reference to 'the four corners of the earth' and 'the islands of the sea', which some may have interpreted as including the British Isles. Certainly John Dury, who was close to John Thurloe, the Secretary of State, and who was also in contact with Menasseh ben Israel, maintained that the Jews needed to be in England

in order to fulfil the prophecies referring to 'the four corners of the earth'.

47   Thomas Tany came to prominence in 1650. He circumcised himself and believed he would lead the Jews back to Israel and would be their king. (He also claimed the thrones of England, France and Rome.) His heretical views of God the Father, Christ, Mary, the Bible, and education landed him in prison. After his release in 1654 he made a single-handed attempt to attack Parliament with a sword. Tany was active until his death in 1655 – he drowned at sea on his way to Holland to call the Jews. John Robins claimed, amongst other things, to be both God Almighty and Adam before the Fall. However, after his imprisonment he eventually recanted.

48   These tribes were carried into exile by the Assyrians after the conquest of the Northern Kingdom (Israel) around 722-1 BCE. Much speculation existed as to where the descendants of the tribes now resided. The discovery of America just over a century before added new impetus to the debate, with some claiming that the American Indians were descended from the Lost Tribes.

49   Menasseh eventually dismissed the link with the American Indians as ridiculous.

50   **Roth**, *A History of the Jews in England*, p 154.

51   **Roth**, *A History of the Jews in England*, p 161.

52   **Wolf**, *Menasseh ben Israel's Mission*, p xxxix (cited in **Pollins**, *Economic History of the Jews in England*, p 32).

53   Cited in **Romain**, *The Jews in England*, p 72.

54   A report of Cromwell's closing speech to the conference, 'coming to us at second-hand', is recorded by W C Abbott in The Writings and Speeches of Oliver Cromwell. Cromwell, addressing the clergy, desired to be informed by them whether it was not their opinion, that the Jews were one day to be called into the church? He then desired to know, whether it was not every Christian man's duty to forward that good end all he could? ... This silenced the clergy. He then turned to the merchants ... He then fell into abusing the Jews most heartily, and after he had said everything that was contemptible and low of them: 'Can you really be afraid,' he said, 'that this mean despised people should be able to prevail in trade and credit over the merchants of England, the noblest and most esteemed merchants of the world!' (Vol IV, pp 51-52 [cited in **Pollins**, *Economic History of the Jews in England*, p 33].)

55   Carvajal was the earliest of the new generation of immigrants to arrive in England (the few Jews who had been living there at the turn of the century having been expelled in 1609 following a bitter internal quarrel in the course of which one party denounced the other to the authorities as Judaizers). He arrived in 1630, interestingly from Rouen, from whence had originated the medieval Jewish community of England a little under six centuries before. Roth picks up the story:

Before many years had passed, he was among the most prominent merchants in the City. He possessed his own ships, trading with the East and West Indies, as well as the Levant, in a large variety of commodities. He imported gunpowder and munitions on an extensive scale, brought large quantities of bullion from abroad, and during the Civil War was grain contractor for Parliament. (**Roth**, *A History of the Jews in England*, p 159.)

56 In fact another influential Jew living in England, Hector Nunez, had acted similarly for Queen Elizabeth three-quarters of a century before, making the government aware of preparations for the Armada (1587-8).

57 It is interesting to compare the influence of the twentieth century Jew, Chaim Wiezmann, on the British government, with that of Carvajal and de Caceres. In 1916 his work as a research chemist led him to discover an efficient method of yielding acetone, a solvent in great demand by the British army during the First World War for use in munitions production. This can only have had a positive effect on politicians such as Lloyd George (minister of munitions) and Winston Churchill (first lord of the admiralty), and may well have helped prompt the Balfour Declaration of 1917 which laid out the government's commitment to seeing 'the establishment in Palestine of a national home for the Jewish people'.

58 Pollins challenges that 'no evidence exists to support the view – put forward by some historians – that Cromwell knew they were secret Jews' (**Pollins**, *Economic History of the Jews in England*, p 32). However, Cromwell certainly would have known once their names appeared as signatories on the later petition of 1656.

59 Roth observes: A primary factor in the foreign policy of the Commonwealth was the protection and encouragement of English commerce. This was the cause of the war with Holland, and it played its part in that with Spain. But negative steps to protect trade were not sufficient. It was patent that Jewish merchants had been very largely responsible for the recent growth and prosperity of Leghorn, of Hamburg, and especially Amsterdam. Were they persuaded to settle in London, they might do as much there as well. (**Roth**, *A History of the Jews in England*, p 158.)

60 **Hyamson**, *The Sephardim of England*, p 13.

61 The following is the text of the petition which was dated March 24th, 1665/6:

To His Highness Oliver Lord Protector of the Commonwealth of England, Scotland & Ireland & the Dominion thereof.

The Humble Petition of the Hebrews at present Residing in this city of London whose names are underwritten

Humbly shoeweth:

That acknowledging the manyfold favours and Protection your Highness hath been pleased to grant us in order that we may with security meet privately in our particular houses to our Devotions, and being desirous to be favoured more by your Highness we pray with Humbleness that by the best meanes which may be such Protection may be granted us in writing as that we may therewith meet at our private devotions in our particular houses without feare of molestations either to our persons, families or estates, our desires being to live peaceably under your Highness' Government. And being we all mortal, we also humbly pray your Highness to grant us licence that those which may die of our nation may be buried in such a place out of this city as we shall think convenient with the proprietors' leave in whose land this place shall be, and so we shall as well in our lifetime, as at our death be highly favoured by your Highness for whose long life and prosperity we shall continually pray to the almighty God.

[Signed:]

Menasseh ben Israel, David Abrabanel, Abraham Israel Carvajal, Abraham Coen Ganzales, Jahacob de Caceres, Abraham Israel De Brito, Isak Lopez Chillon

(Cited in **Romain**, *The Jews in England*, p 77.)

62   **Roth**, *A History of the Jews in England*, p 166.

63   **Pollins**, *Economic History of the Jews in England*, p 37.

64   **Romain**, *The Jews in England*, p 78.

65   In fact king John's declared policy on the Jews, as laid out in the Mandate to the Justices assigned to the Custody of the Jews in 1253, had been that if they could not be of benefit to the Crown they should not remain in England.

66   **Pollins**, *Economic History of the Jews in England*, p 29.

67   **Roth**, *A History of the Jews in England*, p 152.

68   In 1648 the Council of Mechanics passed a resolution in favour of universal toleration for all religions, 'not excepting Turks, nor Papists, nor Jews' (cited in Pollins, Economic History of the Jews in England, p 30), although the final document did not go that far and spoke of toleration only for Christians.

69   **Roth**, *A History of the Jews in England*, p 152.

70   This attention to, even obsession with, appearance continued long after the community was re-established. Even a century later it could be seen, as the wealthy element saw the arrival of increasing numbers of poorer Jews as quite undesirable, since it not only created social problems but also gave a bad impression to the general population.

71   **Pollins**, *Economic History of the Jews in England*, p 31.

72   **H N Brailsford**, *The Levellers and the English Revolution*, p 395 (cited in **Pollins**, *Economic History of the Jews in England*, p 36).

Messianic Jews and the Definition of Jewishness

by Walter Riggans

Terminology

Throughout this essay Jewish believers in Jesus are variously referred to as 'Messianic Jews', 'Jewish Believers' or 'Hebrew Christians'. To a great extent the terms are interchangeable, though they have nuances of their own, and some individuals have personal preferences. We have therefore not used one term exclusively, and the context usually clarifies the choice.

Introduction

It is a truism to state that Jewish people in the westernised, industrialised world are pre-occupied with the issue of Jewish identity. It is a fascination for some, and a source of frustration for others, but for all of them it is of paramount importance. The issues of Jewish survival and Jewish continuity are obviously bound up with this matter of the very definition of what constitutes the essence of being a Jewish person. Not surprisingly, this is also a matter of great concern to the Messianic Jewish community.

In point of fact, the question as to the correct definition of Jewishness has taken on a considerably more intense significance in modern times than it did during the Middle Ages and the pre-modern era. Academic studies, rabbinic discourses, novels, poetry, and debates of all kinds are devoted to this subject in our day. There would appear to be at least six major and complex historical factors which are held by Jewish commentators to have led to the intensity of the debate in the modern Jewish world:

- The rise of post-enlightenment humanistic and individualistic world views which have impacted on the Jewish communities of the industrialised world, producing the process known as secularisation. This process has consequently led, for a high proportion of the Jewish people, to the suspension, and even rejection, of the following of the halakhah as the foundation for Jewish life and identity.

- The opening of the ghettoes and the so-called 'ghetto mentality' of the Jewish people, while bringing clear benefits, has also had a negative consequence in that it has led to the situation where many Jewish people feel no compunction about marrying non-Jews and living a very attenuated Jewish lifestyle. This has momentous consequences for the Jewish lineage and heritage of the children of these marriages, especially if the mother is not Jewish.

- This twin process of secularisation/assimilation has led to the questioning of, and even rejection of, traditional Jewish attitudes to community solidarity, general relationships with the wider society, socio-religious rituals, and fundamental beliefs about God and his relationship with humanity.

- A major part of the Jewish response to modernity has been the growth and blossoming of alternative religious philosophies to that of Orthodox Judaism. In particular, there has been a sustained growth of the various progressive religious communities whose attitudes and practices concerning intermarriage, conversion to Judaism, and even the definition of Jewish lineage are quite unacceptable to those who are trying to maintain the traditional ways.

- The growth and spread of modern antisemitism, incorporating the decades of severe pogroms in Eastern Europe, the Dreyfus case in France and the Nazi era, culminating in the Shoah (Holocaust), has left an indelible mark on the Jewish community. Jewish survival in Europe was seriously under threat at one time, and it will be some considerable time, if ever, before the memory of that trauma will be less searing than it is now. Added to this is the fact that people who are actively antisemitic often work with a looser definition of Jewish identity and nature than the traditional Jewish one, leading to a situation where it can appear invidious to insist on a definition which *thereafter* excludes those who suffered with, and as part of, the Jewish people.

- The birth and establishment of the modern State of Israel has itself had a huge influence on this matter of the definition of who is a

Jewish person. The complexities of Jewish life in the Diaspora and the issue of antisemitism have actually had a significant impact on the policy of the State of Israel regarding who is eligible to be classed as Jewish for the sake of emigrating to Israel as a Jewish person under the Law of Return. Many Jewish communities take their lead in the definition of who is a Jew from the legislation of the State of Israel rather than from the rabbinic traditions. We shall look at this whole complicated issue later on in the essay.

It would certainly be correct to say that this complex matrix of issues has provided the context of the debate which has raged fiercely in the Jewish community since the middle of the last century, reaching new heights in the 1930s and 1940s.[1] However, I believe that it is also correct to say that since the late 1960s a seventh important factor in the debate has developed. I am referring to the increase in the number of Jewish people, indeed a wholly disproportionate number, becoming involved in various religious faiths. Is it in fact a requisite aspect of 'Jewishness' that a religiously-minded Jewish person (and not all Jewish people are religiously-minded) must be restricted to following a recognisable form of *Judaism*? Why can't a Jewish person become a devotee of a Zen master? And even if it were to be said that Jewish people should only express their spirituality through a recognisable form of Judaism, who is to be permitted to decide what would constitute such a recognisable form anyway?

It is clearly of fundamental importance in any exploration of the identity and acceptability of the Messianic Jewish community to examine this issue of the definition of what it is to be a Jew. Especial care will have to be taken when trying to evaluate the role played in this by *religious* motivation and preference. Such care is not always taken, unfortunately, and indeed Henry Feingold objects that the debate has been clouded by those who fail to distinguish clearly between 'Jewishness' and 'Judaism'.[2]

This is certainly a critical matter, and will need careful treatment as we move through this essay.[3] It is a commonplace to state that the defining of Jewishness is a complicated business due to the mix of biological, ethnic, religious and cultural factors involved. It should also be said that not everything which is associated by people today as being of the essence of Jewishness is in fact characteristic of the Jewish people down through the generations. We must beware of stereotypes, short memories and vested interests.

Who Is A Jew? Some Working Definitions

While it is impossible to do an exhaustive analysis of the 'Who is a Jew?' question within world Jewry as a part of this essay, it is important to set something of a context for the Messianic Jewish debate on this vital issue. Generally speaking, there are four types of definition which are commonly found in the discussions:

a) *The biological definition.* A Jew is someone who has a Jewish mother. As we shall see later, some communities accept the Jewishness of either parent as sufficient to determine Jewish lineage. According to the biblical witness it was the father who was the significant parent, and the rabbinic liturgy still echoes with references to the bonding with the three patriarchs, Abraham, Isaac and Jacob. Traditionally, however, it is the mother who has been designated as determining whether or not a person is born Jewish, not least because one can always be sure who the mother is of any baby.[4]

Probably for most Jews the matter of parental determination is the most decisive single factor in the decision about whether or not someone is to be considered as Jewish. For some, indeed, this is enough of a definition, though most would agree that it is only the fundamental part of a more complex whole. Ludwig Lewisohn, for instance, has argued that such a position leads to simplistic ethnic definitions if taken as the sole determinant of a person's Jewishness.[5] Most Jewish believers, however, seem happy to rest their case for acceptance as being Jewish ultimately on this very criterion, perhaps somewhat naively in some cases. Arnold Fruchtenbaum, for example, makes this claim:

> The implication of this definition is that no matter what a Jew does he can never become a non-Jew; no matter what the individual Jew may believe or disbelieve he remains a Jew ... Nothing, absolutely nothing, can change the fact that he is a descendant of Abraham, Isaac and Jacob.[6]

b) *The religious definition.* To be a Jew one must keep Torah in accordance with halakhic definitions. This traditional and 'Orthodox' definition is not accepted by all of modern Jewry, of course. Having said that, though, there is nevertheless a sense in which Masorti (Conservative) and Reform Jews would also insist that they have a loyalty to Torah, even though Torah and loyalty to it are defined, substantially and methodologically, in ways other than by Orthodox Judaism today.[7] One religious perspective which probably would be held in common by very many Jewish people, though, would be that actual conversion to another religion is a violation of any definition of being a Jew. Therefore any such conversion would serve as a disqualification from being considered a Jew. This view is so common that, as we shall see shortly, it has come to play an enormous part in the legislation of the State of Israel *vis-a-vis* the definition of who is to be considered Jewish for the purposes of the Law of Return. Jewish believers reject the accusation that they have converted to another religion, and so generally reject this definition.

c) *The socio-cultural definition.* Being Jewish is primarily about one's socio-cultural commitments and lifestyle within the Jewish community. The Jewish people is seen as essentially an ever-changing and ever-developing civilisation within civilisations. This view typifies the Reconstructionist movement, but it is also the basic perspective of many secularised and Liberal Jews.[8] It is probably the position least discussed by Jewish believers, since the social and community ostracism which follows their confession of faith in Jesus effectively prevents any ease of involvement within the community. It often serves as a self-fulfilling definition, in that the Jewish community excludes Jewish believers from its socio-cultural definition of Jewishness, which consequently excludes them from all meaningful socio-cultural involvement in the community, and thereafter cites as evidence for the fact that Jewish believers have abandoned their Jewishness, their total lack of socio-cultural commitment!

d) *The Nationalist/Zionist definition.* The only true Jews today are those who live in Israel, or who live genuinely self-sacrificial lives for the Zionist cause. It is a moot point whether this is actually held as a real definition for determining Jewishness, or whether it mainly serves to distinguish, for those who so use it, Jews regarded as worthy of the name from decidedly second-class Jewish people. It is a definition most

famously associated with David ben Gurion and his attitudes
expressed at the beginnings of the State of Israel.[9] This Zionist issue is
one which also exercises Jewish believers, as we shall see. Again there
is a serious complication in that the laws of the State of Israel make it
very difficult for known Messianic Jews to make aliya (to immigrate to
Israel) when they strongly desire to do that.[10]

Arnold Fruchtenbaum goes as far as to state that the eschatological
beliefs of the Messianic Jewish community actually give them an
added dimension of support for Israel:

> *The unbelieving Jewish community can only worry and send funds in*
> *hope of Israel's survival. The Hebrew Christian has no fear for the*
> *safety of Israel, since he that keeps Israel neither slumbers nor sleeps*
> *(Psalm 121: 4). All of these current events concerning Israel are*
> *moving toward the events of the Great Tribulation and will culminate*
> *with the second coming of the Messiah ... For the Hebrew Christian,*
> *the beginning of this goal of the Messianic Programme is to be seen in*
> *the present State of Israel ... He is loyal to the state of Israel, upholds it,*
> *and looks forward to greater things to come.[11]*

Suffice it is to say at this point that all four definitions are relevant to
the Messianic Jewish debate over the proper definition of who is a Jew.
Each of them will be referred to and appealed to in different ways in
this essay.

The Halakhah and the Issue of Jewishness

Halakhists are fully aware of the complexity of the question of Jewish
identity, particularly *vis-a-vis* its political importance in the State of
Israel. Reference can only be made here to some of the major discussions among leaders of the Jewish community and Jewish academics.[12]
In his study on rabbinic attitudes to this question, specifically set in the
context of the Jewish-Christian schism of the opening centuries of the
Common Era, Lawrence Schiffman carefully sifts the Tannaitic
materials and concludes that:

> *By the time of the rise of Christianity, the halakhah clearly defined the*
> *Jew by birth as one who was born to a Jewish mother.[13]*

With regard to those who wished to convert to Judaism, which is to say those not born to a Jewish mother, he presents an eight-point summary of the halakhic definitional procedure from the given Tannaitic sources:

- To begin with, Judaism is centred on the Jewish people ...
- If one is not born a Jew ... the halakhah demands the maximum of commitment, for the convert is literally changing his heredity ...
- He must be committed to the acceptance of the Torah ... not only the Laws of the Torah but also the Rabbinic interpretation or Oral Law ...
- He must also identify with the entire historic experience of the Jews ...
- He must at the same time acquire the characteristics of charity and kindness which Jews have been proud to maintain ...
- The male convert must be circumcised ...
- He must purify himself in a ritual bath ... striving to live a life of purity and holiness ...
- Finally he must bring a sacrifice ... he is ready to draw near to the divine presence and to come under its wings as a full member of the people of Israel.[14]

In essence, these eight points continue to determine orthodox attitudes and definitions. Indeed it is probably true to say that the various non-orthodox communities of today are also, in their own ways, basically seeking to re-define or refine that same halakhic system of principles and perspectives. The traditional views are still very much the dominant ones.[15]

At this point it will therefore be instructive to quote the words of Baruch Maoz, a pastor of a Messianic congregation in Israel. He represents many when he asserts that Jewish believers should not take the traditional halakhic position as their basic perspective. In his opinion, to start from the rabbinic definition would be to hand the rabbis the very thing which a growing number of Jews today wish to withhold from them: the right to arbitrate who or what are to be considered Jewish ... The desire to be recognised as a denomination of Judaism standing alongside Orthodox ... is a misguided one. Our aspiration should be to replace these versions of Jewishness, not to stand alongside them.[16]

David Stern is even more peremptory than Maoz. His often-quoted statement cuts the ground from any hint of acknowledging the authority of the halakhah and the rabbinate to rule on the Jewishness or otherwise of Messianic Jewish people:

> *in any case, it isn't the Jewish community that made me Jewish – it's*
> *God who made me Jewish![17]*

Maurice Bowler, for many years a staff worker with the organisation, Christian Witness to Israel, has written that Jewish believers of all persuasions will have to reconcile themselves to the fact that they must carve out their own niche in the Jewish world, in no way relying on the authority of rabbinic Judaism, since they do not wish to be rabbinic disciples but Jesus' disciples:

> *No one can exclude a Jew from his people Israel; even the Talmud*
> *recognises the indelibility of Jewishness. But membership in the*
> *rabbinic community is in the hands of the leaders of that community,*
> *and no amount of cosmetic adjustment to titles and customs will win*
> *acceptance for Hebrew Christians. Only apostasy from Christ would*
> *achieve this.[18]*

Messianic Jews wish to work from what they consider to be the single, pure, biblical basis in their definition of who is a Jew. Of course there is no clear and absolute blueprint to be found in the Bible, and so even Messianic Jews and Hebrew Christians disagree on certain points. As a matter of interest, Christian scholars, who ignore halakhic considerations altogether, also present different opinions on this matter of what is the biblical definition:

> *A Jew is a Jew by virtue of God's special relationship with the people of*
> *Israel in history.[19]*
>
> *A Jew is a member of a people chosen by God for special service whom*
> *He will not allow to fall from His hand.[20]*
>
> *Being a Jew is a matter of the heart, not of the flesh ... Not all*
> *Abraham's descendants are true sons of Abraham ... One is a Jew by*
> *faith, not by works or law. Those who live by God's grace are his*
> *people, whether their roots are Jewish or Gentile ... The biblical refer-*
> *ences to the Jews ... while historical in their day, are actually timeless*

in that they refer to those who in spirit and truth own Jesus as Lord.[21]
... anyone in the line from Abraham, through Isaac and Jacob, is a Jew.
It is nationality based on descent.[22]

Both Verkuyl and Barth anchor their definitions in their reading of the biblical doctrine of election, and disallow the traditional Christian replacement theology which states that election is now only operative in the lives of Christians. On the other hand, Mansell stands within that very replacement tradition, so that in his view people who are born with so-called 'Jewish lineage' are in fact only really Jewish if they are also part of the church. Codrington takes the line that a biological/ethnic definition is the truly biblical one. Each of these Christian commentators is convinced that he is presenting the biblical definition!

Can there be any resolution then of the various definitions? If both synagogue and church are offering different approaches, then is any definition possible by which Messianic Jews can be accepted as Jewish by the Jewish community, notwithstanding their belief in Jesus? As we shall see, the Messianic Jewish community is divided between those who would like, if possible, to receive at least a grudged and tacit 'blessing' from the Orthodox Jewish authorities, and those others who have no such desire, either because they refuse to acknowledge the authority of the halakhah altogether, or because they are satisfied to be simply one of the many Jewish communities, whether recognised or not by the Orthodox Jewish establishment.

Practically speaking, then, what is the Messianic Jewish community's realistic hope of 'rehabilitation' into the Jewish fold? Are they doomed to be forever labelled and treated as 'apostates', or is there any possibility of movement towards acceptability?

Heretics and Apostates

Stuart Charmé has introduced what he regards as a helpful distinction into the debate by distinguishing between what he sees as the Jewish categorisation 'heretic' and a second category of 'apostate'. Slightly different terms are used by other authors, but the distinction to which he draws attention is a substantial one. The question which concerns us is whether in his view Messianic Jews should be regarded simply as heretics, or worse, as apostates. As is well known, the common charge made against Messianic Jews is that they are indeed apostates. Here is Charmé's definition of a heretic:

> Heretics are those who hold to religious beliefs or practices that are at odds with the 'majority position' in their religion ... Nevertheless, heretics identify themselves with their religion and insist that their beliefs are what the religion is truly about.[23]

This concept and definition are supported as being appropriate by Schiffman in his Tannaitic studies. He concludes that:

> A heretic is one whose beliefs do not accord with those of the established religion to which he claims adherence.[24]

Such a 'heretic', may well be cut off from the world to come, in accordance with the passage in the Mishnah which says:

> The following are those who do not have a portion in the world to come; the one who says there is no resurrection of the dead, the Torah is not from heaven, and the apikoros.[25]

But, significantly for our discussion, Schiffman concludes from the evidence in the Mishnah and Talmud that:

> The question of Jewish status, and that of a portion in the world to come are separate issues. The fact that certain heretics are excluded from the world to come in no way implies expulsion from the Jewish people.[26]

Charmé comes to the same conclusion, though he acknowledges that sometimes such heretics are in fact driven out of the community and persecuted by outraged 'loyalists'. Usually, though, the community simply ignores the heretic and the particular beliefs or practices that have been adopted, and often there is subtle bridge-building, in the hope that the heretic can be 'persuaded to repent and return to the traditional perspective'.[27]

Messianic Jews, of course, do not consider themselves to be heretics, and are hardly likely to relish being referred to by this designation. Charmé's point, however, is that perhaps the Jewish community should see them as heretics, and adopt a more open attitude towards them. In my experience over the past twenty years this is in fact an attitude which is being adopted practically by many in the Jewish community, even in the State of Israel. At least it is preferable, so the theory goes, to the other attitude by which Messianic Jews are formally excluded from the Jewish community. Charmé goes on to define apostates as those:

> ... *who totally reject both their old religious beliefs and their old communal identity.*[28]

We have reached an altogether more serious breach of 'orthodoxy' and 'orthopraxy' at this stage. Significantly, this focus on the apostate's desertion from, or rejection of, the Jewish community as well as of its traditional beliefs and perspectives, is seen in the great constitutional feast of world Jewry – Passover. Here is the time when the Jewish people worldwide are celebrating the mercy and sovereign grace of God in rescuing them from slavery and exile, and in creating of them 'a kingdom of priests and a holy nation.'[29] As is well known, there is a vital part of the Seder where four representative 'sons' show the four types of response to the Passover duty and celebration. It is the first two types of response which concern us here. There is a 'wise son' who asks:

> *What are the testimonies, statutes and judgments which the Lord our God has commanded us?*

Then the 'wicked son' asks:

> *What does this service mean to you?*

In both cases the person is addressing the community of Israel in the shape of the family and friends actually there around the Passover table. In both cases the fundamental question is being asked about the meaning and significance of the service. So what is the difference between wisdom and wickedness? When does lack of knowledge and understanding become grounds for alienation? The difference lies in the fact that the wise son acknowledges that it is 'our God' who commands certain beliefs and practices, and who demands obedience to them all from all of 'us'. In other words, he identifies himself with the community and is actively a part of it, though with a lack of complete knowledge and understanding. The wicked son, on the other hand, makes no self-inclusive statement, and the Passover text actually spells this out in its very next words:

> *You, he says, and not himself. Because he removes himself from the community, he has denied a principle of our religion.*

It is this concept of 'self-alienation', then, that is at the heart of the matter. Messianic Jews are traditionally seen as having committed exactly this act of self-exclusion in accepting the New Testament as scripture, and Jesus as their Messiah, Saviour and Lord. In spite of this, as we have seen, Messianic Jews themselves strongly resist the charge that they have forsaken their Jewish identity and status, claiming that, on the contrary, they have been excluded by others, primarily the religious authorities and those who influence the media. Put crudely, and using Charmé's categories, a neutral observer might assume that Messianic Jews would prefer the term heretic to that of apostate, should they ever have to choose between the two! In fact they claim to belong to neither, and prefer to affirm their continuity with God's purposes as seen in the Torah and New Testament.

Before going any further, it will be useful at this stage to examine the contribution of the religious and political authorities in the State of Israel to the overall question of how to define who is to be considered Jewish.

The Role Played by Israel's Legislature and Rabbinical Courts

For many Jewish people today the single most important factor in the debate over who is a Jew is not what Orthodox Jewish leaders say is the halakhic definition, but rather what the State of Israel has decided. It is of course true that religious matters in Israel, including that of the definition of Jewishness, are also dominated by Orthodox Jewish councils and parties, yet a brief account of the process by which Israel's legislation came to be drawn up as it did regarding who is a Jew will be useful in giving a further context for Messianic Jewish attitudes and decisions.

When the State of Israel was established, it became clear that some legislation would be necessary to create a suitably accountable process whereby Jews qua Jews worldwide could emigrate to Israel and become full Israeli citizens. Two laws became the basis of all subsequent legislation in Israel: the Law of Return (1950),[30] and the Nationality Law (1952).[31] These state (and further affirm) that every Jew has the legal right to settle in Israel as an 'oleh', *ie* the technical term for a Jew who emigrates to Israel with the intent to settle there as a citizen. Israel's Prime Minister at the time, David ben Gurion, introduced the Law of Return to the Israeli parliament with words which have become justly famous:

> *This law lays down not that the State accords the right of settlement to Jews abroad but that this right is inherent in every Jew by virtue of his being a Jew if it but be his will to take part in settling the land.*[32]

The matter which concerns us, of course, is whether or not Messianic Jews participate in this legal right, a question we will deal with shortly.

In 1953 a further law of significance for Messianic Jews was created in Israel. It was given the title of Rabbinical Courts Jurisdiction Law (1953),[33] and legislates that marriages and divorces of Jews, as well as other personal religious matters, must be carried out 'in accordance with the Torah' and 'under the exclusive jurisdiction of Rabbinical Courts'. It needs to be stressed that all of these courts in Israel are Orthodox. Matters of personal status are therefore under Orthodox Jewish supervision and control, and the religious issue of who is a Jew is thereby determined in Israel according to the halakhah. Can Messianic Jews be married in Israel? Will the circumcision of their sons be carried out as a matter of course? The answer to both of these questions (and several others relating to personal status) is 'No'. This has an obviously serious affect on the Messianic Jewish community.

A further basic Law which has played a major part in the struggle of Messianic Jews in Israel for acceptance and legal rights is the Population Registry Law (1965),[34] which rules that every Israeli must register, with the Ministry of the Interior, his/her 'nationality and religion'. For instance, an Israeli Arab could write 'Arab' for nationality and 'Muslim' for religion. A Jew may write 'Orthodox' or 'Reform' etc under 'religion'. The question is whether the designation 'Messianic Jew' would be accepted by the Ministry of the Interior as a religious category. In theory this might have been possible before 1970, but since then it has been impossible, though, as we shall see, a challenge to the current laws is being made by Messianic Jews who wish to emigrate to Israel as 'olim'.

> *Both the Population Registration Law and the Law of Return were amended in 1970, the former being amended in the following way:*
>
> *3A (a) No man will be registered as a Jew by nation or by religion if a notice according to this Law or any other registration or public document show that he is not a Jew ...*
>
> *(b) In regards to this Law and any registration or document made in accordance to this Law the term Jew bears the meaning given this term in article 4B of the Law of Return.*
>
> *(c) This article is not retroactive.*

The Law of Return was amended in this way:

> *4A (a) The rights pertaining to a Jew by the Law of Return ... thereby pertain to the children or grandchildren of the spouse of a Jew or ... of a Jew, excepting those (children, grandchildren or spouses) who were Jews and converted to another religion.*
>
> *4B In regards to this Law a Jew is one who was born of a Jewish mother or converted to Judaism, and has not converted to another religion.*

The clear issue facing Messianic Jews therefore became that of whether a Messianic Jew is regarded as a member of another religion. Is becoming a Jewish believer in Jesus a conversion to Christianity? At first glance this may seem to some to be nothing more than a rhetorical question. What else could it be other than conversion to 'another religion'? Is it not self-evidently the case that anyone from one faith community who becomes a believer in, and follower of, Jesus has converted to the new faith called Christianity? Yet this understanding is challenged in the case of Jewish people who believe that Jesus is the very Messiah promised to the Jewish people by God.

In the light of this, there have in fact been several famous legal challenges by Jewish believers to the Israeli legislature. A brief review of these test cases will be instructive, and will also serve to show the context in which Messianic Jews, both in Israel and elsewhere, live and lobby their governments and courts.

The Brother Daniel Case

The first and most celebrated test case was that known as the Brother Daniel case.[35] Brother Daniel was born to Polish-Jewish parents who named him Oswald Rufeisen. From his early youth he was committed to going to live in what was then Palestine, and he joined the local Zionist Youth Movement branch. In 1939 he finished his schooling and embarked on a training scheme which was preparing farmers to go to Palestine and to help create a flourishing community of Jews there. However, the Nazi occupation of Poland put paid to that scheme, and Rufeisen, like so many others, was forced underground. He joined the Jewish resistance movement and was involved in the active and personal rescue of hundreds of his fellow Jews from the Gestapo. Late in 1942 he had to go into hiding altogether, and found himself in a convent, being looked after and sheltered by the authorities there. The short story is that he became a sincere Roman Catholic himself, though consistently seeing himself as, nevertheless, still a *bona fide* Jew, maintaining his links with his family and the Jewish community. In fact he continued to work in the Jewish resistance movement till the end of the war, and maintained his Zionist ambitions.

After the war, he joined the Carmelite order of the church as a full monk, taking the name Brother Daniel. He chose this order because he hoped to be transferred to a Carmelite monastery in Palestine. A decade later, in 1958, he was in fact so transferred, and when he went to the Polish authorities he simply stated that he was a Jew who wished to emigrate to Israel. He, of course, had his birth certificate etc, to satisfy the Poles of his Jewishness, and was duly stripped of his Polish nationality and given a 'Jewish' title on his documents. Upon arrival in Israel he filled out the necessary immigration papers, listing himself as Jewish ethnically but as a Roman Catholic religiously, and claiming his right to citizenship under the Law of Return. This problematic matter was brought to the attention of the Minister of the Interior himself, who in turn asked the government for an authoritative ruling. The forthcoming ruling denied Brother Daniel registration as a Jew. His appeal to the Supreme Court captured the imagination of Jewry worldwide, but with a majority of four to one against, the court rejected his subsequent appeal.[36]

Their rejection was based on two considerations: first, that the Law of Return did not include 'apostates' within its definition of who is a Jew; and secondly, that since religious apostates have by definition deserted their roots and community, then Brother Daniel could not legitimately record 'Jewish' as his 'ethnic group'.

Brother Daniel strongly contested the first point, claiming that he was still a Jew under religious law, and basing himself on the halakhic ruling that 'Israel – even if he sins – is still Israel'.[37] In other words, even should worldwide Jewry disapprove of his 'conversion', and even should that disapproval lead to social ostracism, nevertheless even such a perceived 'sin' did not actually disqualify him from being a Jew according to halakhah. The Justices actually conceded this point, but in a significant precedent they declared this to be irrelevant to the issue at hand, since the term 'Jew' in the Law of Return does not refer to the 'Jew' of Jewish religious law, but to the 'Jew' of secular law.

In other words, the Law of Return was established by legal precedent in the State of Israel to be a secular Zionist Law, and not an halakhic one. Appeal was made in this to the legal fiction of the 'common man', and how he would see the proper definition of who is a Jew. It is important for us to note, then, that biological descent alone was thereby regarded as insufficient grounds for acceptance of Jewish status under the Law of Return. However, it was left as an open question whether being Orthodox or not, 'religious' or not, was itself important for a Jewish person wishing to become an oleh.

This, of course, leads to the second point made by the four Justices who formulated the majority position against Brother Daniel, namely that a Jew who converts to another religion has abandoned the Jewish community, and therefore forfeits any claim to Jewish identity. Rufeisen contested this point as well, and his personal record served to support his counter-claim that he was as actively involved in the Jewish community after becoming a Roman Catholic as he had ever been, and in fact more than many other Jews. Though Justice Cohn accepted this counter-claim, the others did not. In his deliverance, Justice Landau asserted that by conversion, a Jewish apostate:

> ... cuts himself off from his national past ... no longer shares a common fate with the Jewish people ... and erects a barrier against any further identification with the Jewish people.

This case obviously provided a major stimulus for the 1970 legal amendments mentioned above, and it has proven to be decisive for all subsequent controversies. The decision to deny Brother Daniel, or any similar Jewish 'convert', the legal right to be considered a Jew under the Law of Return has affected many Messianic Jews since who have considered emigrating to Israel.[38]

On the other hand, Brother Daniel's application and appeal did serve to highlight the issue in peoples' minds, and there followed a succession of important legal cases, the first of which also played a major part in catalysing the changes in the Laws of 1970.

The Shalit Case

This second, and equally important, stimulus for those amendments came in that very year of 1970 with the so-called Shalit case.[39] This case exercised the Supreme Court between 1968 and 1970, being memorable not only for its role in the process of Israeli Law concerning Jewish identity, but also for the huge public outcry it produced. The vital issue was that of the Jewish identity of the children of a Jewish father and non-Jewish mother who wished (or whose parents wished for them) to be registered as Israelis. Major Benjamin Shalit was undoubtedly Jewish, and indeed an Israeli by birth. He became a career officer in the Israeli army, and while serving in Edinburgh he met and fell in love with a non-Jewish girl. They married, without his wife undergoing conversion to Judaism, and chose to settle in Israel, where their two children were born.

The Population Registry Law demands the legal registration of each new baby, and Major Shalit filled out the requisite forms according to his conscience and convictions. This meant that under the section titled 'Religion' he entered a dash, indicating no religious belief or affiliation, and under the section titled 'Nationality' he entered the word 'Jewish'. However, the official at the registration office refused to accept this classification, and a correspondence began between the outraged Shalit and the Ministry of the Interior.

Eventually Shalit decided to make this a more public matter, convinced as he was that there was a very serious principle involved here for all other secular Israelis, and so he took his case to court. In an unprecedented move, the Supreme Court sat as the High Court of

Justice, with nine of its ten members.

Shalit summarised his case in this way:

> *It is not faith that unites us as a nation. Too many people do not practise religion for that. The cultural and sociological factors are the ones that determine who is a Jew ... My children were born in Israel, speak Hebrew, live in a Hebrew culture, and go to Hebrew schools. They know nothing else. How can the Interior Minister say that they are not Jews?*[40]

The judges were divided in their opinions, and their decision came only with a five-four majority. This majority found in favour of Major Shalit (and his wife) *viz* that the nationality of his children could be registered as Jewish, as he had wished.[41] There are two matters that must be pointed out here. First, the judges tried to avoid being drawn into the wider controversy (both religious and political) about the ultimate definition of who is a Jew. As a point of fact most of them were not prepared even to discuss whether the Shalit children were truly Jewish. They attempted to reduce their remit to the legal technicalities of the case, specifically whether or not registration officials are bound to accept the father's own statements in such cases and, if not, whether they can legally introduce other criteria (eg halakhic definitions and concepts). Their ruling, as we have seen, was that the official must accept the father's *bona fide* registration of 'Jewish nationality' for his children.

Secondly, however, the judges conceded that the time for facing those wider issues was approaching fast. It is clear that they felt that Israel's burgeoning social reality must eventually take precedence over the accepted religious definition that the children of non-Jewish mothers are not Jewish, irrespective of the actual circumstances of each case. One of the judges, Mr Justice Berinson, was particularly concerned with the traditional Orthodox refusal to distinguish between Jewish religion and Jewish nationality. He cited an actual circumstance in Israel where this meant that:

> *... the head of the terrorists in Eastern Jerusalem, born of a Jewish woman and a Muslim father, who tried to kill and annihilate the State of Israel, is considered as Jewish by religion and nationality: while the family of a Jewish Major, fighting the wars of Israel, is considered*

devoid of Jewish nationality.

Considerable political controversy followed the decision of the Supreme Court, and the religious parties put a great deal of pressure on the government of Israel to step in and reverse the decision. The government acceded, and within two months the Knesset had enacted new legislation. This was not, however, retroactive, so that the Shalit children remain registered as Jewish by nationality. But the legislation was able, as intended, to prevent the Shalit case becoming a precedent. Both the Law of Return and the Population Registry Law were amended with respect to the traditional religious definition of who is a Jew. The basic emendation was to create clause 4B in the Law of Return, a clause which reads, as we noted already:

> For the purpose of this Law, Jew means a person who was born of a Jewish mother or has become converted to Judaism, and who is not a member of another religion.

The non-Jewish children of a Jewish father (or even the non-Jewish grandchildren of a Jewish grandfather) are still to be accepted as legitimate olim in Israel, but if they wish to marry a Jewish person in Israel, or if in any other way they have to establish their Jewish identity within the State of Israel, they will have to undergo conversion according to the halakhah. However, in the context of our major interest, the important aspect of this new legislation is the final phrase of the amendment. Presumably this would simply be interpreted to mean that a Jewish believer could not be accepted as Jewish.[42]

The Dorflinger Case

The next important case for Jewish believers was undoubtedly that concerning Esther Dorflinger, brought before the High Court of Israel in 1979.[43] She was an American Jew who became a believer in Jesus while she was living in the United States. Having decided thereafter to make aliya, she arrived in Israel and requested status as a new immigrant. However, the Minister of the Interior denied her request on the grounds that according to article 4B of the Law of Return she could not be considered as a Jew, since she had become a member of another religion. Dorflinger proceeded to petition the High Court of Justice for a ruling in her favour, but the Justices decided against her.

Justice Witkon, who delivered the main opinion of the court, with Justice Asher concurring, said that it was not a question of whether Dorflinger felt Jewish or regarded herself as Jewish, and indeed he said in a public article that he did not doubt that she did feel this way.[44] He insisted, however, that there had to be an objective measurement in this matter, and that it was for the court, not the petitioner, to establish this measurement. The criterion of membership of, or allegiance to, a second religion must guide the court in a case like this. Dorflinger, it was ruled, lived by a faith and lifestyle system which would be considered as Christian by Christian churches anywhere, and when pressed about the nature of her faith in Jesus, she had not been willing to deny the deity of Jesus in front of the court. Therefore the court must decide in favour of regarding her as having converted to another religion.

This decision was particularly significant since Dorflinger was not actually in membership of any Christian denomination or congregation. She specifically refused to join a church, or to assent to any credal statement of faith whatever, and stated to the court that her faith was the result of a direct revelation from God, not as a result of theological instruction or participation in Christian services of worship, or the like. Only the reading of the New Testament, which had been entirely of her own volition and initiative, had played a part in her coming to faith in Jesus as Israel's Messiah. At one point she said:

> Theology and theological creeds are alien to the pure and simple New Testament faith in Jesus. The identity of Jesus is not an issue of theological definitions but one of divine revelation. My understanding of Jesus is not based on theological definitions but on God's revelation to me personally by His Spirit according to his word.[45]

However, Dorflinger had been baptised in a church by an ordained minister, and as Justice Witkon said:

> This is acknowledged by all authorities to be an act symbolising admission to the Christian faith.[46]

Justice Shamgar summed up the court's opinion in a way that found immediate favour with the leading jurists and writers of Israel at the time. He spoke of Dorflinger's desire to be regarded as a Jew in spite of her faith in Jesus, and then went on:

In so doing she has made use of long and tortuous arguments regarding the possible tie of a Jew to the belief in the messiahship of Jesus as though we were still in the beginning of the first millenium of the Common Era, as though nothing had happened since then in regards to the formation of religious frameworks and the separation from Judaism of all those who chose the other way ... However, religious freedom does not mean that the petitioner can force the respondent, who acts on the basis of statutory law, to accept her innovations and definitions that contradict those that are in the law, and to treat her as a Jewess, despite her belonging to a different faith.

In this case, then, we see a further development of the State's determination to base its legislation on what it calls 'objective' data. There is no objectivity in this matter, but the ruling was made that the opinion of the majority is to be taken as the neighbour of objectivity. The integrity of Jewish believers is not challenged, and that in itself is to be recognised and appreciated, but their inner convictions are not held to be relevant for the purposes of legal registration.

The Dahaf Report

Before going on to look at the next – and still current – significant case, a few words must be said about a major initiative taken in 1988 by a group of Israeli Messianic Jews who wished to determine for themselves to what extent, if any, there was indeed public support within Israel for allowing Messianic Jews to make aliya under the Law of Return. So much of the rationale for these court rulings depended on the presupposition that the Israeli man on the street would not be able to countenance Messianic Jews that these believers decided to test the presupposition. Between 17-24 January 1988 the Dahaf Research Institute conducted a public poll of 1,189 Israeli citizens, excluding only members of kibbutzim from their cross-sectional interviews. This Institute functions within Israel in the same way as the famous Gallop Poll organisation, and was led by its Director of Research, Mina Tzemach, who has a PhD in Psychology from Yale University. It is a respected independent organisation, selected by the Messianic Jewish group for its independence and professionalism.

The people interviewed in this case were asked about 10 'categories' of potential olim, in the following order:

1   A person born to a Jewish mother, who does not believe in the existence of God.
2   A person born to a Jewish mother, who belongs to Hare Krishna, Scientology, or a similar cult. (The Hebrew word used for cult was 'kat'.)
3   A person born to a Jewish mother, who believes that Yeshua is the Messiah.
4   A person born to a Jewish mother, who does not believe that the Torah is the words of the living God.
5   A person born to a Jewish mother, who believes that both the Torah and the New Testament are the words of the living God.
6   A person born to a Jewish mother, who was baptised in the framework of a Christian church.
7   A person born to a Jewish mother, who was baptised in the framework of a Messianic Jewish congregation.
8   A person born to a Jewish mother, who believes that Yeshua is the Messiah, considers and feels himself to be Jewish, and was baptised within the framework of a Messianic Jewish congregation.
9   A person born to a Jewish mother, who believes that Yeshua is the Messiah, considers and feels himself to be both Jewish and Christian, and was baptised within the framework of a Christian church.
10 A person born to a Jewish mother, who is faithful to the State of Israel, pays his taxes to the State, serves in the army, celebrates the Jewish holidays, keeps commandments from Israel's tradition, feels that he is a Jew, and believes that Yeshua is the Messiah, but was not baptised into Christianity.[47]

While there is no room here for a full analysis of the results of the poll, nor even for a complete layout of those results, some of the statistics and comments will be usefully included in our survey. Perhaps most germane to this article is the following table, looking at the overall reaction to the 10 'categories'. Here, in simple tabular form, are those statistics given as percentages:

Question number	Has right	Has no right	No response	Total
1	83	13	4	100
10	78	17	5	100
4	73	22	5	100
5	68	27	5	100
7	63	32	5	100
8	61	34	5	100
3	61	35	4	100
2	61	35	4	100
9	54	41	5	100
6	49	46	5	100

The Mishkan report itself highlights several matters, including the following:

An absolute majority of the public (more than 50%) favours granting an immigrant's visa under the Law of Return to all the above mentioned categories, except for the last case. Even in this case, an absolute majority of those expressing an opinion favoured granting the visa (49% to 46%).[48]

The two groups which received the highest support rates may be identified as Jews who do not believe in God at all, and persons ... who keep the Jewish tradition, celebrate the Jewish feasts, and believe that Yeshua is the Messiah.[49]

The two categories with the lowest support rates are those who have been baptised ... in a Christian church framework.[50]

Messianic Jews in Israel were, naturally enough, delighted by the results of this Poll, but there was also some evidence of sober reflection on the ambiguity of much of it. The report nevertheless concludes that the Israeli public seems happy to grant aliya rights to a person born to a Jewish mother and yet who also believes in Yeshua – as long as there are reassurances that this person is not a traitor to his people. These reassurances are to be evidenced by Jewish lifestyle, self-identification with the Jewish people, and loyalty to the Jewish State. This conclusion is drawn from several results of the Poll:

a The very high (78%) support rate given to the believer in Yeshua who pays his taxes, serves in the army, celebrates Jewish festivals, etc. It seems that each point adds more reassurance.

b   A comparison between questions 6 and 9. If all that is known about
a person is that he had a Jewish mother and was baptised in a
Christian church, only 49% support his right to immigrate. But if it
is also known that he considers himself a Jew (even though he also
considers himself a Christian, and the question explicitly states that
he believes Yeshua is the Messiah) then the rate rises to 54%.

c   A comparison of questions 6 and 7. Here the focus is on the context
of baptism. If the baptism is in a Christian church framework the
support rate is 49%, but if it is in a Messianic Jewish congregational
framework the support rate rises to 63%.[51] The whole report can be
found in the sources given in endnote 47, where the socio-religious
breakdowns are also to be found. But enough has been shown here
to suggest the importance of this Dahaf Poll to the Messianic Jewish
movement, and to further suggest, as the Messianic Jewish
community in Israel insists, that attitudes in Israel at least are
changing towards the Messianic Jewish community. Perhaps the
day is not so far off when Jewish believers in Jesus will be tolerated
by the majority within Israeli society.

In short, it would seem that as far as the situation in Israel is concerned,
the work of the legislative authorities has not 'defused' the crisis over
the identity of Jewish believers, but has merely 'lengthened the fuse', to
coin a phrase. In more general terms, the underlying religious issue
goes on unsettled, namely who has the authority to supervise conversion to Judaism and to authenticate true Jewish identity, an issue
which exercises all of the non-Orthodox communities in Israel.[52]

The Beresford Case

And so we come to the latest case to occupy the Israeli legal courts. It
involves two Messianic Jews, a married couple, who wish to make
aliya to Israel. Gary and Shirley Beresford are both South Africans, and
were both born to Jewish mothers from well-established Jewish
families. In the late 1970s they both became convinced of the
Messiahship of Jesus. In 1982 they tried to begin the immigration
process for coming to settle in Israel, but the Israel Agency there in
South Africa turned them down when their faith in Jesus was made

known. After a long period of continued frustration in their efforts, the Beresfords went to Israel on visitors' visas in 1986, and proceeded to re-initiate the aliya process there.[53] At this time they also began attending a Hebrew-speaking Messianic Jewish congregation in Ramat HaSharon, to the north of Tel Aviv.[54]

Their application to become olim was based squarely on the terms of the Law of Return, but the Ministry of the Interior rejected their application on the by now established grounds that they were 'members of a different faith'.[55] They immediately petitioned the High Court for a reversal of this decision on the grounds that they were *bona fide* Jews, and not members of some alien faith.[56] A major part of their argument was that they had never joined a church of any sort, nor were they supported in any way by any Christian group, let alone a Jewish mission of any type or form. Their personal beliefs about the Messiah and his identity were exactly that, beliefs which they maintained were well within the parameters of Judaism.

The High Court, consisting of three judges, Justices Elon, Barak, and Khalima, finally gave their ruling on 25 December 1989. Their 90-page ruling concluded that the Beresfords' beliefs did indeed constitute a voluntary and consistent membership of another religion, *viz* Christianity. Interestingly, Justice Elon took a traditionally Orthodox line of approach, while Justice Barak's view was unreservedly a 'secular, liberal, dynamic one'.[57] Justice Elon wrote:

> *Messianic Jews attempt to reverse the wheels of history by 2,000 years. But the Jewish people has decided during the 2,000 years of history that (Messianic Jews) do not belong to the Jewish nation ... and have no right to force themselves on it.*[58]

Justice Barak's opinion was that since the great majority of Jewish people, and Israelis among them, would reject the beliefs of Messianic Jews as being inconsistent with those of Judaism, then the claims of such Messianic Jews that they are still *bona fide* Jews must be rejected by Israel's legislature.[59]

The Beresford's appeal was therefore turned down yet again. However, all the Justices advised, as had been done before to Brother Daniel, that the Beresfords should apply for citizenship to be conferred upon them by Israel under its Citizenship Law. Unlike Brother Daniel, the Beresfords refused this offer, and formally appealed for a session of the five-member Supreme Court to hear their case one more time. Their lawyer, Joseph ben Menashe, mindful of the precedents, advised them to appeal to the Ministry of the Interior for Permanent Residence status.[60]

We are awaiting the next landmark case, because it will surely come, but it is already clear that an ongoing negative response by the Israeli authorities will continue to make it difficult for Messianic Jews in other countries and contexts to be accepted as fully Jewish by the wider community.

Are Messianic Jews Still Jewish?

The assertion is plainly made by Messianic Jews that a Jewish person does not need to give up being Jewish when he/she becomes a believer in Jesus. Such a person remains Jewish, happily Jewish, and acceptably Jewish – to God at least.[61] David Chernoff states that a major aim of his book is to show that 'historically and biblically it is Jewish to believe in Yeshua (Jesus)'.[62]

There is quite often a feeling expressed by Messianic Jews that simply because they have chosen to identify with their Jewishness, they should have done enough to be regarded as Jewish by other Jews, at least by those who treat their own Jewishness more lightly than does the Messianic Jewish community![63] However, as we shall see, this point is not generally conceded. Rabbi Meir Kahane spoke plainly for many when he proclaimed:

> Let it be known and shouted forth that there are no such things as Hebrew Christians ... Hebrew and Christian are two terms mutually exclusive, mutually contradictory.[64]

Rabbi Marc Tanenbaum has also spoken out firmly :

> They blithely side-step history, ignoring fundamental differences between Christian and Jewish concepts of God, as well as historical factors that have led to the evolution of the two separate systems of belief.[65]

Marshall Sklare summed up a consensus of Jewish voices when he said in 1973:

> Traditionally, of course, Jews have held the Jewish convert to

Christianity in utter abhorrence ... What kind of love is it, Jews wonder, that would deprive a man of his heritage?[66]

There are many Jewish voices, then, which claim that Jewishness and Christian faith are incompatible. Messianic Jews are adamant that they have not ceased being Jews, nor have they been deprived of their inheritance, because of their belief that Jesus is the Messiah. At one climactic point in his work, Hutchens states:

Both Jews and Christians in their particularistic orientations have tra-ditionally said identification with one has required total separation from the other. The two systems of belief are thereby mutually exclusive, so it is reasoned. 'Not so', says the Messianic Jew, 'I am a Jew, I acknowledge and celebrate ... the Jewish calendar. I abide by the dietary laws, I worship on the Sabbath. My sons are circumcised and bar-mitzvahed, my daughters are married under a canopy, my wife lights the candles every Sabbath. I am a Jew, and yet I believe that Jesus was the fulfilment of the Messianic promises.'[67]

This conviction that they are still *bona fide* Jewish persons is expressed strongly by Messianic Jews when it comes to discussing the concept and issue of 'conversion':

A Jew ... is not converted in the ordinary sense of the term. He does not turn around or change direction. On the contrary, he proceeds in the same direction; he advances in faith from the Old Testament to the New Testament.[68]

Don't call me a converted Jew. I never converted from being Jewish, but I was converted from sin – and being Jewish was never a sin![69]

People are to be converted. But they are converted sinners, not converted Italians or converted Spaniards or converted Jews. What must be turned away are sinful habits and desires.[70]

Part of this assertion is the insistence that for a Messianic Jew to be properly so-called, he/she must fully acknowledge himself/herself to be both Jewish and a believer in Jesus. The process known as 'conver-sion' takes place at the 'universal level', as it were, not at the level of one's Jewishness. It is human selfishness which is overturned, not Jewish identity. History has of course shown that there have been many Jews whose 'conversion process' involved a denial of this Messianic Jewish conviction. Such 'converts' were intent, whether from motives of personal aggrandisement or from a real or perceived fear for life and limb, on abandoning their Jewishness. This attitude, while understood in historical terms, is nevertheless roundly condemned as an unacceptable practice by the contemporary Messianic Jewish movement.

As Jacob Jocz wrote at one point:

A Jew who accepts baptism with a view to losing his identity is not a Hebrew Christian, though he may be a Christian ... a Jew who accepts baptism without conviction is not a Hebrew Christian, but a renegade.[71]

Similar passionate sentiments were expressed by Harcourt Samuel:

We are not renegade Jews ... We are not apostates ... We are looked upon as traitors by our own people. We are not. And yet, I am not quite sure if the man who hushes up his Jewishness and is completely absorbed in a largely Gentile Church is not after all a traitor to his people.[72]

This attitude is echoed strongly by Fruchtenbaum, whose own conclusion is that:

If a Jew accepts baptism solely to lose his identity as a Jew, he is by no means to be considered a Hebrew Christian, he is a renegade, a traitor and an apostate. A Hebrew Christian is proud of his Jewishness. He is also proud of his faith in the Messiahship of Jesus ... There is the problem of distinguishing between those Jews who became believers in Jesus by conviction, and those who were forced to convert. The latter can hardly be called Hebrew Christians; there is a world of difference between Jewish Christians and Christianised Jews.[73]

Daniel Juster puts it like this:

Being a Jew is not just a physical thing ... Messianic Jews should be on guard against tailoring their identity to a meaning which is weak in heritage identification because of the influence of Jews who become believers and are themselves weak in their heritage identification. This weakness is to be countered if there is to be a dynamic Messianic

Judaism.[74]

Very often this assertion of Jewishness is accompanied by the personal testimony of Messianic Jews that since becoming believers they identify much more strongly than ever before with their Jewish traditions and roots. A famous expression of this is that of one of last century's most noted Jewish believers, Dr Isaac Da Costa, of Amsterdam. In one of his major works he wrote in the Preface:

> *The sketch of Jewish history presented in these pages, and viewed in the light of Christian truth, may perhaps appear as foolishness, and an offence to my brethren concerning the flesh; but in taking up the book, they will find, nevertheless, that it still bears the impress of its author's Israelitish origin. Surely, in confessing myself, by the grace of God, a disciple of Jesus Christ, I did not cease nay, then I only began to rejoice that I was indeed a Jew.*[75]

David Harley's 1976 British survey of Messianic Jews came across this claim in almost every case, with typical statements being, 'I feel 100% Jewish since I have accepted the Messiah'; 'I feel a stronger and closer allegiance to the Jewish people'; 'I am not now ashamed to be Jewish'; 'I am more proud of my Jewishness and more conscious of it'.[76]

Rachel Kohn says in her summary that while many Jewish people who converted to Christianity in the nineteenth and early twentieth centuries began to lose their Jewish integrity and identification upon baptism:

> *Hebrew Christians proclaimed their difference with a discernable righteousness. Thus it was said of the well-known itinerant missionary, Reverend Joseph Wolff ... that he looks with pity upon those Jews who, though professing Christianity, are ashamed of being known to the world as sprung from the Jewish stock.*[77]

In point of fact, Messianic Jews see a double standard at work when the Jewish community accuses them of no longer being Jewish in any meaningful sense. Charmé mentions this in his study, looking first of all at the issue of a selective religious definition:

> *In short, the Messianic-Jew accuses the Jewish community of selective enforcement of its theology as a means of suppressing one particular*

heretical group. If Jewishness were consistently defined as a religious matter, the Messianic-Jews might be able to see why they are not Jews in the sense that traditional religious Jews are. But they find a religious definition of Jewishness somewhat arbitrary in its application, since not all 'legitimate' Jews practise the religion of Judaism in all its aspects.[78]

Then there are times when the Jewish community tends to define Jewishness:

... in terms of cultural and sociological identification with the Jewish people. The Messianic-Jew claims this identification as much as any other Jew.[79]

How then are Messianic Jews to proceed with their determination to obtain a fair hearing for their case? Is there any realistic possibility that the Jewish establishment will listen to them and consider them as worthy of being called Jewish? The situation is extremely complex. Perhaps the central question here is whether or not a Messianic Jew is to be considered as halakhically still a Jew. Certainly this is where many Messianic Jews focus their attention. Henry Knight, for example writes on this point:

The Talmud states that 'an Israelite (Jew), even though he sin, is still an Israelite' (B San 44a). Most Orthodox authorities accept that this Halakhic rule covers the sin of apostasy, so that membership of another religion, or of none at all, does not exclude the Jew from belonging to the community of Israel. This principle, if evenly applied, means that Jews who have embraced the Christian faith are still Jews.[80]

Menachem Benhayim, emphasises the same point, quoting in the process an article in the Encyclopaedia Judaica:

In an article on 'apostasy' published in the Encyclopaedia Judaica, the writer notes: 'Prevailing halakhic opinion throughout the ages has always considered the apostate a Jew for all purposes of obligations, ties and possibilities given to a Jew, but denying him some specific legal rights, in particular in the economic sphere, and in the performance of certain honorary symbolic acts.'

Benhayim then proceeds to add:

In practice, of course, the 'apostate' was usually ostracised and often mourned for as 'dead' ... yet as a 'dead Jew'; not as a 'former Jew'.[81]

Benhayim implies that being regarded as a dead Jew is preferable, at least strategically, to being regarded as a former Jew. We are not so far from the discussion as to whether it is better to be considered a heretic than an apostate. The Messianic Jewish community is quite convinced that it deserves to be included in the wider Jewish community, and that it is invalid to regard Messianic Jews as 'former' Jews or as 'apostates', since both of these terms presume exclusion from the Jewish community.

Nissim Rejwan seeks, in his article on this question of Jewish identity, to establish that this notion of 'once a Jew always a Jew' is in fact the common presupposition of all Jews everywhere. He refers to the charming and perceptive story by the American Jewish writer, Abraham Cahan, in which a typical New York Jewish mother recovers from the shock of discovering that her daughter wishes to marry an Italian non-Jew. Eventually she agrees, on the firm condition that he converts to Judaism. This he does, supervised by the strictest authorities. When they marry they go to live with the girl's mother, who insists that her son-in-law prays before he gets his breakfast each day. The bride has a brother who also lives in the mother's house, but he is not required to pray before breakfast. After a while the son-in-law asks why this is, and the mother's response is the point Rejwan is seeking to make:

He is a Jew ... I know he is a Jew: You've got to prove it![82]

In this story it is irrelevant to the mother whether her son is a 'good Jew' or not; the fact is that he is a Jew. This is understandably the common denominator of assessment throughout Jewry. But does this allow for the possibility that a Messianic Jew might yet be regarded as halakhically Jewish, albeit a 'bad Jew'? Berger and Wyschogrod seem to suggest this line of thought in their attack on 'Jewish Christianity'. Their final chapter ends with this thought which certainly seems to leave the door open a little for Messianic Jews:

Furthermore, every form of 'Jewish Christianity' in existence today teaches Jesus as God and not only as the Messiah. Any Jew who embraces this belief commits idolatry. While he does not thereby cease

to be a Jew, since a Jew always remains a Jew, he commits one of the
gravest sins of which a Jew is capable. It is imperative that Jews know
this.[83]

That this judgment on Jewish believers, namely that they have become
contemptible sinners, or heretics, to use Charmé's categories, is the prevailing opinion in the responsa on this subject (though not without
exceptions, as would be expected), is the conclusion of Rabbi Walter
Jacob,[84] Stuart Charmé,[85] and Rabbi Louis Jacobs.[86] But having said this,
the extent of the Jewish community's reaction to this 'sin' is such that
social ostracism is the norm for any such Jewish believers. For most
matters they are regarded as effectively excluded from the community
of Israel, even if this is not strictly the case halakhically.[87]

Some authorities, notably among the non-Orthodox communities,
recommend a relatively benign attitude to Messianic Jews. Rabbi
Walter Jacob says in one of his responsa:

We cannot, and should not, exclude such individuals from attendance
at services, classes or any other activity of the community, for we
always hope that they will return to Judaism and disassociate them-
selves from Christianity. But they should be seen as outsiders who have
placed themselves outside the Jewish community ... Such individuals
should not be accorded membership in the congregation ... [88]

On the other hand, some authorities, particularly in the Orthodox
sector, are deliberately severe in their treatment of those they insist on
referring to as 'apostates'. One example is that of the Northern
California Board of Rabbis, who in the early 1970s stated their
'complete intolerance' of Messianic Jews.[89] In 1972 the Massachussetts
Rabbinical Court of Justice ruled that a Messianic Jew might not be
permitted to marry a Jewish person, or to be buried in a Jewish
cemetery. This case caused a furore at the time. Their rationale was
basically that Jewish believers have 'separated themselves' from the
community, and therefore must be treated as no longer part of the
community.[90]

A contemporary example from Britain was presented by Rabbi
Sylvia Rothschild (a rabbi in the Progressive movement) on a BBC1
documentary about Messianic Judaism, entitled: 'King of the Jews?'.

This was screened on Sunday, 31 March 1991. Rabbi Rothschild said there that Messianic Jews were 'the enemy' of those Jews and Christians who were trying to work out a *modus vivendi* at the close of the twentieth century.

Charmé sums it all up like this:

> *The Jewish community finds the Messianic-Jew guilty of both ethnic infidelity (by violating group solidarity) and theological heresy. As far as most Jews are concerned, the interaction of those two elements transforms the Messianic-Jews into apostates, despite the latter's claim to the contrary.*[91]

Samuel Fishman decided in the early 1970s to test this 'self-alienation', as he called it, of Messianic Jews among the college youth of America. In the Introduction to the book which published his findings he wrote:

> *There is little evidence that modern Jewish-Christians are as Jewishly observant as their ancient (ie in New Testament times) counterparts. We find among them that Hebrew is limited, kashrut rare, and Jewish literacy unusual.*[92]

It might be objected that this is the case amongst a great percentage, if not a majority, of American Jews generally, certainly among those at colleges throughout America. However, Fishman concludes that these 'Jewish-Christians', as he calls them, are moving away markedly and alarmingly from their community roots. The responsa literature also seems to focus a great deal on this 'self-alienation' of the 'apostate Jew', concluding that the only appropriate counter-measure, whether severely or leniently applied, is to reinforce that alienation by a policy of exclusion in the hope that the person may come to realise the error of his/her ways and the extent of his/her sin.[93]

A second agreed basis of the Jewish communal treatment of Messianic Jews is that only the Jewish community *per se*, not any individual, nor any lobbying interest group, can legitimately decide who is a Jew. As we have seen, this was part of the decision of the Israeli High Court against Esther Dorflinger. Rabbi Jacob has put it clearly and strongly:

> *Individuals who feel a vague attachment to one or another religion pose no problem for those religious groups that leave identification solely in*

the hands of the individual. Judaism, however, does not do so. It is not
the individual who defines whether he/she is Jewish, but the group.[94]

This would seem to create an impasse for the Messianic Jewish movement. The Jewish world may be embroiled in its own impasse over the proper criteria for deciding who is a Jew, but as long as the various authoritative groups are agreed that none of the definitions should include Jews who believe that Jesus is Israel's Messiah, then Messianic Jews will be effectively excluded by 'the Jewish community'.

It would seem that the most controversial aspect of the whole debate over the integrity and acceptability of the Messianic Jewish movement is this very one about the nature of authentic Jewish identity. Who is a Jew? What determines who is a Jew? Who decides what determines who is a Jew? If it be conceded for the moment that the great majority of Jews work with the Orthodox interpretation of who is a Jew, whether by conviction or by default, then is there such a thing as a critical mass of like-minded Jewish people, people who do not conform to that Orthodox interpretation, but whose self-designation and self-definition may yet be accepted by a majority within the Jewish community, even if that acceptance is given grudgingly? Is this, in effect, what has happened with the whole range of non-Orthodox 'denominations' within Jewry, like the Conservative, etc.? And if so, what is that critical mass likely to be?

These are important questions facing the Messianic Jewish community today. Whether or not the time will come when their numbers, public profile and good reputation become such that they have to be recognised and accepted as part of the Jewish world, we need to wait and see. But it certainly looks more likely now than it did even ten years ago.

Joy Davidman was an influential writer in Christian circles of a generation or two ago. She herself was a Jewish believer, and proud of both her Jewish heritage and her Christian faith. Her husband, C S Lewis, was also deeply influenced by his wife's integrated identity, and in a foreword to one of her books he wrote something which has touched many since with its simplicity and charm:

In a sense the converted Jew is the only normal human being in the
world. He has taken the whole syllabus in order, as it was set; eating

the dinner according to the menu. Everyone else is, from one point of view, a special case, dealt with under emergency regulations.[95]

Although the phrase 'converted Jew' would not be appreciated by Messianic Jews, the overall sentiment certainly is. Jewish believers deserve to be heard fairly by both the Jewish and the Christian communities. They are, by definition, a challenge to synagogue and church, but this should not be presented as a disqualification from the right to justice and the presumption of integrity. There is surely no excuse for the marginalising of these Messianic Jews by the larger communities to the extent that they are not even allowed a fair hearing in today's society.

In the light of today's increasing polarisation between the Orthodox and non-Orthodox communities in the Jewish world it is not difficult to realise that the Messianic Jewish community still has a very long way to go in being accorded the presumption of authenticity – at least by the Orthodox Jewish community. In the meantime, personal and communal integrity and a wise choice of strategies for the purpose of being accepted as Jewish will go a long way in helping the Messianic Jewish community to achieve that goal.

Notes

1   On this see the useful article by **Michael Oppenheim**: *Modern Jewish Identity: The Prominence of the Issue*, Forum 51/52, Spring/Summer 1984, pp 95-103, and the literature referred to there. See also **Elliot Dorff**, *The Meaning of Covenant: A Contemporary Understanding*, in **Helga Croner and Leon Klenicki** (eds), *Issues in the Jewish-Christian Dialogue*, Paulist Press, NY 1979.

2   **Henry L Feingold**, *The Jewish Role in Shaping American Society*, in *A Time To Speak: The Evangelical-Jewish Encounter*, ed by **A James Rudin** and **Marvin R Wilson**, Eerdmans, Grand Rapids, 1987, pp 45f.

3   Apart from specific reference materials cited in this article, see also the following useful article on the modern Jewish debate over Jewish identity as seen from the viewpoint of Reconstructionist thought: **Leslie Simon**, *A Perspective On Intermarriage And Conversion*, The Reconstructionist, Vol 46, No 10, February 1981, pp 7-14. A recent article which sets out the complexity of the issues involved in the debate very well is **Stanislaw Krajewski**, *Jewish Identity in a Non-Jewish World*, Christian Jewish Relations, Vol 20, No 3, 1987, pp 8-25. The somewhat complex situation in the early centuries of the Common Era is also noted by Rabbi Norman Solomon in his lecture, *Division and Reconciliation, The London Diocesan Council for Christian-Jewish Understanding*, 1980, pp 7f. A contemporary Christian treatment of this distinction between 'Judaism' and 'Jewishness' is that of **A Roy Eckardt**, *Jews and Christians, The Contemporary Meeting,*

Indiana University Press, Bloomington, 1986, esp pp 37-61.

4   A thorough analysis of this matter is found in the special Winter 1985 edition of the Journal, Judaism, Issue 133, Vol 34, No 1, entitled *Children of Mixed Marriages: Are They Jewish?*

5   **Ludwig Lewisohn**, *What is the Jewish Heritage?*, New York, B'nai B'rith Hillel Foundation, 1954, pp 1-6. Stephen Brook presents a rich selection of minimalist definitions of being Jewish by prominent Jewish figures in Britain, all of which have this simplistic ethnic basis. See his *The Club: The Jews of Modern Britain*, London, Pan Books, 1989, chapter thirteen, 'Being Jewish'.

6   *Hebrew Christianity: Its Theology, History and Philosophy* (rev Ed, San Antonio, Ariel Ministries, 1983), p 8. In note 15 the references to the Reform Jewish community in the USA will discuss the official Reform position which accepts both patrilineal as well as matrilineal descent in the determination of whether or not a person is genetically Jewish. This is now also the official position of the British Union of Liberal and Progressive Synagogues, as expressed in their pamphlet Liberal Judaism and Jewish Status (London, no date).

This acceptance of either parent as being a legitimate channel for the biological aspect of the definition of who is a Jew has been accepted in turn by the International Messianic Jewish Alliance, and by many Messianic Jewish groups, eg Beth Messiah Synagogue, Virginia Beach, U.S.A., whose eighth article of Faith states that: 'Jews according to the flesh (descendants of Abraham through Isaac, whether through the blood line of the mother or of the father) who place their faith in Israel's Messiah, Yeshua ... remain sons and daughters of Israel.' This position is also basically accepted by **Daniel Juster**, *Jewish Roots: A Foundation of Biblical Theology for Messianic Judaism*, Rockville, Md, Davar Publishing, 1986, p 192.

7   See **Leon Roth**, *Judaism: A Portrait*, Faber, London, 1960, p 15 for a strong statement that the Jewish religion is the primary determinant of what it is to be Jewish. Fruchtenbaum rightly points out that if a strict Orthodox definition of what it is to be a religious Jew is to be called upon as a means of barring Jewish believers from being considered to be acceptably Jewish, then that definition will rule out most Jews today. See his *Hebrew Christianity*, *op cit*, p 2.

8   For a rhetorical and poetic expression of this position see the famous statement of **S Dubnow**, *Nationalism and History*, ed Koppal S Pinson, Jewish Publication Society of America, Philadelphia, 1950, pp 1f.

9   See **Fruchtenbaum**, *op cit*, p 3.

10   See **Fruchtenbaum**, *op cit*, p 116.

11   Op cit, p 117.

12   Important articles include the following: **Mordecai Roshwald**, *Who Is A Jew In Israel?*, The Jewish Journal of Sociology, Vol 12, No 2, December 1970, pp 233-266. (He analyses eight aspects of definition); **Charles S Liebman**, *The Present State of Jewish Identity in Israel and the United States*, Forum, Vol 27, No 2, 1977, pp 22-34. The attitude of tertiary level education students is analyised by **Chaim I Waxman and William B Helmreich**, *American Jewish College Youth: Changing Identity*, Forum, *ibid*, pp 35-44, and also in the influential book by **David Caplovitz and Fred**

Sherrow, *The Religious Drop-outs: Apostasy Among College Graduates*, Beverly Hills, Sage Publications, 1977.

13 **Laurence H Schiffman**, *Who Was A Jew? Rabbinic and Halakhic Perspectives on the Jewish-Christian Schism*, Ktav, New Jersey, 1985, pp 9-16.

14 Ibid, pp 19-39. See here also the book by **Nicholas de Lange**, *Origen and the Jews*, Cambridge University Press, Cambridge, 1976, pp 29-37.

15 For the Conservative re-definition, see **Donald Frieman**, *Conversion or Convenience?*, Conservative Judaism, Vol 24, No 4, Summer 1970, pp 36-42; **Morris S Goodblatt**, *Converting Because Of Marriage Motives*, Conservative Judaism, Vol 28, No 3, Spring 1974, pp 30-40; **Edward M Gershfield**, *Hillel, Shammai And The Three Proselytes*, Conservative Judaism, Vol 21, No 3, Spring 1967, pp 29-39; **Theodore Friedman**, *Conversion And Conservative Judaism*, Conservative Judaism, Vol 28, No 3, Spring 1974, pp 21-29.

The Reform re-definition is discussed by **Robert P Jacobs**, *Rabbi Schindler's Call To Convert: Are We Ready?*, Journal of Reform Judaism (J R J), Vol 27, No 2, Spring 1980, pp 30-39; **Richard G Hirsch**, *Jewish Peoplehood: Implications for Reform Judaism*, Forum 37, Spring 1980, pp 123-133; **Manfred H Vogel**, *Some Reflections on the Question of Jewish Identity*, J R J, Vol 30, No 1, Winter 1983, pp 133; **Raphael Jospe**, *The Reform Movement and Jewish Status: Some Observations*, J R J, Vol 32, No 1, Winter 1985, pp 52-63. See also the Responsum #38, in Contemporary American Reform Responsa, *op cit* , pp 61-68.

Reconstructionist revisions are found in discussions by **Mordecai M Kaplan**, *Religious Imperatives Of Peoplehood*, Reconstructionist, Vol 25, No 9, June 15, 1959, pp 3-9; **Ronald A Brauner**, *Who Are We?*, Reconstructionist, Vol 41, No 5, June, 1975, pp 27-30; **Rami Shapero**, *Conversion: Considering a New Paradigm*, Reconstructionist, Vol 51, No 8, July-August, 1986, pp 13-17.

In Britain, the Union of Liberal and Progressive Synagogues has taken its lead from the worldwide Reform movement, though it is on the liberal wing of that, and it has published a substantial pamphlet on the issue of Jewish identity, with definition and rationale, entitled Liberal Judaism and Jewish Status (n.d., but 1980's, copies available from the U L P S).

Modern halakhic discussions are analysed in the articles by **Eliezer Berkovits**, *Conversion According to Halakhah – What Is It?*, Judaism, Vol 23, No 4, Fall 1974, pp 467-478; **J David Bleich**, *The Conversion Crisis: A Halakhic Analysis*, Tradition, Vol 11, No 4, Spring 1971, pp 16-42; **Marc D Angel**, *Another Halakhic Approach to Conversions*, Tradition, Vol 12, Nos 3-4, Winter-Spring 1972, pp 107-113.

16 **Baruch Maoz** *Who Is A Jewish Christian?*, Unpublished MS, nd, p 7.

17 Said in an interview on the video, Messianic Revival, produced in Los Angeles by The Union of Messianic Jewish Congregations, 1990.

18 **Maurice G Bowler**, *Messianic Assemblies and the Bible*, in Mishkan, No 10, Spring 1989, p 15.

19 **J Verkuyl**, *Contemporary Missiology: an introduction*, Eerdmans, Grand Rapids, 1978, p 141.

20 **Markus Barth**, *De Jood, Jezus, en het Geloof der Joden*, Verkenning en Bezinning, December, 1972, p 2. For the same point see **Alan P F Sell**, *Reformed Theology and the Jewish People*, Geneva, World Alliance of

Reformed Churches, 1986, pp 32ff.

21   **David Mansell**, *Who Are The Jews?* Restoration Magazine,
     September/October, 1983, pp 6-9.

22   **Reginald G Codrington**, *An Appraisal Of Modern Jewish Evangelism – with
     special reference to Southern Africa*, Publications of the University of the
     Western Cape, Cape Town, South Africa, 1983, p 13.

23   **Stuart L Charmé**, *Heretics, Infidels and Apostates: Menace, Problem or
     Symptom?*, Judaism, Winter 1987, p 17. His categories remind one of the
     distinction between 'sect' and 'schism' which was drawn, for similar
     purposes, by **Salo W Baron**. See his standard work, *A Social and Religious
     History of the Jews*, Philadelphia, 1958, Vol 2, p 63.

24   **Laurence H Schiffman**, *Who Was A Jew?*, N.Y., Ktav, 1985, p 41. See also
     Aharon Lichtenstein, *Brother Daniel and the Jewish Fraternity*, Judaism,
     Vol 12, No 3, Summer 1963, pp 265ff.

25   Sanhedrin 10: 1. While there is a certain variation among the MSS, the
     overall thrust of these words is consistently presented. For discussion see
     the references given by Schiffman, *op cit*, p 90, note 1.

26   **Schiffman**, *op cit*, p 46.

27   **Charmé**, *op cit*, p 18.

28   *Ibid*. See also on this point the article by **H G Kippenberg** on *Apostasy*, in
     Mircea Eliade (ed.), *The Encyclopedia of Religion*, NY, Macmillan, 1987,
     Vol1, pp 353-356.

29   Exodus 19: 6.

30   5710-1950; 4LSI 114.

31   5712-1952; 6LSI 50.

32   A fuller quote is to be found in the *Encyclopedia Judaica*, Vol 10, p 1486.

33   5713-1953; 7LSI 139.

34   5725-1965; SH 466, p 270.

35   Three articles, one from each decade since the Brother Daniel Case in
     1962, will suffice to show how the case continues to occupy the attention
     of Jews worldwide. **Aharon Lichtenstein**, *Brother Daniel and the Jewish
     Fraternity*, Judaism, Summer 1963, Vol 12, No 3. pp 260-280; **Mordecai
     Roswald**, *Who Is A Jew In Israel?*, The Jewish Journal of Sociology,
     December, 1970, Vol 12, No 2, pp 253-255; **Nissim Rejwan**, *Who's a Jew:
     Two Famous Non-Questions Answered*, Midstream, August/ September,
     1985, Vol 31, No 7, pp 39ff. The actual legal decision is recorded as 16 PD
     2428; SJ (SV) 1.
     The whole story of Brother Daniel has now been told for the first time by
     an American Jewish scholar, **Nechama Tec**, in her biography, *In The Lion's
     Den: The Life of Oswald Rufeisen*, OUP, Oxford, 1991.

36   The articles in note 35 give details of the case of course, but the members
     of the court were Justices Silberg, Landau, Berinson and Many, who
     formed the majority, and Justice Cohn who wrote a dissenting opinion.

37   Sanhedrin 44a.

38   Two further reflections on the Rufeisen case which come from the
     Messianic Jewish community are the following: There is an essay, *Who Is
     A Jew?* by **Arthur Kac**, in the anthology which he compiled and edited,
     The Messiahship of Jesus, Chicago, Moody press, 1980, pp 136-139 (Kac
     comes from a perspective of Evangelical Protestant scholarship).

Representing Roman Catholic Jewish believers is **Father Elias Friedman**, O D C, whose essay, *What Is A Jew? The Fr. Daniel Case*, was published in The Southern Cross, January 2nd, 1963, pp 1-4.

39 Recorded as 23 P D (2)477;S J (S I)35. See **S Clement Leslie**, *The Rift in Israel: Religious Authority and Secular Democracy*, Routledge and Kegan Paul, London, 1971, pp 39-41.

40 Quoted in **Fruchtenbaum**, *Hebrew Christianity*, *op cit*, p 4.

41 For notes on this decision and its impact see the *Israel Law Review*, Vol.5, No 2, April 1970, pp 259-63; *The Jerusalem Post*, 25 January, 1970.

42 For general material on this case see the *Encyclopedia Judaica*, Vol 10, pp 1485ff, 63ff.

43 Recorded as HCJ 563/77 33 (2) PDY97, 100-102

44 *The Jerusalem Post*, April 4, 1979.

45 Statement of Esther Dorflinger – Before The Israeli High Court of Justice, mimeographed sheets prepared by Ole Kvarme, Spring 1979, as quoted in **Emmanuel M Gitlin**, *Little Flock: Jews in the Church of Christ*, Privately published MS, 1981, p 42.

46 See note 41. For discussion of the issue of baptism from the perspective of Messianic Judaism see **Moishe Rosen**, *Y'shua: The Jewish way to say Jesus*, Moody Press, Chicago, 1982, p 78-81. For the traditional Christian view, as interpreted by Jewish tradition, see **Marc Saperstein**, *Moments of Crisis in Jewish Christian Relations*, SCM Press, London, 1989, p 15.

47 The translation here is taken from the full translation and commentary found in Mishkan, No 10, Spring 1989, pp 79-90. Further comments can be found in **Menachem Benhayim**, *Public Opinion Poll*, The Hebrew Christian, Vol 61, No 4, December 1988 – January 1989. pp 107f.

48 Mishkan, No 10, *op cit*, p 84.

49 Mishkan, No 10, *op cit*, p 85.

50 *Ibid.*

51 Mishkan, No 10, *op cit*, p 86.

52 See the discussion in **S C Leslie**, *The Rift in Israel: Religious Authority and Secular Democracy*, Routledge and Kegan Paul, London, 1971, pp 44-48.

53 See the article, *Changing Faith*, by **Jon Immanuel** in the *Jerusalem Post International Edition*,13 January, 1990, pp 9-10. This case was also mentioned in the *Jewish Chronicle*, 5 January 1990. A full discussion of the whole affair and the issues raised by it is to be found in the *LCJE Bulletin*, no.20, May 1990, which is devoted to the Beresford Case.

54 This information was reported by **Menachem Benhayim** in his *News from the Homeland*, The Hebrew Christian, Vol 63, No 1, April-June 1990, pp 15-16.

55 See the *Jerusalem Post International Edition*, 6 January 1990, in an unattributed item, *News Report*.

56 *Ibid.*

57 *Ibid.*

58 *Ibid.* This is clearly a reference to, and reiteration of, the opinion of Justice Shamgar in the Dorflinger Case.

59 *Ibid.* We have here a continuation of the basic line of argument taken in the Brother Daniel Case. It is of some interest that both Justices Elon and

Barak dismissed the significance and the actual findings of the Dahaf Poll, though it was presented to the court in anticipation of an appeal to the opinion of the man in the street. See the LCJE Bulletin, No 20, *op cit*, pp 9, 10f.

60   This information comes from a report in *The Hebrew Christian*, Vol 63, No 4, Dec 1990-Feb 1991, p 106.

61   For a statement of this which is actually contained in a Confession of Faith, see the Confession adopted at a special meeting of the American Fellowship of Christian Jews, May 2nd, 1949, published as *The Confession of the Christian Jew*, Sar-Shalom Publications, New York, 1949.

      The conviction among Messianic Jewish pastors in Israel today is that if Jewish people must give up their Jewishness by believing that Jesus is the Messiah of Israel and the Son of God, then that can only mean that Jesus is an imposter, but since they know that Jesus is decidedly not an imposter, then their Jewishness is intact. See **Baruch Maoz, Avner Boskey and Joseph Shulam**, *Israel Today and Tomorrow*, Presented privately at Manila for Lausanne II, 1989, p 9. This point is debated by **Rabbi Klenicki and Rev. Neuhaus** in their book, *Jew and Christian in Conversation*, Grand Rapids, Eerdmans, 1989, pp 27-30.

62   **David Chernoff**, *Yeshua the Messiah*, MMI Publishing House, Haverton, Pa, 1983, p 6. Such statements are very common from the pens of Jewish believers, so only a few references are given here, each by representa-tives of characteristic positions: **Charles Kalisky**, *Who is a Jew?*, a tract in the series, What Every Jew Should Know, (No, 30), published by Sar Shalom Publications, NY, no date; **Victor Buksbazen**, *The Hebrew Christian and Israel*, a tract published by Spearhead Press, Philadelphia, no date; **Jacob Blum**, *What is a Hebrew Christian?*, a tract published by the American Messianic Fellowship, Chicago, no date; **Abram Poljak**, *The Cross in the Star of David*, The Jewish Christian Community, London, 1938, p 2.

63   See **Walter Barker**, *Messianic Judaism*, Unpublished MS, CMJ Office, 1988, p 150.

64   See **James Milton Hutchens**, *A Case for Messianic Judaism*, Private Publication of a doctoral thesis, Fuller Theological Seminary, 1974, where this is quoted on page 9.

65   Quoted on page 10 of Hutchen's work, *op cit*.

66   Quoted on page 35 of Hutchen's work, *op cit* See also **A Roy Eckardt**, *Jews and Christians: The Contemporary Meeting*, Indiana University Press, Bloomington, 1986, pp 69-70, 88.

67   Hutchens, *op cit*, pp 83f.

68   **Arthur W Kac**, *The Messiahship of Jesus, op cit*, p 99. See also *Introducing the Jewish People to their Messiah*, American Board of Mission to the Jews, NY, 1977, p 5; **Lev Gillet**, *Communion in the Messiah*, Lutterworth Press, London, 1942, pp 195f.

69   **Moishe Rosen**, quoted in *The Hebrew Christian*, Vol 55, No 1, Spring 1982, p 13. See also **Jacob Jocz**, *The Jewish People and Jesus Christ*, Grand Rapids, Baker Book House, 1981, pp 210, 218; **Elizabeth M Miller**, *Discourses on Judaism and the Jewish People: From Mission to Dialogue*, Unpublished doctoral thesis, University of Aberdeen, 1984, p 320; **Marvin R Wilson**, *Our Father Abraham*, Eerdmans, Grand Rapids, Michigan, 1989, p 46.

70   **John Bell**, *How To Be Like The Messiah*, Orangeburg, NJ, Chosen People

Publications, 1987, p 62. See also **B Z Sobel**, *Hebrew Christianity: The Thirteenth Tribe*, NY, John Wiley and Sons, 1974, p 261; **Moishe Rosen**, *Y'shua: The Jewish Way To Say Jesus*, Moody Press, Chicago, 1982, pp 82ff.

71   **Jakob Jocz**, *The Jewish People and Jesus Christ*, op cit, p 230. See also **Abram Poljak**, *The Cross in the Star of David*, p 3.

72   **Harcourt Samuel**, *Why Hebrew Christian?*, number 2 of the Centenary Booklets published by the Hebrew Christian Alliance of Great Britain, London, May 1966. An interesting view of the effect of such nominal conversions upon the Hebrew Christian community is given by **Menachem Benhayim**, *Marginals*, in The Hebrew Christian, Vol 62, No 4, December 1989 – February 1990, pp 114-116.

73   **Arnold Fruchtenbaum**, *Hebrew Christianity*, op cit, pp 13, 43.

74   Op cit, pp 194f.

75   **Isaac Da Costa**, *Israel and the Gentiles*, London, James Nisbet and Co., 1850, pp ix-x. For other such testimonials, gathered by a scholar who is himself unsympathetic to the Messianic Jewish phenomenon, see **Robert E Blumenstock**, *The Evangelization of Jews: A Study in Interfaith Relations*, Unpublished thesis, University of Oregon, 1964, pp 163ff.

    Further examples of this claim of the fulfilment of their Jewish faith and self-understanding are extremely numerous. Many have been collected by **Sandra Jane Lawliss**, *Messianic Judaism: An Argument for Contextualising*, Unpublished MA Thesis for the Columbia Graduate School of Bible and Missions, Columbia, S Carolina, 1983, pp 39-47. Some specific sources are: **Abe Cohen**, et. al.: *More Jewish than ever – We've found the Messiah*, Christianity Today, Feb. 1st, 1974, pp 12f; **John Vinocur**, *A Most Special Cardinal*, The New York Times Magazine, March 20th, 1983, pp 29ff; **John Bell**, *How To Be Like The Messiah*, op cit, p 9.

76   Op cit, pp 10f. *Examples of Messianic Jews*, professional people, with the same testimony are gathered by Kac, and in fact his examples come from both Western and Eastern Europe. See his *The Messiahship of Jesus*, op cit, pp 140f. The same conclusion is presented by **Eliezer Maas**, *Stand Firm, A Survival Guide for the New Jewish Believer*, Lansing, Il, American Messianic Fellowship Publications, 1990, p 22. See also the testimonies in **Robert Winer**, *The Calling: The History of the Messianic Jewish Alliance of America*, 1915-1990, Wynnewood, PA, MJAA Publications, 1990, p 46.

77   **Rachel Kohn**, *Ethnic Judaism and the Messianic Movement*, Journal of Jewish Studies, t.cit, p 86. For more examples of this attitude see further in Kohn's article, pp 86ff. See also **Jakob Jocz**, *The Church of Rome and the Jews*, International Review of Missions, Vol 51, No 203, July 1962, pp 323f, for treatment of Jews who became Roman Catholics, also becoming spokespersons for the retention of their Jewishness. For several examples of statements of Messianic Jews that before their commitment to Jesus as Messiah they saw Judaism and the Christian faith as mutually exclusive, whereas now they see the perfect harmony between them, see **Astrid Berner**, *Messianic Jews in Israel*, M.A.Dissertation, unpublished, The Queen's University of Belfast, 1989, pp 24ff, 33.

78   **Stuart L Charmé**, *Heretics, Infidels*, art cit, p 24.

79   *Ibid*.

80   **Henry Knight**, *The Role of Messianic Congregations in the Body of Christ* (Unpublished paper, 1986), p 2.

81   **Menachem Benhayim,** *Refutations,* art cit, p L.

82   **Nissim Rejwan,** *Who's a Jew?,* art cit, p 40.

83   **Berger and Wyschogrod,** *Jews and 'Jewish Christianity',* NY, Ktav, 1978, p 66. Cf Gitlin, *op cit,* pp 13-15 for the same perspective.

84   **Walter Jacob,** *Status of a Completed Jew in the Jewish Community,* Journal of Reform Judaism, Vol 32, No 1., Winter 1985, pp 88-91.

85   **Stuart L Charmé,** *Heretics, Infidels,* art cit, pp 22f. He deals primarily with the views of Rashi.

86   **Louis Jacobs,** *Theology in the Responsa,* London, Routledge and Kegan Paul, 1975. Jacobs obviously cites opinions which differ on the decision appropriate to this question. The key references are as follows: Geonic period, pp 26f; eleventh century, pp 30, 33, 34; thirteenth century, pp 52, 75f, fifteenth century, pp 108f.

87   See **Charmé,** art cit, p 23; **James W Wood Jr,** *Jewish-Christian Relations in Historical Perspective,* Journal of Church and State, Vol 13, No 2, Spring 1971, p 195.

88   **Walter Jacob,** *Status of a Completed Jew,* art cit, p 90.

89   This case is discussed by **Edward E Plowman,** *The Rabbis Aren't Smiling,* Christianity Today, April 28, 1972, pp 34f.

90   *Ibid.*

91   **Stuart L Charmé,** art cit, p 24. Cf Jewish Exponent, Vol 171, No 5, 1982, *op cit,* p 48.

92   **Samuel Z Fishman,** *Jewish Students and the Jesus Movement,* Washington, D C, B'nai B'rith Hillel Foundation, 1973, p 47.

93   **Louis Jacobs,** *Theology in the Responsa, op cit*: eleventh century, pp 33f., 36; twelfth century, pp 50f.; sixteenth century, pp 136, 142; nineteenth century, pp 207f, 209f, 220, 222; twentieth century, pp 307f, 318. For Rabbinic authorities who press for a process akin to conversion for any who wish to rejoin the Jewish community by renouncing Christianity, see **Walter Jacob,** *Status of a Completed Jew,* art cit, p 89. See also his *Return to Judaism of a Baptised Jewish Girl,* Journal of Reform Judaism, Vol 33, No 4, Fall 1986, pp 69f.

94   **Walter Jacob,** *Status of a Completed Jew,* art cit, p 88. See also **Balfour Brickner,** *Christian Mission-aries and a Jewish Response,* Worldview, May 1978, p 38.

95   **C S Lewis,** in his Forward to the book by **Joy Davidman,** *Smoke on the Mountain,* London, Hodder and Stoughton, 1955, p 8.

Appendix 1

 Pardes, The Centre for Biblical and Hebraic Studies

This collection of essays is co-published by *PWM Trust* and *The Centre for Biblical and Hebraic Studies* in England. The primary aim of the Centre is to explore the Hebraic culture and background of the Gospels and New Testament writings and to offer teaching to a wide range of people of all ages and at different stages of spiritual maturity. The Centre offers facilities for those who wish to study the Second Temple period in the history of Israel which forms the background to the teaching of Jesus in the Gospels and the writings of the Apostles. The Centre also offers facilities for those who wish to specialise in New Testament scholarship through Hebraic roots research and those who have a general interest in reclaiming the original Hebraic understanding of the New Testament.

There are institutions in Israel and in the United States with a similar purpose which are well established and well respected for their scholarly standards of work. Until 1995, when *The Centre for Biblical and Hebraic Studies* was founded by David Forbes, there was no similar institution in Britain. David Forbes' personal interest in exploring Hebraic roots stretched back many years and throughout his ten years of ministering with the Prophetic Word Ministries team he developed and extended that interest.

Since David's death the Centre has been led by the Rev John Fieldsend, himself a Messianic Jew. The Centre regularly offers Teaching Days on a variety of themes; residential courses; a number of distance learning programmes, at access, intermediate and college level, on a wide range of subjects, including 'The Jewishness of Jesus and the Gospels', 'The Prophets of the Old Testament', 'The Second Temple Period' and 'The Festivals of Israel'. Most of the Jewish Festivals are celebrated with appropriate teaching at the Centre which also offers facilities for sabbaticals and private study with tutorial help available, and we are gradually building up a comprehensive library.

A Bursary Fund has been established in David's memory to assist a wide range of people to take advantage of the Centre's services.

More information about the work of the Centre and the facilities it offers, is available from :

The Centre for Biblical and Hebraic Studies
The Park
Moggerhanger
Bedford
MK44 3RW
United Kingdom

Telephone: 01767 641400
Fax: 01767 641515
email: pwm@the-park.u-net.com

Prophetic Word Ministries Trust is a Registered Charity No 326533.

Appendix 2

Prophetic Word Ministries Trust

Moggerhanger House, the home of Prophetic Word Ministries Trust, offers fellowship facilities for groups who wish to use the house and grounds for conferences, retreats or community facilities. The Centre for Biblical and Hebraic Studies is part of the ministry of the PWM Trust which is based at The Park, Moggerhanger, near Bedford, forty-five minutes north of London. The Park is a beautiful country house estate with extensive parkland, walled gardens and woods at the heart of which is a Grade I listed Georgian mansion, designed by Sir John Soane RA, the architect who designed the Bank of England in 1777. The original house is much older but Soane recast it in 1792 for the Thornton family who were Governors and Directors of the Bank of England and had connections with the Clapham Sect, whose most famous member was William Wilberforce. The house and grounds are full of historic interest and provide a beautiful setting for the Centre.

More information about the House, and the family of Ministries based there is available from:

Prophetic Word Ministries Trust
The Park
Moggerhanger
Bedford
MK44 3RW
United Kingdom

Telephone: 01767 641400
Fax: 01767 641515
email: pwm@the-park.u-net.com

Prophetic Word Ministries Trust is a Registered Charity No 326533.

Index of Biblical and Early Jewish Writings